THOMAS MORE

A Lonely Voice Against the Power of the State

by Peter Berglar

English translation by Hector de Cavilla

Scepter

Text design: Carol Sawyer/Rose Design

Scepter Publishers, Inc.
P.O. Box 211, New York, N.Y. 10018
www.scepterpublishers.org

Printed in the United States of America

ISBN: 978-1-59417-073-7

Library of Congress Cataloging-in-Publication Data
Berglar, Peter, 1919–1989.
  [Stunde des Thomas Morus. English]
  Thomas More : a lonely voice against the power of the state / by Peter Berglar ; English translation by Hector de Cavilla.
    p. cm.
  Originally published as: Stunde des Thomas Morus. Olten : Walter, 1978.
  Includes index.
  ISBN 978-1-59417-073-7 (alk. paper)
  1. More, Thomas, Sir, Saint, 1478–1535. 2. Great Britain—History—Henry VIII, 1509–1547—Biography. 3. Henry VIII, King of England, 1491–1547—Relations with humanists. 4. Great Britain—Politics and government—1509–1547. 5. England—Intellectual life--16th century. 6. Christian martyrs—England—Biography. 7. Statesmen—Great Britain—Biography. 8. Humanists—England—Biography. I. Cavilla, Hector de. II. Title.
  DA334.M8B4713 2009
  942.05'2092—dc22
  [B]
                                        2009038676

Contents

Foreword

The words that give this book its title refer to two things. On the one hand, they signify the highest point of Thomas More's life, the culmination of his personal development, his career, and his destiny, within the era in which he lived. They also suggest something transcending time, an undefined quality that makes *his* hour *our* hour too. It is that dimension beyond the here and now that justifies the book's subtitle: *A Lonely Voice Against the Power of the State.*

Thomas More was a family man and a humanist writer, a defender of the Church of Rome, a lawyer and civil servant in a state passing from the Middle Ages to modern times amidst the radical transformation of Europe. I hope to convey all this in the pages that follow.

More's story, a fascinating one, deserves telling simply as the biography of an outstanding historical figure. But it also is more than the story of one man's life, for its timeliness, in the best sense of the word, can touch us personally. This English statesman not only lived in the thick of a battle of intellects, opinions, and events, but also went head to head against the physical might of a state that thrust itself into his life in the persons of Henry VIII and Thomas Cromwell—as well as the docile social-political cadres who bent their knees before them.

The specific issue they were grappling with was, strictly speaking, the king's divorce and second marriage. Related to that was the separation of the English Church from the Church of Rome. More generally, what was involved was the breaking away of society and the state from the medieval political order and the birth of the modern concept of independent nationhood. But something else also was implicated in these events, namely, the state's ambition to impose not just de facto obedience but also active assent. Now, for the first time in history, simply tolerating the unilateral decisions of an establishment was not enough; explicit approval was demanded, and not only defiance but personal opinion were subject to persecution, with nonconformity treated as the equivalent of rebellion.

In the cradle of modern Europe, then, we witness a power struggle to preserve the freedom of the individual in the face of organized power, something not always or necessarily identified with the state. Thomas More set very modest standards of personal liberty for himself. Religious reasons or, more precisely, faith, forbade him to assent to Henry's divorce and remarriage and the separation of Christian England from the universal Church of Rome and the pope. Here was an affront to conscience that did not permit him to act against faith by swearing an oath of obedience, even as a pure formality, to such laws against God.

This clear divide between the dictates of faith and those of conscience is very significant, but often it is not seen clearly enough. More's inability to consent to the king's divorce and remarriage (in other words, to recognize the supremacy of Crown over Church) because it offended against the concept of justice, was not a matter of "conscience" but a consequence of faith, whereas acting in accordance with the faith and not casting it aside was, in effect, an act of obedience. Because of that obedience, which Thomas More was not prepared to abandon even if it cost him his life, he was fated to mount the steps to the scaffold.

In the Western world today the scope of personal freedom is incomparably broader than it was in Thomas More's day. Besides refusing assent to what offends against justice or, more generally, to what runs counter to our convictions, we can go further and actively defend our own opinions, without the make-believe of nonexistent agreement. Plainly this is not the case everywhere in the world, and even in our free and open society there is a growing tendency to impose uniformity on conflicting points of view—at least, those voiced in public—while allowing everyone to think whatever they like as long as they say only what is acceptable. Coercion to standardize behavior and thought, without taking into account inner convictions and the authenticity of the individual, is growing all over the world, nor is it restricted to the physical exercise of political power.

So the "hour"[1] of Thomas More provides both an example and an agenda for our time as well. There will never be a shortage of state power bent on forcing total submission. Five centuries after this brave Englishman lived and died, we need to face the fact that the time may yet come when we shall be forbidden to fight for our convictions. Perhaps we will

---

1. "Hour" refers to the title of this book in the original German: *Die Stunde des Thomas Morus* (*The Hour of Thomas More* or *Thomas More—His Hour*).

be allowed to remain outwardly silent yet inwardly faithful. But perhaps we will be forced even to speak and act against our beliefs.

"A Lonely Voice Against the Power of the State"—these words too have been chosen deliberately. Thomas More stood alone, first, because conscience is something altogether personal, but above all because those who follow their consciences often are few. Where circumstances require it, obedience to conscience also implies the capacity for steadfastness in the face of an overwhelming majority that thinks or decides otherwise. Despite that, all of us deep in our hearts would all secretly like to be counted among the "few." In the final analysis, however, that depends on grace, a gift bestowed on Thomas More to which he responded with fidelity. Fortitude of conscience made it possible for him not to betray his faith, and deep faith empowered him to obey his conscience even unto death.

Finally, this "Thomas More"—His Hour," which touches all of us personally, refers not only to the moment of truth of an ultimate life-or-death decision but also to this man's role as an example: in his family life, in his relationship with his children, in his educational principles, his professional diligence, his intellectual flexibility, in the human virtues of prudence, justice, temperance, charity, and fortitude, and, also in his abundant sense of humor and the succinct sharpness of his wit. In sum, More's "hour" also is the hour of his love of God and mankind—an hour in reality eternally present.

PART ONE

The Upward Climb

When the sick see they are being treated by physicians whose state of health is even sadder than their own, they rebel and turn pigheaded, whereas in a healthy physician, on the other hand, they place their trust entirely.

— Thomas More to John Colet, October 25, 1504

CHAPTER ONE

The Epitaph in Chelsea

Cemeteries and burial sites are not only places of repose but sometimes of shock and occasionally horror. They have inspired philosophers, poets, and painters; and those who read an epitaph inevitably read it as an epilogue rather than a prologue.

In the case of Sir Thomas More, a humanist among humanists, who called himself "Morus" (fool), we find the happy instance of an utterly sincere, modest, and down-to-earth man, who wished to give an account of himself in the inscription on his grave—a biography in an epitaph, an entire life in the words carved on a sepulcher. Historians wisely mistrust autobiographical testimonials because they know that people consciously or unconsciously tend to regard themselves more positively than they deserve and to portray events accordingly. With Thomas More, however, it is otherwise. From all we know of him, including his letters and the writings and testimonies of others, he was not at all pretentious. Indeed, he was so genuinely modest that the celebrated Chelsea epitaph can be taken as an understatement of the typically ironic and modest British sort.

This epitaph will serve as our guide, then, as we look into questions of motive, background, and consequences.

CHAPTER TWO

A Statesman and Writer

1.

The Old Church in Chelsea containing More's tomb and epitaph was destroyed in an air raid in April, 1941. It was rebuilt in such a way that the burial chapel became the head of the principal nave, while the epitaph, on a black marble plaque bearing the inscription, was placed in the sanctuary to the right of the altar.

More moved to Chelsea in 1524 from Bucklersbury, in the center of London. Chelsea too has for a long time been part of the city center, but at that time it was a town on the banks of the river Thames outside the city walls. Thomas was already into the final phase of his life when in 1532[1] he composed his epitaph. He had given up his post as Lord Chancellor of the Realm on May 16 because he could approve neither the breaking away of the English Church from Rome nor Henry VIII's divorce and remarriage, which took place in 1533. He was by then a man of fifty-four, stripped of all influence, with a state of health that left much to be desired and a worrisome financial situation. He sensed what the future held for him, a black and anguishing prospect filled with unsuspected imponderables over which he would have no control. He may not have foreseen his death at the hands of the executioner, but he undoubtedly saw the end of the line ahead.

That he should have composed his epitaph then, having quit the service of Henry VIII after fourteen years, suggests that, whatever other reasons may have been operative, he anticipated a need for it in the not too distant future.

᜕ ᜕ ᜕

---

1. The full text of the epitaph was sent by Thomas More to his friend Erasmus in a letter written in June of 1533.

"Thomas More was born in London of a known, though not noble, family. He was somewhat brought up in learning. After spending several years in his early life as a defense lawyer in court, having first been a judge and later sub-Sheriff in his native city, the invincible Henry VIII summoned him to the royal court, that King, unique among monarchs, to whom was granted the honor of bearing the title of "Defender of the faith," a title gained by the sword and the pen. He was received at Court, elected a member of the Privy Council, ennobled, appointed Vice-Chancellor and later Chancellor of the Duchy of Lancaster and, finally, by the special grace of his sovereign, Lord Chancellor of England."

⁓❧ ⁓❧ ⁓❧

Thomas had been born in London, probably on February 6, 1478. There is no absolute certainty about the date. According to a note left by his father, John More, which came to light about a hundred years ago, the years 1477 and 1478 and the sixth and seventh of February fit as the date of birth. It is a happy portent that, as Chambers points out,[2] the first book printed in England appeared at the same time as little Thomas. With this advent of printing, a new era was born, surpassing in significance the voyage of Christopher Columbus and Luther's theses in Wittenberg; if anything is especially important in the life of Thomas More, it is books.

Although a fair amount is known about Thomas's father, John More (we shall be alluding to him when we come to interpret the epitaph), little is known about his other forebears. His grandfather was probably an accountant and personnel supervisor for the Corporation of Lawyers in Lincoln's Inn;[3] he became a member of this association in 1470. With Thomas, then, the third generation of this family was to be in the service of the judiciary. His maternal grandfather, Thomas Granger, after whom the boy was named, was a respected and wealthy citizen of London. Appointed Sheriff in 1503, he was still alive when his grandson was making a name for himself as a lawyer and a Reader at the Law School in Furnivall's Inn, and, by 1510, was starting a family.

The epitaph's second phrase mentions, though very much in passing, the literary interests of Thomas More, before even enumerating

---

2. Cf. R.W. Chambers, *Thomas More. Ein Staaatsmann Heinrichs VIII* (Munich-Kempten, 1947). (The author cites this German translation. The English original was published in London in 1935. From here on it is simply cited as Chambers.)

3. One of the "Inns of Court," the law schools of London.

the principal stages of his career as a lawyer, which carried him steadily to the very pinnacle of his profession. Those laconic words "He was somewhat brought up in learning" take in the whole of his literary output, from the earliest epigrams of the youthful author to the great debates with Tyndale, leader of Luther's followers in England (although it is admittedly problematic whether More would consider these works of theological controversy to be literature).

Look back on a life and body of work, and it is very easy to see early works as daring in their vision; nor can it be denied that early indications sometimes hint at what is to come. Sometimes, but not always.

People have also wished to find elements of autobiography in More's epigrams.[4] They stigmatize the King's tyranny, poke fun at clergy unfit for the episcopacy, ridicule self-regarding behavior and ludicrous emulation of the French. But even though all these concerns are found in the life of Thomas More, that is not reason enough to speak of autobiography, since they are common to many cultured people of his time. Moreover, social criticism has been a classic ingredient of the epigram from ancient times to the present.

Although the aims of this book do not permit us to linger on miscellany, one of More's four youthful works in English that have been preserved deserves mention. It was written around 1503 and has become a curiosity for adopting something like an old man's perspective transposed to the time of his youth. The work in question, *Nine Pageants*, is composed of nine stanzas, eight in English, one in Latin, that comment on nine images of a "beautiful tapestry painted on an exquisite canvas" which Thomas says he designed for his father's house. The motifs are conventional: a child at play who wants all books thrown into the fire; a man on horseback who runs the child down because he feels superior to him; love triumphant that makes the man regress to childhood; the wisdom of old age that conquers love; old age overcome by death; death overcome by posthumous glory; glory conquered by time; and, finally, time conquered by eternity. The last image shows the poet seated in a chair and drawing the moral "All is vanity" in Latin.

The striking thing about the text is that its common knowledge, drawing on universal human experience and universally applicable, takes on in More's hands the dimension of the human relationship with God, steeped in humility.[5] In a sense the tapestry depicts his own life.

4. Chambers, 100.
5. See in this respect, the Epilogue of this book.

Still, the directions of that life were not predetermined at the start. For Thomas, would it be the world or the monastery? How strong was the youth's inclination to the religious state? Why did he opt for the lay state? These are crucial questions. To find answers, we must look more deeply into the decisive factor suggested by the epitaph's "brought up in learning." Specifically, we shall have to examine his interest in the person and work of Pico della Mirandola.

As is the rule in biographies of those times, we know little of the infancy of Thomas. He was a second child. There was an elder sister, Jane, born in 1475, and four younger siblings: his sister Agatha, who died at an early age (b. 1479); brothers John (b. 1480) and Edward (b. 1481), the first of whom lived more than thirty years and for a time was Thomas's secretary; and, lastly, a younger sister Elizabeth (b. 1482), who married John Rastell and was the mother of William Rastell, printer, lawyer, judge, More's biographer and publisher of his complete works.[6] Thomas's mother, Agnes, died before 1490. She was followed by three stepmothers, the third of whom survived Thomas by nine years. He was a good son to his stepmothers and applauded his father's fourth marriage at the age of about 70, even though this meant a reduction in his inheritance.

Thomas attended the renowned old St. Anthony's School in London and there acquired his basic knowledge of Latin, the language he was to use throughout his life as his second mother tongue. He then went into service as a page at the residence of the Archbishop of Canterbury, John Morton, who at that time was also Lord Chancellor, and later was to become a cardinal. "There," Chambers writes, "he had occasion to observe how of all the grandees of the Realm" conducted themselves.[7] In his *Utopia*, More recorded his gratitude to the prince of the Church who introduced him to the social and political milieu in which he himself was to move for the next quarter of a century.[8]

At the age of fourteen—not unusual for the time—he entered Oxford University, where the Archbishop had obtained a place for him in Canterbury College, which was under the direction of the

---

6. Chambers, 30–36. His biography of Thomas More, preserved only in fragmentary form (*The Rastell Fragments*) was published as an annex to the edition of Harpsfield (cf. note 15). Rastell in 1557 published the works of Thomas More written in English (these are cited as: *Works*).

7. Chambers, 63.

8. Thomas More, *Utopia* (the author cites the German translation by Gerhard Ritter [Berlin, 1922]), p. 14 (cited hereafter as *Utopia*).

Benedictines. Greek was especially cultivated there, having been "redis-covered" as part of the great humanist movement, and young More studied the language too, though without mastering it as he had Latin or as well as his friend Erasmus.

The next stage in his career, almost two years later, was spent at New Inn, a kind of professional school for lawyers. Shortly after, in 1496, he went from there to Lincoln's Inn. The decade that followed was one of growing and maturing, probably difficult and uneven, of which we know little more than that it ended in his complete dedica-tion to the world, his marriage, and his debut in Parliament in 1504. During these years the study of law, ancient languages, and classical literature, teaching, and an intense spiritual life all coalesced for More. In November, 1501, he wrote one of his scholarly friends, a professor of Latin named John Holt: "You ask me how my studies are going? Splendidly! Couldn't be better! I have given up Latin and now devote myself to Greek. I shall probably forget the former and never master the latter."[9] The irony here, as so often aimed at himself, and the under-statement are among More's typical traits that make him so attractive.

Friendly relations with the humanists, to whom we shall refer again in the chapter on Erasmus, and studies like those mentioned did not keep him from dedicating himself seriously to jurisprudence and theology. While still a student himself, he taught at the law school in Furnivall's Inn and also lectured on St. Augustine's *City of God* at St. Lawrence's, parish church of his teacher and friend William Grocyn. These lectures were very well attended, as we know from Erasmus. Grocyn himself expounded in St. Paul's Cathedral on his critical appreciation for the ancient Christian writer then believed to be Dionysius the Areopagite,[10] and More comments drily: "It is difficult to tell whether he thus renders a greater service to his own celebrity or to his listeners. His pupils attend en masse; if only they were as learned as they are numerous! Of course, the common herd attended too, many of them attracted by fascination for novelty; others to pretend they understand something of the mat-ter. Those who consider themselves wiser stay at home so as not to give

---

9. Letters of Thomas More (the author cites the letters from the German edition: *Die Briefe des Sir Thomas More*, edited and with an introduction by Barbara von Blarer, [Einsiedeln/Cologne, 1949]), 16 (hereafter cited as Blarer).

10. Cf. Acts of the Apostles 17:34; converted by St. Paul, it seems that he was the first Bishop of Athens and a martyr. Using his name, an unknown Syrian author, perhaps the Patriarch Peter of Antioch, composed a series of writings of a neo-Platonic type around the year 500, the so-called Pseudo-Dionysius.

anyone occasion to suppose that there are gaps in their culture."[11] We can imagine that More entertained a similar opinion of his own audience.

Here at the dawn of the sixteenth century, there was as yet no parting of the ways between faith and science, piety and philology, the humble acceptance of the divine mysteries, and the aspiration to reestablish in their original purity the sources from which Holy Scripture has come down to us. The inquiring humanists are at the same time men of the Church—priests and orthodox spiritual leaders, in particular More's friends William Grocyn, John Colet,[12] Thomas Linacre, and William Lily.

There was no contradiction at all between the study of antiquity and the ideal of priesthood, between mastery of Greek and its integration into the doctrine of the Church. Potential conflicts were not yet visible. Humanism labored to purify and strengthen faith by the new means supplied by classical culture; it had not yet become, either in intention or by a process of evolution, an alternative to the faith.

Thus, More's eventual decision in favor of the lay state was unrelated either to his interest in the new learning or to some contradiction between that learning and the spiritual life. The process by which he reached his decision may indeed have involved the young man's subjective uncertainties, but that is not reason for making the decision itself seem more complicated than it was.

Between 1499 and 1503, More lived in the London Charterhouse, a Carthusian monastery with a guesthouse.[13] The Carthusians had arrived in England in the days of King Henry II (1154–1189), who built the Witham monastery for them, probably as a token of repentance for having instigated the assassination of the Archbishop of Canterbury, Thomas à Becket. In 1349, as a plague was wreaking havoc in London, the bishop had acquired a large plot of land for use as a public cemetery, and it was here that the Carthusians' "Annunciation to the Mother of God" monastery was erected. The guesthouse formed part of the monastery complex, which included the church, the cells (the monks' individual living quarters), and the common rooms (for

---

11. Blarer, 16.

12. Ibid., 17.

13. The Carthusians are a contemplative order of hermits, founded by St. Bruno of Cologne. They take their name from their first monastery, La Grande Chartreuse, founded in 1084 between Grenoble and Chambéry in the Alps. Around 1500, they had some 200 monasteries. Each Carthusian lived in his own small house, with only the lay brothers living a community life.

the lay brothers). Young More lived there despite the rule of the order prohibiting any except religious from residing in the monastery. In 1490, a general chapter of the order had allowed unmarried males to live there as guests. These men were incorporated into the community without taking vows or making promises or assuming obligations—yet absorbed, so to speak, into the daily spiritual routine. Thomas participated in Holy Mass and the meditations, readings, and penitential routines of the monks, serving God alongside them, while pondering the question of whether that was the way of serving God that God had in mind for him or whether he was called to live in the midst of the world, pursuing a profession and fulfilling social, matrimonial, and family responsibilities.

But why did a young man enter a monastery even as a guest? Few people today would even understand the question. By the end of the twentieth century, the monastic ideal was marginalized in social consciousness. In More's day, though, the situation was very different. The world was teeming with clerics, especially monks and friars of contemplative and mendicant orders, and they were an abundant source of scandal, not only because their numbers and character seemed—and probably were—unhealthy in relation to the secular clergy and the laity, but also because too few seemed worthy of their own calling.

But even more important—and the real difference between subsequent eras and our own secularized times—was that everybody, young or old, rich or poor, then regarded it as normal and natural to choose between remaining in the world or giving it up, starting a family or becoming a cleric—a secular or religious priest or brother. Medieval society was the product of two distinct types of training: spiritual and worldly. Each had its own economic, social, and cultural conditioning and consequences, and everyone had to choose between them. To the financial advantages (the benefice system), social privileges (cultural opportunities and prospects for advancement), considerations of power and influence (episcopal sees and membership in cathedral chapters allotted according to political, dynastic, and family considerations) were added pastoral demands, selfless service of God and man, and the priestly vocation. Here was a mix to challenge and sometimes subvert the uprightness of the choice. On the other hand, this interaction of the two states of life also meant that both individual lives and the entire socio-political and cultural reality of Latin Christianity were permeated with religiousness to an extent now difficult to imagine.

To repeat, then, there is no need for a tortuous investigation of why Thomas More was led to reflect on whether he had a vocation to the religious life. This was the normal career route for countless young men, and there was nothing strange about his considering it for himself. Indeed, it would have been surprising for a young man like Thomas, well brought up, with an inclination toward the sciences and a natural and healthy piety, not to consider the clerical state. As a general rule, after all, it was thought imperative to withdraw from the world in order to attain the fullness of Christian life.

A very different question is whether Thomas felt a strong inner impulse toward the priesthood and religious life, and had to overcome a conflict between this impulse and the law studies his father had imposed on him. John More had no sympathy for his son's "modern" wish to acquire a philological and philosophical education. Erasmus wrote to Hutten: "As a young man Thomas devoted himself to the study of Greek and philosophy in which his father, otherwise a prudent and honest man, gave him so little support that it would be more correct to say that he abandoned him completely. It even seemed as if he had disowned him because he had got the impression that Thomas wanted to disavow the career followed by his father, whose professional training was in English jurisprudence. The legal profession had nothing to do with science as such, but in England the authorities in this particular discipline enjoy a very high reputation."[14] In other words, the father exerted such heavy pressure on the son, withholding financial assistance and otherwise showing disapproval in no uncertain terms, that Thomas dedicated himself to studying law, since in those days it was almost unheard of to go against one's parents' wishes.

Of course this tells us nothing about what actually went on in the depths of the soul of the Carthusians' guest. That he did not become a priest or monk simply to obey his father, to whom "man of letters" and "cleric" meant the same thing, is a very superficial suggestion, and Erasmus gives far too simplistic an explanation, probably due to his own antipathy for the religious life. Something far more complex appears to have been at work in More's heart and troubling his conscience. Later, he was to pay with his life for his loyalty to the

---

14. Erasmus of Rotterdam, *Letters*. The author cites these from the German edition, translated and edited by Walther Köhler (Wiesbaden, 1947), 254. This is from a letter of July 23, 1519, written in Amberes. (The collection will be cited as Köhler.)

hierarchical order of obedience, and it is reasonable to suppose that just as he obeyed God rather than the King, so thirty-two years earlier he would have obeyed God rather than his father if he had really been called to the priesthood.

But it was just this "really" that cost him years of inner turmoil. His son-in-law William Roper[15]—who lived under his roof, knew him at close quarters, and is an excellent witness—relates that More lived the religious life in the Charterhouse "dedicated to devotion and prayer, but without taking vows."[16] Erasmus, writing to Hutten, gives more details: "During that time, he concentrated entirely on the pursuit of piety: keeping vigil in prayer and preparing himself for the priesthood with other similar exercises. This was much more sensible than the procedure of those who throw themselves without more ado into such a difficult way of life, without putting themselves to the test beforehand. Nothing prevented him from devoting himself to that kind of life except the inability to shake off his yearning for a good woman. He preferred being a chaste husband to being a dishonest priest."[17]

This last expression alludes to the circumstances of the time when many priests violated their vow of celibacy and people were up in arms about it. The point is touched on, though only in passing, earlier in the same letter, which is in effect More's first biography: "When the time was right, he did not resist respectable flirtations in which he was happier when the females themselves opened their hearts to him than when they had to be 'conquered,' and he also preferred to be captivated by intellectual interplay rather than by the physical relationship."[18]

In sum, this was a young man attracted to modern scholarship through his dedication to classical languages and early writers, but also because of the great Christian tradition, the study of Holy Scripture and the Fathers of the Church; and so also attracted to the clerical state, where he might have combined all these things. More importantly, he was filled with a yearning to love God and give himself completely to

---

15. In regard to Roper, see Chambers 19–26. The first critical edition of *The Life of Sir Thomas More*, by Roper, by E. V. Hitchcock, was published in London in 1935 (it will be cited as Roper). The book *The Life and Death of Sir Thomas More*, by Nicholas Harpsfield, was edited by E. V. Hitchcock and R. W. Chambers in London, in 1932 (cf. Chambers, 26–32).

16. Andrés Vázquez de Prada, *Sir Tomás Moro* (Madrid, 1975), third ed., 86. Cited as Vázquez de Prada.

17. Willehad Paul Eckert, *Erasmus von Rotterdam. Wirk und Wirkung*, 2 vols. (Cologne, 1967), vol. 2, 447 (cited as Eckert).

18. Ibid., vol. 2, 443.

him. But that would have meant renouncing a human love, marriage, and having a family; and this, he came to realize, he ought not to do.

In his biography of More, Vazquez de Prada notes that Thomas, failing to find inner peace in the Charterhouse, toyed for a time with the idea of entering the Franciscans. The Spanish historian writes: "Another young man, lacking the same uprightness of character and perseverance, would have been totally discouraged after four years. But Thomas, generous where God was concerned and honest with himself, felt a mysterious, unabating restlessness in his heart, without the consolation of clearly seeing his way."[19]

How and when, then, did everything become clear to him?

More threw himself into his "dual life"—the contemplative and ascetic regimen of the Charterhouse together with close contact with the outside world: choir and canonical hours, Mass, spiritual exercises, and fasting, on the one hand; legal studies and the practice of law, lectures, discussions with friends, and social life, on the other. "Somewhat brought up in learning," says his epitaph. It was the encounter with learning that served as context for his realization that he was not called to be a priest: no tragic discovery in the circumstances, yet one that probably caused a painful twinge in some corner of his soul. The decisive moment, as suggested above, came with his encounter with the figure and work of Giovanni Pico della Mirandola.

This Italian count, who died at the youthful age of thirty-two (1463–1494), was part of an illustrious circle gathered around Lorenzo the Magnificent, a duke of the Medici family of Florence. Pico himself was a key figure in the Italian renaissance. A man of noble lineage, rich, handsome, and of great charm, possessing wide-ranging culture, outstanding intelligence, and conversational brilliance, he was the very archetype of the new age, the *homo magnus*. In a sense, he sought to break free of the medieval-Christian vision of the world as a place illuminated only by the supernatural light of God, filled with terrestrial night, and enmeshed in suffering construed as the transition into the Kingdom of God. He transforms that panorama into a radiant landscape of man's creative power, proclaiming a Kingdom of human perfection come down to earth. He was moved by an ecstatic fervor of a sort: he might gladly have put into God's mouth the ancient words of the serpent, "*eritis sicut Deus*" (You will be like God).

---

19. Vázquez de Prada, 90.

Delighted with the knowledge that Greek and Latin classicism had revived, he wanted to be more than just a connoisseur of antiquity. Not content with rediscovering the ancient writings and studying them according to philological criteria, nor complacent about his knowledge of Hebrew and his familiarity with Arab sciences and the secrets of the Eastern world, he "reached down to the deepest roots of the human psyche and the divine," as his nephew's biography of Pico puts it. In 1486, having composed his magnificently ingenuous synthetic text on human dignity (*Oratio de hominis dignitate*), Pico set down nine hundred theses containing something like the sum total of his vision of the cosmos, and, "bursting with pride on discovering the mysteries of the Hebrews, Chaldeans, Arabs, and the obscure teachings of Pythagoras and Orpheus,"[20] he invited all the learned men of Italy, and "the whole world even," to attend a scholarly disputation in Rome. (In 1487, Pope Innocent VIII declared some of his theories to be heretical and thereby put a stop to the first international academic congress.)

It was not this Pico, introduced to More by a reading of the biography, who impressed and influenced him, but the transformed and penitent Pico della Mirandola, overcome by the love of Christ. This figure, also portrayed by the nephew's book, entered into the insecure heart of Thomas. He translated the Latin biography, actually a prologue to Pico's published works, into English[21] and sent it, together with his translation of selections from the works, to a friend of his youth, Joyeuce Lee, who had become a nun of the Order of St. Clare. "Dear sister," he wrote, "of all the books that have come into your hands, this may well be the most profitable. It teaches moderation in happiness, and patience in misfortune. Nowhere will you find anything better on the rejection of worldly goods and the pursuit of eternal happiness."[22]

The biography tells how one day, strolling with his nephew, Giovanni Francesco, Pico della Mirandola turned to him and said: "Nephew, keep to yourself what I am about to reveal. I have decided to give to the poor the goods I have left, embrace the cross, and go barefoot through every city and into every castle preaching Christ."[23] Different though More's situation was, he was moved by these words

20. Ibid., 106.
21. It was published under the title *The Life of J. Picus, Earl of Mirandola*, in London in 1510.
22. Blarer, 22.
23. Vázquez de Prada, 106.

precisely because they were not spoken by a cleric but by a man of the world, who had abandoned himself wholeheartedly to worldly pursuits like ambition, sensual pleasure, and sublime intellectual joy. Pico had his "Damascus"—his total conversion to Christ—in an encounter with Girolamo Savonarola, the Dominican friar of Florence whose fervent piety swept people along with him through sheer perseverance. Yesteryear's Don Juan, who moved in the most exalted circles of society wherever he went, had become a disciplined man who observed strict hours of prayer, practiced self-mortification, and despised the worldly honors that formerly he had passionately coveted.

The realization that this converted man was happy and inwardly liberated impressed Thomas deeply. For the first time, he had seen in Pico della Mirandola's example that it was possible for the laity too to give themselves to God in the midst of the world. Vazquez de Prada notes the profound relationship between the commentaries on the psalms—Pico's prayers and meditations in his latter years—and those of Thomas More near the end of his life while imprisoned in the Tower of London.[24] Under Savonarola's influence, Pico, like More, had thought of renouncing the world and entering a monastery. But, again like More, he did not. There, though, the similarities ended. Had Pico lived longer, he might well have followed the path indicated by his spiritual guide. More was confirmed in his decision not to go in that direction, although he could never entirely shake off a hankering for it.

The passages we have quoted from Pico della Mirandola are from his *Twelve Rules*, the work of the Italian which, together with the biography, More had translated. They comprise a set of suggestions to help with the inner struggle to resist the temptations and seduction of sin— they are an anticipation of the *Twenty-Two Rules of the Enchiridion militis christiani* ("Brief Manual of the Christian Soldier") by Erasmus, published in 1501. After the *Twelve Rules*, which with notable brevity seek to facilitate liberation from the things of this world, come *Twelve Conditions* that those who long to be near God—to love the Love— must satisfy. The first condition is: *Amare unum tantum et contemnere omnia pro eo*. More paraphrases this as:

> The first thing is to love only one love.
> And for its sake abandon all others. . . .

---

24. Ibid., 104–114.

How can a divided love satisfy
The One who is undivided Love?[25]

The undivided love that had once taken hold of and transformed Pico della Mirandola was not yet developed fully in the young More, but it was growing slowly and unobserved in his soul.

The encounter with the work of Pico served to influence his ambitions and literary creativity in his *Utopia*, his *History of Richard III*,[26] and, essentially all his works.

We know that More entertained the idea of writing something like a contemporary history of England extending to the death of Henry VII in 1509. But his only effort along these lines were of Richard III, last king of the House of York—an unhappy and criminal king whose defeat in the struggle against Henry Tudor and death in the battle of Bosworth in 1485 brought to an end the era of the "War of the Roses." The work, begun in 1514, remained fragmentary because the writing of *Utopia* in 1515/1516 prevented its completion and because Thomas may well have reasoned that his way of writing history by portraying kings as weak, fallible beings and reproaching them for their sins may not have been altogether prudent just then. So he abandoned the project.

More's treatise *The Four Last Things*, written in December, 1522, also remained unfinished and was unpublished until the complete edition of his works appeared in 1557. The text provides an unusual insight into a man who had been in the service of the King for the past four years and for one year was Vice-Chancellor of the Exchequer. In this latter capacity he performed with the utmost discretion and skill the substantial role as official channel of communication between sovereign and chancellor. Henry VIII held him in high esteem, while the Chancellor, Cardinal Wolsey, used him and protected him. He spent many days at Court, away from his family, in a setting governed by the whims of power.

The pedagogical nature of this treatise deserves consideration. Deeply involved in the education of his favorite daughter, Margaret, More challenged her to a literary contest in which father and daughter

---

25. *Works*, 25; Vázquez de Prada, 109.
26. *The Yale Edition of the Complete Works of St. Thomas More*, Vol. 2: "The History of King Richard III," ed. by R. S. Sylvester (New Haven-London, 1963). This Yale publication of the *Complete Works* will be cited as *CW*.

would commit to writing their thoughts on the grand theme of *The Last Four Things*. This was nothing unusual either for More or for the times. *Memento mori* ("remember that you have to die") has been a preoccupation of men of all ranks throughout the centuries. In particular, the late Gothic era, the fading Middle Ages, and Renaissance (though the latter more as a necessary curb on its arrogant denial of the inevitability of dying) were accustomed to stage performances of the Dances of Death. As a child, More had fearfully watched those highly realistic performances in London's St. Paul's Cathedral. Now he saw life as a kind of stage setting in which both the drama of history and all it's individual acts ended in a dance of death. At the same time, death was the divinely ordained transition into the "great rest" of eternal peace in reality and not just inside a theater.

Even some people close to More later suspected him of having a scrupulous conscience together with a pride concealed behind the mask of conscience and something akin to spiritual arrogance. But More knew how to strike an inner balance between fear and hope. He was convinced that man is born with the possibility, though not the certainty, of salvation. Though an intellectual, he did not despise the spiritual means equally available to ordinary people: Holy Mass, regular prayer, contemplation of the mysteries of redemption, reciting the psalms and the Rosary, asceticism. Although cheerful and sociable, for the love of God he suppressed the slightest sign of sensuality or egocentrism. Among outstanding traits of his character was a simplicity never coarse in its ingenuousness and childlike but not childish.

The Old Testament Book of Ecclesiastes provided a model for *The Four Last Things*. No other text in Holy Scripture focuses so forcefully on mortality and death. This iron law of life on earth is the measure of worldly things and of oneself. "All is vanity," the leitmotif at the core of the sayings of Solomon, the Preacher in Ecclesiastes, was the governing principle of Thomas More's life. Dying and death, just like birth, are summonses from God. Whether death be quick and painless or difficult and agonizing, it is always the call of Love. Such was Thomas More's faith, a faith that never wavered, expressed in letters and writings like the ones that concern us here, and later in the *Dialogue of Comfort against Tribulation*, as he awaited a death he expected to come in a most cruel form.

Thomas tells us to think frequently and realistically about our own deaths.

You must visualize yourself lying on your deathbed—the moribund heart beats excessively, and the blood pumps unrhythmically in your veins—your back is aching and your head is splitting open with fever—the death rattle is gasping in the throat and your flesh shakes with the shivers and, as life ebbs away, a stiffness takes hold in your legs; the breath shortens, your strength dissipates and your fingers grope in search of an impalpable handgrip that is not there.[27]

More had no illusions. Life is "an incurable illness," and once we realize that, we should look on death "not as a stranger but as our next-door neighbor,"[28] something that, properly understood, is not particularly difficult or frightening but perfectly natural. On May 17, 1521, two weeks after his appointment as Vice-Chancellor, More had witnessed an instance at close range.

Edward Stafford, Duke of Buckingham, was beheaded in the Tower of London for high treason. It was the beginning of a long series of judicial murders, including eventually that of More himself, ordered by the system of justice during the reign of Henry VIII. The indictment, trial, and sentence passed on the Duke, the most powerful nobleman in England after the King, were fabricated around events that supposedly took place eight years earlier, when Princess Mary, the future Queen, had not yet even been born. Tittle-tattle and calumnies fueled rumors that the Duke, a descendant of Edward III and a relative of Henry, clung to the hope of succeeding him should the Tudor king die without issue.

On Henry's part, the question of succession was breeding concern and irritation that culminated in despotic action. Apart from one daughter, his wife, Catherine of Aragon, had given birth only to children who were either stillborn or soon died. In those days the idea of a succession via the female line was totally alien and unthinkable, so that the King's extreme sensitivity on this point is not hard to understand. But this hardly seems sufficient to warrant an execution. A degenerative process was gradually becoming apparent in Henry's personality. Lack of sexual moderation and resulting cruelty, an attractive, regal persona, fawning adulation from courtiers, the renaissance notion of royal power, and an ethos of opportunism all combined to encourage the monarch in the exercise of power. The young, handsome, apparently sensitive

---

27. *Works*, 77; Vázquez de Prada, 254.
28. *Works*, 81; Vázquez de Prada, 255.

and pious, picture-book King was transformed into a figure with tiny, malevolent eyes set in the plump face we know so well from portraits.

Not just this aspect of the Stafford case must have made the author of *The Four Last Things* shudder, but the speed with which the wheel of fate revolves: from heights to depths, from wealth and splendor to wretchedness and proscription, from the lifestyle of a magnate to a criminal's death on the scaffold. "All is vanity"—and here was a graphic illustration of Solomon the Preacher's words. Thus More speaks of the powerful Duke, who, at the moment of expecting to see his daughter wed, suddenly found himself in prison, his court dispersed, his goods confiscated, his wife flung into misery, his children disinherited, and himself judged without further inquiry—his coat of arms dishonored, his gilt spurs broken to pieces, and he hanged and quartered.[29]

Conscience did not allow More to wait idly for death and the hereafter, but spurred him on to prepare for it. That meant seeking and following Christ, which for him meant loving his neighbor in everyday life by conscientiously fulfilling his professional duties, goodness in family life, work that strives to achieve the physical, intellectual, and spiritual welfare of one's neighbor. And something more: living at close quarters with Jesus Christ in prayer, Holy Mass, the sacraments, and sacrifice. This unity of Christian life[30] was ingrained in him—a cheerful dinner companion who was also a deep thinker, an intellectual polemicist and valued jurist who was a humble man of prayer and preferred mercy to strict justice, a generous and practical family man who yearned for the stillness of a cloister. This servant of the King served the King of Kings at Mass; beneath the trappings of office, this courtier wore a penitent's garment that caused sores; this successful literate man offset the favor of his sovereign and popularity with the public by fasting, going without sleep, and caring for the poor. For him, *memento mori* was never separate from *memento vivere* ("remember that you live").

Before going briefly into the details of his life, More's epitaph mentions the stages of his career. A few words ("after spending several years of his youth practicing as defense lawyer in the courts, having first been a judge and later sub-sheriff in his native city") cover nearly a decade and a half. The barrister becomes a judge, the judge becomes an officer of the Crown and Head of Government.

---

29. *Works*, 81; Vázquez de Prada, 255.
30. In regard to this, see the Epilogue to this book.

In this transition from the Middles Ages to early modern times, men trained in the law were rapidly assuming positions previously held by clerics. A state in the process of secularizing, separating itself from the Church, and becoming an autonomous network of power relationships more and more required its own staff of civil servants. The movement toward State absolutism was underway throughout Europe—a movement that in time would give rise to the modern state, with its civil servants and bureaucrats.

In England, the start of this evolution can be dated with pinpoint accuracy, summed up by two names. In 1529 the Lord Chancellor, Cardinal Wolsey, after fourteen years of virtually single-handed government, was succeeded by Thomas More, Chancellor of the Duchy of Lancaster. For the first time, a layman held the highest administrative office in the land, and from then on, that would always be so.

Erasmus took a dim view of law: "This profession has nothing to do with science as such, but in England anyone who has acquired authority in that discipline enjoys very high prestige, and there no one is considered learned in matters of law unless he has sweated over them for many years. More, who was made for better things, in spirit abhorred his law studies, yet he became such an expert in the subject that not even those dedicated solely to the profession could boast a better practice."[31] Bremond shares this disdain. "We do not need to waste time on his career in the courts, for it is not there that we find the real More. Like so many other people, he devoted the best years of his life to a profession he did not love."[32]

Is this true? I am not aware of any evidence pointing to the repugnance for the study of the law of which Erasmus speaks, or suggesting that he practiced his profession half-heartedly or under constraints, as Bremond seems to suggest. True, More so loved the rediscovered treasures of classical culture that sometimes he had to snatch time for them from what should have been hours of sleep; and now and then he lamented not being as free to engage in scholarship as his learned friends were. But this does not conflict with dedication to his profession. It

---

31. Desiderius Erasmus, *Opus epistolarum*, published by P. S. and H. M. Allen, H. W. Garrod, 12 Vols., (Oxford 1906–1958), IV, 999, 17 (referred to as: Allen, volume, number of letter and page). Cf. Chambers, 95; Eckert vol. 2, 444.

32. Henri Bremond: *Le Bienhereux Thomas More* (Paris, 1904). The author quotes from the German edition: *Thomas Morus, Lordkanzeler, Humanist und Martyrer*. Published by Johannes Maria Hocht and Rudolf von der Wend (Ratisbon, 1949), 51 (referred to as: Bremond).

was precisely the memory of an honorable barrister, a just judge, a man known and respected by all, that his fellow countrymen kept for decades after his death. Spiritual life, professional pursuits and private studies never became mutual obstacles.

In his epitaph, More makes no mention of his parliamentary debut in 1504. He had been admitted to the bar in 1501,[33] while living in the London Charterhouse and wrestling with the question of whether he had a religious vocation. Quickly acquiring prestige, he was elected a member of the Parliament opening in January, 1504.

The twenty-six-year-old parliamentarian caused Henry VII a few headaches. The King, a very thrifty, not to say stingy, individual, had the right to exact financial assistance from Parliament for certain matters related to the royal household. Now, as Roper relates, he was demanding ninety thousand pounds for his son Arthur, the Prince of Wales, who had died in 1502, aged fifteen, and his daughter Margaret, who had married King James IV of Scotland in August, 1503. Parliament understandably balked, and in the forefront was young More, who "put forward such convincing arguments and reasonings that the King's demands were roundly reduced to tatters."[34] Having to make do with half the sum he had demanded and learning that it was a young man barely old enough to shave who had demolished his plans, Henry VII flew into a rage. According to Roper, he took vengeance not on Thomas but on his father, John More, whom he imprisoned in the Tower of London in 1503/4, on some pretext sufficing, and kept him there until he paid a hundred pounds.[35] Whether this incident happened exactly as Roper tells it is uncertain, but in any case the father/son relationship did not suffer because of it.

The young man's upward trajectory was steady and straight. In the spring of 1505 we find him a member of the Mercer's Company, a reliable man whom the London cloth and silk merchants trusted with their legal affairs. In January, 1510, as one of the representatives elected by the City of London, he entered the first Parliament of Henry VIII, who had come to the throne the year before. Eight months later he was appointed sub-Sheriff of London, one of two officers with a legal background who assisted the Lord Mayor in all hearings that came

---

33. Germain Marc'hadour: *L'Univers de Thomas More, Chronologie critique de More, Erasme et leur epoque (1477–1536)*, (Paris, 1963), 115 (referred to as: *L'Univers*).

34. Roper, 7; Chambers, 97.

35. Ibid.

within the municipal jurisdiction. For eight years, until the summer of 1518, when he transferred from the municipal to the royal service, he held a court session every Thursday morning. Of his activities as barrister and subsequently as judge, which earned him wide popularity, Erasmus observes: "Despite making his living from his law practice he gave everyone his affable and honest advice; he was more concerned about the benefit to his clients than to himself: as a rule he persuaded them against litigation, as it would be cheaper that way; and when he did not succeed in this, he would show them the least costly way to sue, for there are people who take delight even in litigation. In London, his native city, he presided as judge in the civil tribunals. Nobody saw as many cases through to term, or more incorruptibly, as he did. He used to return his fees to the majority of litigants."[36]

Looking at the seemingly endless catalogue of posts and duties entrusted to him by election or appointment during those years, one gets some feel for the high degree of trust he enjoyed. He is Justice of the Peace in Hampshire, frequently a professor in Lincoln's Inn school of law, a governor of this renowned academic institution, a teacher in the Furnivall's Inn school of law, and a member of the Doctors' Commons association of scholars (1514) composed almost entirely of barristers. He is responsible for the Christmas and Epiphany festivities in Lincoln's Inn (1510); concerns himself with fishermen's problems, with drainage canals (1514), is in charge of controlling weights and measures (1517) and regulating food prices (1516). He is also a mediator or arbitrator, in 1517, in a dispute between two of St. Vedastus' parishioners and the guild of leather-workers. He serves as legal adviser and spokesman for delegations of municipal judges, bakers, and guilds of London's artisans. When the latter rioted against foreigners, he helped calm the situation, afterwards obtaining clemency for those thrown in jail and setting up an inquiry into the causes of the riot.[37] From this incomplete list it is clear that More enjoyed a special reputation as a prudent and sincere representative in a variety of contexts, including the Court, the Council Royal, and the House of Lords.

Official and informal contacts at Court and, above all, with the head of government, Cardinal Wolsey, led almost naturally to More's

---

36. Allen, vol. 4, 999, 20; Chambers, 118; Eckert, vol. 2, 448f.
37. *L'Univers*, 169–267.

summoning to the King's service. According to Roper, More had caught the King's eye, not for the first time, in the midst of an international litigation. A papal vessel had been seized by order of Henry VIII, and More defended the Pope's side. The settlement, which More worked out in a manner satisfactory to all, as well as his positive performance as part of a legation to Flanders in 1515 and a commercial delegation to Calais in 1517, convinced Wolsey and the King that they needed the services of such a man. The transition took place gradually. Since his first annual salary was paid in the summer of 1518 retroactive to the previous autumn, his new position can be dated from then; in July, 1518, he resigned as sub-Sheriff of London, though that in no way affected his close links with the city in whose interests he continued to act repeatedly as representative and spokesman.

Still, it was impossible to serve city and Crown simultaneously without conflicts arising, and it was easy to see why he opted in favor of the latter: the difficulty or virtual impossibility of declining a call from Wolsey and the King; the high esteem it implied; desire for a better position; service beyond the regional level; and material progress. But he understandably felt some sadness, distress, and anxiety as well. The Archbishop of Canterbury, William Warham, Lord Chancellor from 1504 to 1515 and Wolsey's predecessor, had given up the office at his own request; he was a generous, pious, incorruptible servant of Church and Crown. More wrote him in January, 1517: "If a man relinquishes such an honor of his own free will, surely this is a sign of great modesty and even greater integrity. I know of no one who would have been so modest as to give up of his own volition such an exalted and brilliant post; nobody is so above all ambition that he can value at so little the post of Lord Chancellor!"[38] Yet More, for reasons deeper than Warham's, would resign it in time. The letter goes on to compare the leisure time and freedom to devote to spiritual and scholarly pursuits now enjoyed by Warham with the writer's own situation: "But the more I go on emphasizing the pleasant aspects of your life, the more conscious I am of my own lamentable state: for although I am not entrusted with important business affairs, my scant capabilities tend to dissipate my energies in trivialities; I am always too busy; I cannot set aside a quiet moment all to myself."[39]

38. Blarer, 48.
39. Ibid., 49.

Was More able to reconcile his desire for the contemplative life, scholarly and literary pursuits, and high public office? On October 25, 1517, More writes to Erasmus from Calais, where, accompanied by Sir Richard Wingfield and Dr. William Knight, he is engaged in negotiations with French merchants: "You do well to keep away from the vainglorious activities of princes, and the fact that you should desire to see me free of them too shows the affection in which you hold me. You would not believe how utterly tired I am of all these things. Nothing could be more detestable to me than this mission. If I already loathe legal affairs in my own country, where at least I earn money thereby, you can imagine how intensely they bore me here, where, on top of everything else, I am losing money."[40]

But did More really abhor "legal matters" or is that only half the story? Certainly it pleased Erasmus that his British friend assured him repeatedly that he envied his way of life, free of so many worries, and wished he could lead a similar life. And undoubtedly, More meant it. But in fact he had chosen a different life for himself, that of a working horse in harness.

"Only reluctantly have I accepted a post at Court," he wrote to John Fisher, Bishop of Rochester, immediately after taking office in 1518, "Everyone knows that, and the King sometimes in jest chides me for my aversion."[41] Remarks like this usually involve some posing, and More was not entirely exempt from doing that. In belittling his merits, dismissing promotions and tributes, and praising what others did as more important that his own achievements, he did so in a style that to present-day tastes appears exaggerated; but he was simply following the social etiquette of his day, when rhetorical courtesy and ritual often coexisted with extreme coarseness and people admired, vilified, adulated, and hated each other passionately and without restraint. In More's case especially, all these conflicts and contradictions, internal and external, came together in the peace of divine filiation—not just theoretical knowledge of oneself as a creature of God and therefore his son, but becoming a child of God really and existentially, innocent and trusting, quickly comforted, soon made happy and cheerful after sadness and fear. All these qualities were present in Thomas More in the last years of his life, particularly at times of danger and persecution and also in his martyrdom.

---

40. Allen, vol. 3, 688; Chambers, 183.
41. Blarer, 52.

But these traits were not fully developed in More at the outset. They grew gradually, overcoming opposed tendencies such as that of poking fun at intellectual and cultural inferiors, like his second wife, Lady Alice, or the monks who scorned the new scientific spirit of the times; his excessive esteem for classico-philological erudition, and, most seriously, his ironic streak. Irony, something very different from humor, can be a defense mechanism or a mask, disdain for others or the only weapon of defense against the power of the mighty; but always it expresses a high degree of self-awareness and is the polar opposite of ingenuousness. Irony and innocence are almost always mutually exclusive, and this makes More's irony a key issue. He possessed a marvelous and deeply pious adult ingenuousness, and that was his state of mind in setting out on the final road to his death. Thus the question is how his sarcasm was transformed into the simplicity of a humble heart—or whether what to us seems to have been irony was not that at all.

The puzzle can be illustrated by a passage in More's epitaph: "The invincible Henry VIII called him to his Court, that King unique among kings, to whom had been granted the honor of bearing the title 'Defender of the Faith,' a title won by the sword and pen." Surely there is a bitter laughter here, occasioned by the fact that Henry in 1521 had received from Pope Leo X the title *Defensor Fidei* in recognition for his book against Luther, the *Assertio Septem Sacramentorum* (Defense of the Seven Sacraments). When More wrote those words in 1532, the King was already divorced from his wife Catherine and on the eve of marrying Ann Boleyn, and the clergy, under pressure, had accepted him as Head of the Church of England. Complete separation from Rome and total disintegration of the Catholic Church in the kingdom could already be foreseen. Thomas had no illusions, and against this background deferring to the defense of the faith by sword and pen (an allusion to the execution of heretics) and calling "invincible" a sovereign with few successes in war looks a bit like black humor.

2.

To understand it, we need to look back to the history of England as it passed from the fifteenth to the sixteenth century, and to the person and policies of the second Tudor monarch. The Hundred Years War (1338–1453) between England and France had decisive consequences for both sides. The attempt by England, a country created in 1066 by

Norman conquerors, to regain the land of her origins, uniting both countries and peoples under one crown, had failed. But the war had the effect of reinforcing national identity in both France and England. The national unity of England, already very advanced during Henry VIII's times, had its genesis in the internecine battles known from Shakespeare's plays, to which the name "the Wars of the Roses" was given. These were the immediate continuation and consequence of the foreign wars that had ended in defeat and withdrawal. The bloody and brutal struggle for the Crown pitted against each other the Houses of Lancaster and York, known by their respective Red Rose and White Rose insignias.

In this conflict lasting for decades Edward IV (1461–1483), of the House of York, finally got the upper hand in 1461, thanks to the help of Burgundy and, more importantly, of the wealthy middle-classes. In a way similar to the France of Louis XI (1461–1483), exhausted by the Hundred Years War, Edward IV, in an England exhausted by the civil wars, sought to shore up the position of the Crown, but with less success. In France, from the second half of the fifteenth century onward, royal power became increasingly secure, despite setbacks under the last of the Valois,[42] the Huguenot wars, and the feuding nobility, leading to the absolutism of the era of Richelieu and the Bourbons. But the similar attempt in England failed. Despite the apparently limitless power of Henry VIII or Elizabeth I, England does not continue along the road of European absolutist monarchy. As in the days of Magna Carta, the monarchy retains ties with Parliament, though now via the middle-classes rather than the great lords of feudal times.

After decades of passivity in her foreign policies, as a result of the Hundred Years War and internal disorders, the England of the first Tudor king, Henry VII, took her place in the triangle of tension and conflict formed by England, France, and Spain. This triumvirate was to determine the course of European and transatlantic history well into the eighteenth century. At first, England was content to pursue an opportunistic policy, given that the conflicts—struggles over Italy, Burgundy, the Low Countries—involved France and the House of Austria which, besides the imperial crown and her own territories, had obtained the Spanish crown by inheritance along with its possessions in the New World. England made sure that her support for one side or the

---

42. The children of Henry II and Catherine of Medici: Francis II (1559–1560), Charles IX (1560–1574), Henry III (1574–1589).

other should be well rewarded. The success of this policy of changing alliances depended on betting consistently on the winner, while seeking at all costs to prevent a lasting reconciliation between the other two great powers.

The first phase of this game was marked by the Anglo-Hispano alliance. Spain, under attack from France in Italy, looked for relief and assistance to an English attack in the northeast of France. England, which still dominated Calais and had not yet abandoned dreams of recovering her lost power on the other side of the Channel and of appropriating Brittany, saw in Spain a natural ally, particularly since trade between the two countries was flourishing. Already in 1489, in Medina del Campo, marriage had been arranged between four-year-old Catherine, younger daughter of Isabel of Castile and Ferdinand of Aragon, and Arthur, heir to the English throne and not quite two years old. The wedding took place in 1501, but Arthur died five months before his sixteenth birthday. In 1503, Catherine, eighteen by now, was betrothed to Arthur's younger brother, Henry, then aged twelve. None of the aspirations and objectives of that alliance were fulfilled. In the event, England did not conquer Brittany nor did Spain find relief in its fight against the French invasion of Italy (from 1495 onward). But the marriage between Henry VIII and Catherine of Aragon was to have far-reaching consequences, becoming a matter of life or death for many.

As the medieval political system, with its personalized and transcendent orientation, gave way to the state apparatus of the Modern Age, with its all-embracing and secular character, steadily growing importance was attached to logical, reasonable norms of law. This development took place in tandem with the acceptance of Roman Law, superimposing itself on the ancient rights of both individuals and communities, and ensuring the gradual disappearance of the latter. The actions of the state were held to require a formal legal basis. Thus, Henry VII sought legitimization of his authority by lawful means instead of assassinations and cloak-and-dagger intrigues. Not that injustice and crime now vanished—they abounded in the reigns of Henry VIII and Elizabeth I—but they became "legalized," enshrined as matters of public law. The first Tudor king did not permit himself to be carried away by the ideal of holiness of Edward the Confessor (1042–1066), the chivalry of Richard the Lion-Hearted (1189–1199), or the thirst for power of Richard III. Instead he was guided by calculated profit motives.

A Privy Council commission charged with securing power by legal means went on to become the Supreme Court of the Realm, the Star Chamber, so-called because of the design on the ceiling of the hall where it met. In its very close relationship with the King, it personified the new system of justice. The function of this body, which worked swiftly and thoroughly, consisted in stopping private wars among the feudal lords, eliminating private armies, prosecuting sheriffs' crimes, the bribing of municipal judges, and the bending of the law by those who held local power. The preferred penalties for crimes like these were heavy fines that imposed appreciable losses on existing or potential enemies.[43] Above all, it was the landed gentry, the rich merchant urban middle class, and the small rural nobility who benefited from this new legal regime. Finding judicial support in the Star Chamber, they increasingly went on to assume responsibility for local administration and jurisprudence. From among their ranks were recruited the Justices of the Peace, including, for many years, Thomas More. The gentry showed their gratitude for this royal favor by paying heavier taxes, and the wealthy bourgeoisie even paid special taxes "voluntarily." Henry VII's outstanding ability to find new sources of funds permanently boosted state revenue. This acute awareness of the link between power and money, coupled with shrewdness in exploiting it in a calculating, businesslike manner, justify us in calling this first of the Tudors a modern ruler, though without, of course, stretching the idea too far.

But the king's modernity had limits. He appears not to have grasped the significance of the discoveries occurring overseas. He rejected Columbus's offer to undertake the great voyage westward in his name. In 1497/1498, following the discovery of America, Giovanni Caboto (John Cabot) of Genoa was commissioned to make two trips intended to find the western route to China that was ardently sought at the time. Cabot reached North America, but he brought back nothing of value, and interest in the New World ebbed in London.

In 1509 the founder of the Tudor dynasty lay dying at the age of fifty-two after a reign of almost a quarter of a century. During this time the position of the Crown had become secure and the foundations of a modern state had been laid, but the Crown's power was very far from

---

43. Ernst Schulin, *England und Schottland vom Ende des Hundertjahrigen Kieges bis zum Protektorat Cromwells (1455–1660)*, in *Handbuch der eurospaischen Geschichte*, edited by Theodor Schieder, vol. 3: "*Die Entstehung des neuzeitlichen Europa*," edited by Josef Engel, 907.

being absolute, while the state remained deeply steeped in the conventions of the Middle Ages. Although it had learned how to dominate the high nobility, the English monarchy, unlike its counterparts in France and Spain, did not dominate the nation as a whole. In finances, the Crown remained dependent on Parliament, particularly the House of Commons, and the gentry. Creation of a centralized administration for the whole country by the Royal House never got beyond initial proposals and first steps. The rural nobility maintained their position, and the Justices of the Peace also enjoyed substantial autonomy in relation to the King.

As with the development of the state and society, so too in the case of the Church in England, religious, social, and political factors had by this time become intertwined. Although the break from Rome in 1535 was a violent event deeply linked to Henry's personal and dynastic problems, it was far from unrelated to the evolution that the relationship between Crown and papacy had undergone during the previous two centuries.

Despite occasional quarrels with the papacy and the Church, the English bishops, clergy, and senior nobility were all loyal to the Pope. (The gentry are another story: for intellectual and economic reasons they harbored a traditional enmity toward Rome.) It is therefore a remarkable fact that, with few exceptions they now followed the King, without resistance or demur, acquiescing with something akin to resignation. And yet, there were historical reasons. The argument that even after separating from the Pontiff, the English Church remained Catholic at first inasmuch as no one had schism in view, is not tenable. For one thing, a church separated from Peter is no longer the one instituted by Christ, as Thomas More and his friend John Fisher, Bishop of Rochester, saw quite well. For another thing, the nation in general readily accepted the changes entailed in "Protestantization," so that thirty years after the Act of Supremacy, England was a Protestant country even if the vestments and liturgical forms had not changed. Evidently, despite more than a millennium of instruction by the Church, the faith, in all its fullness and integrity, had not taken root in souls to the extent that might be supposed by someone viewing the Middle Ages superficially. Much medieval devotion failed to rise above the levels of custom, traditions, and social convention. And this, one might say, has been the common state of affairs in the Church, from the first Pentecost until now.

Pope Boniface VIII's exaggerated claims of spiritual and moral dominion, as expressed in the bull *Unam Sanctam* of 1302, were soon followed by the papacy's decline. Rome had managed to maintain for hardly more than a half century the independence it had won in a struggle with the emperors of the Holy Roman-Germanic Empire extending over the previous century and a half. For those with eyes to see, it should have been apparent that the clash with peoples on the way to nationhood, in particular France and England, would be no less violent, passionate, and dangerous than the struggle with the universal empire of the Germans had been.

The Avignon exile or "Babylonian captivity" of the Church (1308 to 1377) and the subsequent Great Schism (1378 to 1415) caused the papacy a tremendous loss of authority. The simultaneous presence in the field of several claimants to Peter's throne in practice left it to the sovereign of each territory to decide which one to recognize, so that the rival "popes" naturally courted the sovereigns. At the same time, the local episcopate and local sovereign of each territory were drawn closer together by the common effort to establish who would be pope for their country.

Pope and anti-Pope alike had to pay for support by relinquishing rights. Strong monarchies attempted to reduce political and legal influence from Rome, while subjecting the episcopate to Crown and state, and as far as possible exercising dominion over the Church. A weak monarchy, on the other hand, sought to make common cause with the See of St. Peter and courted the bishops to secure their help, instead of demanding their subservience. Thus, the state increasingly became the auxiliary of the Church, as was evident in England. In the days of the Great Schism and the strong kings of the House of Plantagenet, Henry IV (1399–1413) and Henry V (1413–1432), the Church depended on the Crown. A few decades later, with the weak kings of the House of Lancaster during the War of the Roses, the relationship is reversed: papal authority gains strength, while the English episcopate becomes the most important power center in the realm and plays a decisive part in governing it.

Relations at the highest levels of Church and State, among the King, the Pope, and the bishops, were of great importance in pushing through the Tudor reform, but even more important was the relationship between Church and society. In 1221 and 1225 the Dominican and Franciscan mendicant orders[44] had established themselves in England; they became the driving force in religious renewal and the growth of piety, as well as the critics of a worldly, feudalist hierarchy enmeshed in politics, and of social poverty; in More's times, they even became a source of scandal. Although steadfast in their faith and loyal to the Pope, they thus prepared the ground for rebellion, without intending to. Meanwhile, the decay of discipline in other congregations persisted: Their members lived like secular clergy and their abbots resembled members of the rural nobility, more outstanding for producing wool than praying the canonical hours.[45]

Over and above all this was the painful situation of the secular clergy. Their numbers, too, were excessive. "Almost ten thousand priests had no regular pastoral work," Kluxen reports. Of the eight to nine thousand parish posts, half were tied to monasteries, cathedrals, and "colleges," administered by curates earning only a pittance.[46] One result was that all those who could afford it, especially the wealthy brotherhoods and artisans and merchants' guilds, had their own chapels, with priests to say Mass, preach, and pray. These private chapels became centers of personal religious practice and widespread criticism of the Church.

John Wycliffe (1320–1384) anticipated not only the ideas that Martin Luther was to announce a century and a half later, but the whole of the doctrine and preaching of the Protestant reform. This included views on the Church, the papacy, grace, free will, justification, sacraments, priesthood, and many other matters. In the same way, too, the religious rebellion of Lutheranism in time was transformed into a social revolution of rural wars and the Anabaptist movement. Wycliffe's overall assault on the faith and constitution of the Church tended toward Lollardism.[47]

---

44. Mendicant orders are those in which not only the members but the Order dispenses with all possessions. They began in the thirteenth century, mostly through the activities of St. Francis of Assisi; over time, the prohibition of owning assets weakened. Another essential difference between them and the older orders lies in the connection between convent life and extramural pastoral activities and also their centralist constitutions. Strictly speaking, nowadays the Franciscans and Capuchins are mendicant orders, though in a wider sense Augustinians, Dominicans, and Carmelites could be considered such.

45. Kurt Kluxen, *Geschichte Englands* (Stuttgart, 1968), 155.

46. Ibid.

47. The name comes from a Dutch expression for members of a sect pejoratively called "Lollards" either analogously with "luller" (i.e., those who sing with low voices) or with the followers of Walter Lollard, burned at the stake as a heretic in 1322 (Kluxen, 160).

Although the ecclesiastical and secular powers, making common cause, succeeded in defeating the great peasant revolt of 1381, purging the University of Oxford, intellectual center of Wycliffe's partisans, and driving the Lollards underground, Wycliffe's followers did not disappear. Their ideas on things like a universal priesthood, equality among all sinners, lay Masses, putting the assets of the Church to use for the common good, and so forth entered into the intellectual currents of the time and spread throughout western and central Europe, particularly in Bohemia, where Hus had declared himself a partisan and successor of Wycliffe.

In the fifteenth century, the Crown and the episcopate succeeded with difficulty in silencing Wycliffe and Lollardism. State and Church had combined to rescue one another. No longer, however, were they partners of equal strength or equally in need of assistance; rather as the unity and discipline of the faith continued to crumble, and the authority of the Church over Christians declined, the alliance between Church and state was being transformed into a protectorate of state over Church. This redistribution of power was not acknowledged as long as the Crown and Parliament saw preserving the dual order as necessary to survival; but once the outlines of a new, different, secular, and emancipated order were discerned, the powerlessness of the Church, Rome, and the papacy, lacking means of their own to retain authority, suddenly became apparent. Thus the third decade of the sixteenth century was the dawn of a long era for Europe in which the will of the sovereign decided which religion his subjects were to embrace.

❧❧❧

There appeared to be no doubt about this where Henry VIII was concerned. The young sovereign behaved as if he were not merely faithful to Rome and the Pope but indeed strictly orthodox and, for many long years, a supporter of the Holy See. When Henry became King at the age of eighteen in 1509, nobles, clergy, gentry, and above all the learned humanists and all those avid for exploits, fondly imagined that a golden age for the happy island had begun. "The heavens smile and the earth rejoices," Lord Mountjoy writes to his old teacher, Erasmus, in Rome, inviting him to visit England, where "everything is full of milk, honey and nectar. Greed has fled the country. Our King aspires to possess neither gold, jewels, nor precious metals, but virtue, glory, and immortality instead."[48]

---

48. Mentioned in Chambers, 114.

More sincerely shared this opinion. On the occasion of the coronation of Henry and Catherine in June, he was not the only one to compose a poem of homage. His was called *Carmen Gratulatorium*, and in it, with considerable audacity, he celebrated the end of tyranny, the coming of liberty, the return of justice, the King's noble philosophical and artistic formation, his hugely promising provenance,[49] the fidelity and courage of the Queen, and their future sons and grandsons, who would provide continuity to the dynasty. It was a flattering, conventional poem in the contemporary manner, by a young jurist of good repute, cultured, and well versed in literature, a member of a generation of humanists, relishing the best in life, seeking to call his new sovereign's attention to himself. In an accompanying letter, the author emphasizes his classical background by quoting a passage from Suetonius. He ends with the hope that his congratulations, though arriving *post festum*, "may not be deemed ill-conceived. I am protected against such a failure by the enormous happiness of all at Thine accession to the throne, the remembrance of which has remained deeply engraved in every heart; the enthusiasm it has brought about will neither grow old nor ever fade away."[50]

Of course, More was wrong about that, as were so many of his contemporaries; but many years were to pass before the monstrous nature of the King would make itself patently obvious—though it was already present in the young monarch, wearing its comely face. His figure, afterwards voluminous and obese, was still trim and athletic. The thin mouth and tiny eyes, at once cruel and effeminate in the later portraits, were merely delicate. Sensuality, later marked by psychopathic lust, was open and attractive. The regal pride, which later would lose all semblance of moral sensitivity and become despotism, was captivating still, easily mistaken for the conceit of a young prince whom nature and destiny had too much favored. Here was the very prototype of an ideal sovereign in those times.

Henry was superb at jousting, a tireless horseman, a master at archery; he had a good humanist education, spoke Latin, French, and Italian, and possessed an excellent knowledge of theology. He seemed at first to see his task as ruler not as the formulation and imposition

---

49. More stresses the prudence of the father, Henry VII, the goodness of the mother, Elizabeth of York, the piety of the paternal grandmother, Lady Margaret Beaufort, and the noble warrior sense of the maternal grandfather, Edward IV. Chambers, 112.

50. Blarer, 29.

of policy down to the level of everyday affairs, but as being a kind of kingly Sun, the radiant center of a circle of optimistic, capable, and ambitious men of the new era.

To be the living icon of that era of change and that nation at its zenith was a full-time occupation, even if daily political tasks were delegated to the Lord Chancellor—until 1515 Warham, Archbishop of Canterbury, later Wolsey, Archbishop of York—and their people. Hunting, jousts, court festivities, disputes with scholars, audiences with envoys, correspondence and consultations completely absorbed the king's time. Yet while allowing his Chancellor great freedom of action in the first decade, Henry was well informed.

The Papal Nuncio in England, Chieregati, described an audience the King granted him in 1516: "One day the King summoned his envoys and invited them to eat in his chambers. The Queen's presence was something altogether exceptional. After the meal, the King began to sing and play musical instruments, exhibiting thus some of his extraordinary talents. Finally, he danced, doing some marvelous things."[51] The same witness tells of a joust in which the King, dressed in silver lamé, "came up to the barrier and presented himself to the Queen and ladies; then performed innumerable pirouettes in the air and, after exhausting his horse, retired to the tent and mounted another; he continued thus, appearing in the tournament over and over again. This was followed by a banquet that went on for seven hours. The King at one point dressed in a white damask, after the Turkish fashion, later in a garment embroidered with roses of diamonds and rubies, and finally in official regal clothes, lined with gold brocade and trimmed with ermine fur, which reached down to the ground."[52]

⚜ ⚜ ⚜

History tells us of other powerful public men like this: Sardanapalus, Nero, Goering. How dangerous they are depends on their inner restraint and the external barriers to their boundless thirst for power and homage. In Henry's case, both inner and outer regulators were either weak or else entirely lacking, and so he became a despot of an almost oriental sort. True, his theological training and obvious religious zeal were expressed in correct devotional observances, persecution

---

51. *Heinrich VIII, von England in Augenzeugenberichten*, published by Eberhard Jacobs and Eva de Vitray (Dusseldorf, 1969), 54 (referred to as Jacobs).
52. Ibid.

of heretics by the state, and the defense of traditional doctrine and the Pope; but it would be a mistake to take these as expressions of an interiorized Christianity acting hand in hand with humility and truth, and to suppose that they guaranteed the security of the Church in England. When Luther shook the edifice of the Church, it pleased the young King's vanity to act as its defender and protector in the eyes of the whole world, demonstrating that he was as adept in theological debate as in jousting or playing the lute. But when it occurred to him that instead of being named Defender of the Faith by the Pope, or struggling with the Pontiff over his plan to divorce Catherine, he could make himself pope and then do as he liked, he found that prospect even more gratifying. As Chesterton says, he cut off St. Peter's head and transplanted his own.

By 1515, Henry, anxious not to be outdone by the German emperor or the king of France, was angling for some lofty title signifying special approbation by the Holy See. The occasion presented itself in 1520, in the form of a book by Luther, *Of the Church's Babylonian Captivity*, attacking with huge virulence the very foundations of the Church. It said nothing new, however, being only a grandiloquent rehashing of the doctrines of Wycliffe and Hus. Henry seized the opportunity by undertaking to rebut "the grand master of heretics." Richard Pace, a cleric in the service of Wolsey, on April 16, 1521, reported to his superior that the King had conveyed to him his desire to defend the Church of Christ with the pen, and to that end would be completing in a few days a tract titled *Assertio Septem Sacramentorum* (In Defense of the Seven Sacraments).[53] A month later the royal author dispatched the work to Pope Leo X, remarking that the Holy Father could see that "he was prepared to defend the Church not only by taking up arms but with the spirit also."[54] In September, the English envoy, at a private audience, handed the Pope the luxuriously bound book, "which today" as the historian of the popes, Ludwig von Pastor comments, "can be seen exhibited in the Vatican Library, side by side with the love letters from Henry VIII to Anne Boleyn."[55] The dedication reads: "Henry, King of England, sends this work to Leo X as a token of faith and friendship."

---

53. Ibid., 78.
54. Ibid., 81.
55. Ludwig von Pastor, *Geschichte der Päpste seit dem Ausgang des Mittelalters*. Vol. 4: "Geschichte der Päpste im Zeitalter der Renaissance und der Glaubensspaltung (1513–1534)," 1st. Section: Leo X (Freiburg im Breisgau), 9th edition, 596ff.

The Pope was impressed. Urged repeatedly by Wolsey and recognizing the political advantages of a close relationship with the English Court, he granted Henry VIII, by a Bull dated October 25, 1521, the title of "Defender of the Faith." Kings and Queens of England bear this title to this day.

It can be said with certainty that the book was essentially written by Henry. Very probably, he sought guidance from ecclesiastical scholars, for instance, Bishops Fisher and Tunstall and perhaps also the Lord Chancellor, Cardinal Wolsey. In keeping with the bad practice of the time, the volume is not sparing in verbal insults. In opposition to Luther's opinions, it defends the divine institution of all seven sacraments: Baptism, Holy Eucharist, Penance, Confirmation, Matrimony, Holy Orders, and Extreme Unction. (Luther maintained that only the first three—later it was to be two—were instituted by Jesus Christ, with the remaining four—later five—introduced later by the Church.) The King also emphasized the origins of papal supremacy, precisely the point that Thomas More would bring forward twelve and a half years later in his own defense. In March, 1534, More wrote to the royal secretary, Thomas Cromwell, that in publishing the original version of his celebrated book, the King had ignored his advice to clarify some passages.[56] At the time, More pointed out, that suggestion could easily have done him more harm than good by annoying Henry.

This was not the only headache the King's theological-literary ambitions were to give his chancellor. After the *Assertio Septem Sacramentorum* was published in German, Luther took up the pen, and if the King's tract had been coarse the reply was coarser by half: a rough pamphlet, *Contra Henricum Regem Angliae*, followed shortly by the German version: *Antwort teutsch auf König Heinrichs Buch*. The response forced the King's defenders to speak out on his behalf, since royal dignity forbade him to trade insults with someone of such low rank.

It was necessary that those repulsing the German's counterattack in what was by then a high-profile public issue be loyal and respectable subjects.[57] Only the two most cultured men in England could be considered for this task: John Fisher and Thomas More. The work was divided as follows: the Bishop of Rochester would be responsible for

56. Blarer, 137. Letter dated March 5, 1534, from Chelsea, six weeks before his arrest.
57. *CW*, Vol. 5, *Responsio ad Lutherum*, edited by John M. Headley (New Haven-London, 1969), 730f.

the theological aspect of the defense, presented in his book *Defensio regiae assertionis contra Babylonicam Captivitatem*; while More would handle the more or less controversial part aimed at Luther personally. We do not know whether he volunteered or the King gave orders. In due course we shall discuss the *Responsio ad Lutherum*, of which there are two versions: the earlier one, composed under the pseudonym "Baravellus," and a later, longer one, under the name "Rosseus." They were published in May and September, 1523, respectively.

The question still stands: Was More being ironic in saying no king had ever been more truly "Defender of the Faith"—in sword and pen—than Henry VIII? Lawyer that he was, Thomas knew how to measure his words with clinical precision. In the 1532 text, he does not say the King deserved his honorary title just then but at the time when it was granted him. The reader of the epitaph can draw his own conclusions. In any case, he remained utterly loyal to his King even at the most difficult times, when any other normal person would have loathed him. The epitaph expresses the ingenuous simplicity that is one of his most endearing traits.

~✦~✦~✦~

But what does "invincible" mean, applied to Henry VIII? Is this just more Court language for a ruler in those times, or does the word stand for something of substance here? It speaks not of a victorious king but an invincible one, suggesting something more than "undefeated." Unquestionably, had the young sovereign wanted to stand forth to the world as a military hero, he would have been delighted to boast of reconquering France, supposing this to have been easily and quickly done; but the moment for doing it had passed irrevocably. The Anglo-Franco war of 1512–1514 brought victory in the "Battle of the Spurs," fought at Guinegate in 1513, and the conquest of the Tournay fortress. But, for the most part, Henry's reign brought no battlefield triumphs comparable to those of Carlos I of Spain (i.e., Charles V) or Francis I of France. In the decade-long struggle between these two over dominion in Italy and supremacy in Europe (and on the French side, resistance to being surrounded by the House of Austria), England sometimes took one side, sometimes the other, but in either case her interventions were ordinarily superfluous and wrongheaded.

Still, England was involved without exerting any decisive influence on the outcome of events, and on more than one occasion the two great adversaries were glad to make use of their ally. Nevertheless, as the pendulum of victory swung between the Spain of Austria and France, England, failing to move fast enough, repeatedly ended up on the losing side. Geography—England was after all an island nation—and her gradual assumption of the role of balance in the "balance of power" saved her from paying too heavily for her mistakes, as would remain true for a long time to come. It appears then that in calling Henry "invincible," More was not so much flattering his King as stating a political fact grounded in this power balance.

3.

During his first three years in the King's service, 1518 to 1521, More was Master of Requests. Among Wolsey's achievements was the improvement of the legal system and, above all, the legal protection of the poor, the so-called common people. Among the royal courts of justice he introduced was the Court of Requests already mentioned, the offshoot of a royal commission set up to deal with the complaints of humble people. This was a tribunal which followed the King as he moved from one castle to another, especially Woodstock and Greenwich.

But Thomas More's activities at Court were not limited to being a judge. From the outset, one of his duties was to be something like a special secretary to the King. From some letters of his written in 1519 to the Lord Chancellor, Cardinal Wolsey, we know that the King availed himself of More's writing skills to communicate his will. So, for instance, in a letter dated July 5, 1519, More conveys to the Cardinal Henry's very firm instructions concerning a dispute between two Irish cities; then he added a good-natured comment by the sovereign: "When, on my return, I conversed with the King, His Majesty was very glad to hear from various quarters that you are in such good health, despite the constant work with His Majesty's affairs, in which, as he said, you have more to do than may appear to those who only see you in Westminster or in Council. His Majesty is of the opinion that you should be grateful for his advice that you frequently interrupt taking the usual medicine, for thereby you shall not be short of good health, which, it goes without saying, may God graciously protect. Woking, July 5. Your most obedient servant, who keeps you in his prayers."[58]

---

58. Elizabeth Frances Rogers, ed., *The Correspondence of Sir Thomas More* (Princeton, 1947), letter 77 (referred to as: *Corr*).

The responsibility of transmitting delicate and often difficult messages to the Cardinal on the King's behalf could easily have tempted More to overvalue his own opinions or hatch court intrigues. But he never sought to put himself first. His discretion earned him universal confidence. To the very end of his life everyone trusted his loyalty and affection, including even those who plotted his downfall, certain he would never retaliate against them with weapons like the lies and false testimony they employed against him.

On May 2, 1521, at the age of forty-three, More was appointed Assistant-Treasurer and Vice-Chancellor and simultaneously granted a title of nobility. Sir Thomas, as he is now addressed (in official documents, he usually puts the title Knight after his name), ranks after the Lord High Treasurer, the Chancellor of the Treasury, who is the Duke of Norfolk. The latter, who in December 1522 would hand over his post to his son Thomas, Earl of Surrey, was responsible for diplomatic representation, but the real work and ultimate responsibility fell to More. For almost five years, up till January 24, 1526, when he was succeeded by Sir William Campton, More would run this department, which was of particular importance in the early stages of a modern state apparatus and functioned as a sort of forerunner of the ministries of the Exchequer and Treasury. Four months before giving up the post, on the wedding day of his daughters Cicely and Elizabeth, he was designated Chancellor of the Duchy of Lancaster. This well-endowed and honorable appointment, as the head of a historic dukedom[59] with Westminster as its capital, brought More his highest post prior to his elevation to Lord Chancellor of England on October 25, 1529.

More's personal opinions on specific day-to-day issues during much of his royal service are virtually unknown. No doubt he kept them to himself to a much greater extent than is the norm nowadays. His ready acceptance of the role of second fiddle, his total lack of arrogance, and his capacity always to place loyalty before self-promotion were noteworthy. Yet, it was precisely because of such qualities, especially by comparison with his predecessor, Wolsey, that the King entrusted the

---

59. The marriage of Blanche, the Lancaster heiress, descendant of Henry III, to John of Gaunt, fourth son of Edward III, brought the latter the title of Duke of Lancaster. The descendants of both had been English kings, from 1399 to 1461 and in the conflict against the House of York (the " White Rose") they fought under the emblem of the "Red Rose." In 1471 the male line of the House of Lancaster disappeared.

Seal of the Realm to him, even though by then it was obvious that Thomas would not approve of, much less support, Henry's plans for divorce or would allow himself to be used as a pawn in the King's power game. But his loyalty and discretion were rock solid. Thomas More, so Henry thought, would carry out his responsibilities without personal political ambition, and be no impediment to the King's goals. Henry did not want a Lord Chancellor who would control policy. He would take care of that himself, with the sycophantic helpers, while More lent an appearance of legality to the burgeoning depotism.

Henry's calculated trust in Thomas More nevertheless rested on a false assumption. Precisely because he kept himself at arm's length from the King's designs and apart from feverish political intrigue, More could tell precisely when remaining in the government would mean collaborating with the sovereign's intentions and rendering himself liable. More stayed in his post as long as there appeared to be a glimmer of hope that Henry's divorce and remarriage could be prevented and he would give in to the Church. On becoming Chancellor, he wrote Erasmus: "Some of my friends are full of joy at my appointment and they even congratulate me. You, who contemplate the fate of a man with great prudence and much discernment—do you feel sorry for me, perhaps? I intend to keep on top of the situation; I am pleased with the great favor and honor our prince has granted me. I make the utmost efforts not to disappoint the extraordinary expectations that the King has of me, for I lack altogether the skill and other qualities that would be particularly useful in my new post, but I propose to compensate for this with the utmost diligence, fidelity, and good will."[60]

Was More really so naïve as to believe he could satisfy those "extraordinary expectations" with diligence and good will? Knowing what those expectations entailed, he must have known better. Not very long after his appointment, according to his great letter of justification dated March 5, 1534, to the King's private secretary, Thomas Cromwell, the King had advised him to ponder his "great issue," the question of the divorce, and consider every aspect without prejudice. "He promised to include me among his most trusted advisers if the arguments succeeded in convincing me of the rectitude of his opinion."[61] The new Chancellor understood immediately that behind this invitation,

---

60. Blarer, 81. Letter dated October 28, 1529, from Chelsea.
61. Ibid., 141.

extended in an almost friendly and confidential manner and seemingly allowing him complete freedom of action to decide for himself while promising a special reward if he reached the right decision, lay a highly dangerous threat. The danger was in no way diminished by the King's promises: to respect More's conscience, not place pressure on him in the event of a negative reply, never raise the subject again, and put him to work exclusively on other matters.

Henry stood by his promises as long as More kept quiet and continued to do his job. Serving the government in such a high-visibility post meant toeing the royal line without necessarily being at one with it. But for the same reason that the King was prepared to tolerate and even retain him in his position, More felt compelled to resign. He was no spontaneous "confessor of the faith" nor did he choose open battle. But the silence of a silent chancellor would have been the silence of an accomplice, whereas the silence of the resignee, the humanist Thomas More, a man respected in England and the whole of Europe, was interpreted as a "No" standing as an obstacle to the King. In the end, Henry needed a loud and clear "Yes" from More.

On May 16, 1532, the British bishops caved in to Henry VIII, accepting him as the head of the Church in England, albeit with the reservation "insofar as the law of Christ permits"—words that were soon to be suppressed. No longer seeing any way out, humanly speaking, More now decided to return the Seal of the Realm to the King. Whether he sensed that the final choice was drawing near—to submit or die—we do not know.

But his lucid intelligence grasped full well that the options open to him could be counted on the fingers of one hand. One was his own death from natural causes. Wolsey had died on the way to the Tower of London prior to the trial which, we may suppose, would have ended with his execution. Fate might have the same merciful release in store for Sir Thomas too. Be that as it may, he wanted neither to anticipate nor avoid his destiny. He did not quit the political scene with a declaration of principle but a medical statement. He wrote to Cochlaeus: "I have not been feeling very well in my health for the past few months, although my appearance was not such that people might have taken me to be seriously ill. I was feeling very bad indeed, and I would probable have got worse from one day to another had I continued to carry the Chancellor's burden. The physician did not want to guarantee an improvement fearing that I might not retire completely; even if circumstances changed he felt he could not promise me a complete cure."[62]

In a letter to Erasmus written the same day, More is more specific about his illness: "Some sort of chest ailment has laid hold of me; and the discomfort and pain it causes do not bother me as much as the worry and fear over the possible consequences."[63] Some sort of psychosomatic cardiac asthma? But Thomas knew what was really dragging him down, and his heart was filled with foreboding.

---

62. Ibid., 85. Letter dated June 14, 1532.
63. Ibid., 86.

CHAPTER THREE

Political Practice

1.

Curiously, More's burial inscription omits from its catalogue of activities and appointments his service as High Steward, *Patronus ac Sensor*, first of Oxford University and then of Cambridge. The posts were filled by election, reflecting the esteem in which he was held in scholarly circles.

In the case of Oxford, Thomas in 1518 had played some part in a not particularly pleasant affair. Whereas at Cambridge, where Bishop Fisher was Chancellor, the study of Greek flourished, in Oxford a campaign had been launched from the pulpit against that "pagan devotion." More, who repeatedly reacted vehemently with a sharp and scathing irony to such attacks, attributed this one to lack of culture on the part of the monks, especially when they sought to find fault with his friend Erasmus for his Greek edition of the New Testament. Acting on the King's orders, he wrote a strongly worded letter to the university, for "Henry," as Erasmus remarks, "who is not an illiterate and by his own hand protects scholars, got to know of the dispute and decreed that all who so desired could study Greek at the university."[1] More took the occasion to lash out forcefully, indeed harshly, against anyone who objected to the winds of change blowing through learned studies, particularly objections advanced in the name of the faith. The objections raised were often presented with little skill, and, More's reply is not always fair-minded. "I am sure that you will understand better than I that if you do not deal root and branch with troublemakers, a dangerous malaise could spread and that, in that event, people

---

1. Allen, III, 948, 182–219. More's letter dated March 29, 1518 to Oxford University is among *St. Thomas More: Selected Letters*, published by E. F. Rogers (New Haven-London, 1961), referred to as *SL*, letter No. 19, pages 94–103; *Corr.*, 60.

from outside the university might feel obliged to take it into their own hands to help the good and the wise among you. I am sure that the venerable father who occupies the episcopal See in Canterbury, who is our Primate and also Chancellor of your university (i.e., Warham), will not be derelict in his responsibilities and will act as he must. Be it in favor of the clergy or yours, he is right to feel responsible for preventing the degeneration of culture, and culture will surely succumb if the university continues to put up with arguments among lazy madmen and allow the Arts to suffer injury unashamedly."[2]

After threatening Wolsey's intervention, and hinting at the loss of royal favor, including the possibility of the end to subsidies, More closes on a note of hope, provided the letter's recipients behave themselves:

> I have no doubt that in your wisdom you yourselves will find a way to put an end to squabbles and silence those simple people, and that you will take care not only to protect Arts from all ridicule and contempt but also maintain them with dignity and respect. Through such endeavors you will gain enormous benefits for yourselves; I find it almost impossible to describe what great prestige you will achieve in the eyes of your prince and of the aforementioned venerable fathers. You would forge a marvelous link between yourselves and me, and it is because of my love for you that I wanted to write all this by my own hand. You know that my services are at the disposal of each one of you. May God graciously preserve your magnificent mansion of culture from all harm, and may He continue to grant that you prosper in virtue and in all the sciences of the spirit.[3]

Thomas More visited both universities often, sometimes for personal reasons, other times in an official capacity; he involved himself in scholarly disputations and took a personal interest in students, as we know from Roper and More's letter to Bishop Fisher dated June 1521. Given his close relations with the universities and their chancellors, Archbishop Warham and Bishop Fisher, it is not surprising that More was elected High Steward of Oxford in 1524 and Cambridge in 1525.

The holder of this office was the chancellor's right hand, responsible for the administration and oversight of the university. More found these duties a source of joy and also occasional vexation, as he

---

2. *SL*, 19; *Corr.*, 60.
3. Ibid.

sought to settle quarrels and protect the schools' legitimate interests while operating in a delicate no man's land between the two poles of power, King Henry and Cardinal Wolsey, while serving both loyally and conscientiously.

2.

Two areas of political activity are mentioned in More's epitaph: parliamentary and diplomatic. Although he held professional positions in many fields, the only ones he considered it worthwhile commending to posterity's notice were his election as Speaker of the House of Commons and his role as an envoy, especially as part of the delegation that negotiated the peace treaty of Cambrai.

The opening session of Parliament over which the King presided on April 15, 1523, was the fourth since Henry ascended the throne. The King was eager that fresh funds be approved to conduct the war with France declared the previous year. But unrest in the House regarding the war in particular and Wolsey's policies in general was already present and growing constantly. The Speaker had an important role to play, not only in presiding over Commons but serving as its mouthpiece before the government and the King. (In those days, the functions of the executive and legislative branches were not so sharply distinguished, so that somone like More, in the service of the king, could also be Speaker of the House of Commons.)

More enjoyed the trust of both the King and Wolsey, and also of the Commons. On April 18 he was introduced to the King as the new Speaker. After Thomas had described himself, as usual, as unworthy of such an honor, and after Wolsey had replied in the name of the King, describing the choice, as was customary, as the best one possible, More delivered a speech whose candor stands out in so conventional a setting as this:

> Bearing in mind that in Your Majesty's Parliament only weighty and important matters relating to Your Realm and Your own royal state are discussed, many members of the House of Commons, intelligent and experienced, would find themselves, to the serious detriment of the common good, prevented from expressing their advice and opinions, if each and every one of your members were not free from the fear that something of what they said might be taken badly by Your Majesty. Wherefore may it please Your Majesty to graciously

grant, most benevolent and pious king, indulgence and pardon to the Commons here present, so that each one may fulfill, freely, and without fear of Your awesome wrath, the obligations of their consciences and be able to express their views without let or hindrance on anything that might arise between us. May anything that may be said by any one of us be graciously accepted by Your Majesty, seeing the words of all of us, however stupid they may be, as an expression of our commitment to the prosperity of Your Realm and the glory of Your Royal person, whose well-being and continuance is what we, Your loyal subjects, wish and petition, and naturally uphold.[4]

Here is the first known testimony in support of freedom of expression in Parliament that goes beyond rhetorical formulas. By no means was this freedom then taken for granted. Even in England, centuries had to pass before it could be institutionalized; and under the Tudors, especially Henry VIII, the self-respect, dignity, and liberty of Parliament all declined.

But now More had an opportunity to show his diplomatic skill in a risky situation. After Wolsey declared the government's imperative need for not less than £800,000 to finance the war against France, More, repeating his superior's position, declared it the duty of citizens to accept that extraordinary tax, though it may be supposed that he did not share that view himself.

Since Commons showed no inclination to accept such economic bloodletting to support an unpopular war, the Cardinal now sought to put certain members on the spot with a point-blank demand that they say how they meant to vote. This was provocative and showed contempt for the House, whose task was to deliberate and reach a decision, subsequently to be announced through the Speaker. More now was in a very delicate situation—which he resolved by not entering into the material aspect of the matter, an approach typical of him. Roper says he knelt down and begged pardon for the silence of the members, noting that the presence of such high authority would silence the wisest and most learned of men. He then "set out, with many and intelligent arguments, that it would not be in accordance with the ancient customs of the House that members should reply individually,"[5] adding that he himself would be unable to report adequately to the Honorable Cardinal in a

---

4. Roper, 15; Chambers, 244.
5. Roper, 18; Chambers, 246.

matter of such outstanding importance "without the Honorable members pouring their intelligence into his own poor head."[6] Here is the quintessential More: genuine humility humorously turning the tables on an arrogant interlocutor. His words can be taken either as praise of the all-powerful cardinal or censure of behavior ill-befitting a prince of the Church. This Christian irony, intended to appeal to the Cardinal's sensitivity and capacity for self-criticism, is characteristic of More and, one might say, a typically English ingredient of his sanctity.

Offended that his financial policy seemed to carry no weight with the Commons, Wolsey exclaimed, according to Roper, "Wish to dear God that you had been in Rome when I appointed you Speaker!" But of course it was not he who had appointed More Speaker but the Commons which had elected him. It appears that arrogance had begun to cloud his grasp of fact.

⚘ ⚘ ⚘

Thomas Wolsey, More's senior by five years, lived from 1473 to 1530, that is, to exactly the same age. There comparisons end. His career followed a much more brilliant course, although, as is always pointed out, "he was only a butcher's son." Chaplain to the court of Henry VII, in 1509 a member of the Privy Council, where he stood out for his resourceful ingenuity and energy, Wolsey for the first time distinguished himself in matters of great weight when in 1512 he organized the army and navy for the war against France and Scotland, traditional anti-British allies. England defeated the Scots; King James IV fell in the autumn of 1513 during the battle of Flodden. His widow, Margaret, sister of Henry VIII, assumed the regency on behalf of James V, then a minor (ninety years later his descendants would replace the Tudor dynasty).[7] The king, grateful for the happy outcome of this his first war, named Wolsey Lord Chancellor in 1515. That same year Pope Leo X confirmed him as Archbishop of York and elevated him to the cardinalate.

It is often said that starting then Wolsey "governed" in England for almost fifteen years, but this must be understood as meaning only

---

6. Ibid.

7. Margaret, daughter of Henry VII, married James IV of Scotland; the son from this marriage, James V, died in 1542; his daughter, Mary Stuart, had to give up the throne in 1568 and, after a long imprisonment, was beheaded in 1587. The son from Mary's marriage to Lord Darnley, James VI, acceded to the English throne after Elizabeth I's death in 1603 and, as James I, became the first king of England and Scotland.

that the King took no exception to his practices in internal politics, his prebendary dealings, which he negotiated unscrupulously, and his ruthless collection of monies, not just for the state but also for his personal enrichment. Henry also accepted his Lord Chancellor's ideas on foreign policy. But as scholarly examination of the sources now makes clear, the King was perfectly well informed on all political affairs, including the most insignificant. Neither at Court nor within the government was any action or decision ever taken without his knowledge and approval. Nothing concerning the state or the Church lay beyond his influence. It is true that Wolsey steered the country with a great measure of independence, but independence at the King's pleasure, which he could withdraw at any time. The Cardinal governed as long as Henry let him, and he fell when Henry determined to exercise the practical and technical aspects of power himself.

It is not surprising that the King accepted Wolsey's ideas on foreign policy. Both men were ruled largely by a longing for prestige. Henry dreamed of being heir to the Holy Roman-German Empire; he decorated himself with the title "Defender of the Faith" and sought to be arbitrator between the rivals Francis I of France and the Emperor Charles V. All was well for the Cardinal as long as he could keep up the appearance that his King was the most brilliant and most important figure in European politics of that entire era. But when the question of the divorce made it obvious that Henry was a much smaller figure on the world stage, and especially in Rome, the humiliated King was unforgiving toward his Lord Chancellor.

Wolsey's own ambition had a specific goal: he aspired to the papal throne. To have to preside as Archbishop of York over an ecclesiastical province neither as large nor as significant as Canterbury was a disadvantage for which he compensated by his position as *legatus a latere* (special legate of the Pope),[8] making him in 1518 papal representative to the Church in England and in 1524 representative for life, something highly unusual. In effect, he was the de facto regent of the Church in England, able to convene all of the English bishops and do very nearly as he liked in local Church affairs. This gave him a decisive role at a time when the Church's reform, unity, and very survival were live issues.

---

8. Each of the ecclesiastical provinces had its own "convocation," that is, an assembly of suffragan bishops and abbots. The Pope alone was lord of all the Church in England. Many monasteries were "exempt" and depended directly on Rome.

But instead of fostering the well being of the Church and promoting sound relationships with Rome and with the Crown, Wolsey abused his position. Greed, a passion for luxury and pomp, and the intoxication of power led him to do all those things for which the Church was then reproached, thereby undermining its prestige and credibility. This included accumulating ecclesiastical positions, with little regard for the duty of residence and supervision, unjustified interference in dioceses, manipulating episcopal appointments, doing away with assemblies, transgressions against celibacy—the Cardinal himself had several children—and a generally unworthy life for a priest. His autocratic policies, based on the power vested in him by the Pope, soured the bishops and distanced them from Rome,[9] and this is a key to understanding the passivity and lack of resistance with which the English episcopate a decade later greeted and even supported the separation from Rome.

Even the King thought of this "regional pope" as someone who knew and could do everything. But this was an illusion. Wolsey could not win the Pope's approval for an "elegant" dissolution of the King's marriage, and when Henry saw clearly that this was so, he took revenge on his creature and destroyed him.

～～～～

When Thomas composed his epitaph, he was confident that the Cambrai peace would endure. It ended a thirty-year war between France and the House of Austria and signaled a decade-long period of peace. As a witness at the celebration of the treaty and its solemn promulgation in the cathedral of Cambrai, he considered it a shining event that overshadowed everyday affairs.

Two years earlier, in 1527, More, together with the dukes of Norfolk and Suffolk, had been part of a delegation charged with negotiating a "permanent peace" with France, and in the cathedral at Amiens he was next to his Cardinal Lord Chancellor when it was signed. In 1525, we find him beside Warham, Archbishop of Canterbury, Bishop Nicholas West of Ely, and the Duke of Norfolk on the commission for the Anglo-French armistice. A few years before that, we find him a member of commercial delegations in Bruges, discussing business matters with representatives of Hanseatic and Flemish merchants.

---

9. Kluxen, p. 181.

Thomas More accompanied Wolsey to Calais, moving in the highest secular and ecclesiastical levels of society; he negotiated with members of the senior nobility of France, Spain, and Venice; held discussions with the King of France; gave the address of welcome when Charles V visited London in 1522. He accompanied the royal couple, Henry and Catherine; enjoyed the Queen's trust and Henry's esteem. His sovereign strolled with him, arm over his shoulder, in the garden in Chelsea and sat at his table. His income continued to rise, and in 1527 reached three hundred and forty pounds. Though upset with this Speaker of the House of Commons, Wolsey asked the King for a bonus for More (August 1523) "because he tends not to look after his own interests."[10] The 1525 treaty with France brought him a French pension. In 1522, Henry made his sub-Chancellor a gift of the farm in Kent in the south of England, among the assets confiscated from the executed "traitor" Buckingham. Three years later he was given farms in Ducklington and Fringford in Oxfordshire,[11] and in November 1526, the King granted him, against his will, a prebend [an ecclesiastical income connected with a cathedral].[12] Presumably, More was not equally happy with all these rewards, and he never coveted any. What came his way as a politician and statesman was nothing out of the ordinary. It simply expressed the King's satisfaction with and liking for a proven, honest, and discreet helper, who inspired neither fear nor envy.

It is difficult to say whether More found satisfaction in the thousand and one details of administrative and political life. Quite possibly, in making the transition from municipal responsibilities to the service of the Crown, he entertained hopes of exercising a creative influence, at least in the first few years, by carrying out policies on behalf of peace abroad and political reform at home. His writings and letters make it clear that, although he could laugh at the world at times, he worried and suffered both for the present and the future on many counts: from the continual senseless wars, the religious schism, the personality of his King, the divorce, the feud with Rome, and, sometimes very likely, his own Lady Alice. But never from any unsatisfied egotism.

---

10. *Corr.*, 278; *L'Univers*, 337.

11. *L'Univers*, 363.

12. Ibid, 387.

Germain Marc'hadour has documented a remarkable diversity in the tasks and activities of Sir Thomas.[13] As was mentioned, administrative lines and responsibilities proper to each position were not clearly delineated, and people working around the King and the Lord Chancellor—lay and (even more numerous) religious counselors, secretaries, titular heads of posts at Court or those temporarily in favor—depended entirely on the royal person or his representative. In theory, More served the state or the Crown only indirectly, but in fact he served Henry VIII and, for eleven of those fourteen years, Cardinal Wolsey as well. Both gave him a multiplicity of tasks: counselor, correspondence secretary, enforcer of orthodoxy and battler of heresy, diplomat and second-tier courtier. Cultured, ingenious, good humored, and kindly, he was equally at ease dealing with foreign envoys and participating in a festive reception or royal supper.

The letters that have been preserved record his role as go-between for Henry and Wolsey. Their specifics—day to day political trivia—are of less interest than what they tell us about More. While maintaining the style required by court protocol, he enlivens this by quoting from conversations or accompanying the obligatory flattery of the Cardinal with his own opinions, in passing as it were. When Henry toys with the idea of siding with the Emperor in 1522 and dreams of reconquering France, More remarks to Wolsey: "I beseech God that it may be so, if it will profit Your Lordship and this realm; otherwise I beg God to grant him an honorable and fruitful peace." More obviously knows how to handle his master: "This morning I also read to His Highness the directives given personally by Your Lordship, so wisely drafted and so elegantly couched."[14] Or this: "His Highness is so delighted with your letter that I can think of none that has pleased him as much. If I am able, with God's help to rely on my poor intelligence, such praise is certainly well founded, for your communication, both in content and style, is among the best I have ever read."[15]

---

13. The book *L'Univers de Thomas More* is structured so that for each year and, where possible, each month or day, on the left side are listed the political events and, on the right, those relating to Thomas More and Erasmus. At the end of every year the principal books published are given. An excellent introduction, numerous notes with explanations, a bibliography, and an index make this an extraordinary working tool.

14. *Corr.*, 110, 261–265; Thomas More to Wolsey dated September 21, 1522, from Newhall.

15. Bremond, 125.

From the correspondence with Wolsey, it is apparent that More's job involved much tension—at the beck and call of two masters, ordered hither and thither, not always in matters of high politics but frequently having to do with monetary transactions[16] or personal whims. These latter could have some curious features, as when More notifies the Cardinal: "Perhaps Your Lordship would like to be informed that His Highness the King took me aside on his way to supper and charged me to write as follows: 'The Lord having called unto Himself the late Mr. Myrfyne, London town councilor, His Highness wishes that Sir William Tyler marry the widow of the said councilor, wanting thereby to grant him a favor. To bring this about, His Highness counts on your discretion and proven loyalty. With this, His Highness says, Your Lordship would afford him great pleasure, and oblige the said Sir William to say prayers throughout his lifetime for Your Lordship.'"[17]

Henry was used to having his way, and Wolsey's unconditional obsequiousness during almost a decade and a half confirmed him in this. But a sovereign favor, purchased and maintained with unlimited docility, is not a solid foundation for retaining power. The second Tudor might in any case have become a vicious tyrant and imposed himself on the realm; but the Cardinal's absolute servility accelerated this process. "If I had served God as diligently as I have the King he would not have handed me over in my grey hairs,"[18] lamented Wolsey as he was about to be taken to the Tower of London. Unlike More, who considered his own suffering a final, exhausting stretch before reaching his final goal of union with Christ, and therefore something for which he was grateful, Wolsey could only see his fall from grace as a disaster.

Still, it would be unfair to judge the Cardinal's personality and chancellorship only in a negative light. He was generous and understood gratitude, and was capable of kindness. After quelling the uprising of May 1517, he obtained the King's mercy for four hundred prisoners, as the Venetian envoy to London relates.[19] His merit in improving the judiciary, speeding up trials and improving legal protection of the poor and humble, as well as the proper conduct of hearings by the Star Chamber is fact. But the positive features were devalued, their effects undermined,

---

16. *Corr.*, 137; from Hertford, November 29, 1524.

17. *Corr.*, 122; from Easthampstead, September 17, 1523.

18. George Cavendish, *The Life and Death of Cardinal Wolsey*, published by R. S. Sylvester (London: EETS, 1959), 243; Chambers, 188.

19. Jacobs, 63.

and the whole of his mandate poisoned by the same vice: his boundless vanity. "His garments were all made of scarlet taffeta or fine vermillion or red satin, with velvety black cebelline fur around the collar." Thus Cavendish, the chamber assistant and biographer, describes his appearance: "In his hand he carried an orange stuffed with a sponge soaked in vinegar, or some other liquid, to fend off the contaminated air, and when irked by the presence of too many petitioners he very frequently put it to his nose. The State Seal of England and the Cardinal's hat[20] were carried in front of him." Such outward trappings might arouse no more than head shaking and ridicule. But Wolsey's remark to the French chancellor, that the Duke of Buckingham had been executed because he had rebelled against the Cardinal's policy, reveals something pathological, as does his affirmation, when trying to ingratiate himself with the French, that "he had been the first to adduce reasons in favor of the divorce so as to isolate England from Spain and thus unite her with France."[21]

Judging from his character, this may be true. If so, Wolsey encouraged the King's request to obtain the divorce in order to be the one who made the royal wish come true—the "fixer" who made himself indispensable to his sovereign and the Boleyn clan, and then became his own first victim. This would explain More's attack on the disgraced Cardinal before Parliament. A man who had abused his office to scheme and intrigue in an affair that not only would cause very deep suffering to Queen Catherine, but also persecution, misery, and death for many of his countrymen and the destruction of the Church in England, did not deserve the treatment accorded to a gentleman.

Be that as it may, the relationship between More and his superiors is not altogether transparent and may give rise to certain doubts concerning his character. Certainly, many daring replies by More have come down to us: as when in the Privy Council he contradicted a proposal by the Chancellor, whereupon the latter reprimanded him severely, and More replied: "Ah, Most Reverend Sir, how I give thanks to God that there is only one lunatic in the King's Council."[22] On the other hand, More was accustomed to flattering Wolsey's vanity, which he recognized as a flaw in the latter's personality, while at the same time enjoying and accepting the Cardinal's protection.

---

20. Ibid., 62.
21. Chambers, 193.
22. Bremond, 123.

Thomas More's behavior conformed to the norm of his time. Highly original as a writer and speaker, he otherwise made no effort to be unusual, realizing that a man of the world who sought to follow Christ had to do that tactfully, without notable eccentricities. Hairshirts are worn, after all, next to one's skin, not over one's cloak.

Over a century ago, Henri Bremond wrote: "Those who from an aversion to Wolsey want to distance him at all costs from More have to acknowledge that they ran neck and neck when the Cardinal was Chancellor, and More in his shadow was moving swiftly through all levels, if not of power, certainly of honor. The one supported himself with unquestioning trust in his faithful protégé who he knew would not deceive him; and the other was filled with respect for a master whose worth he knew and whose influence delayed the complete victory of certain pleasure-seeking friends of the sovereign."[23] Three decades later, Chambers said: "We have grounds for supposing that he (More) thought of Wolsey as being the perverse spirit of Henry and England, as the man who had impoverished his country through senseless wars against France, and that he later entangled him in a conflict with Charles V, who represented the traditional ally of England, the House of Burgundy. Without any doubt, Wolsey had done so, and it was sufficient to provoke the odium of which More might be capable."[24] Bremond, who understood More's sanctity more deeply than Chambers, nevertheless has less appreciation of him as a human being. Chambers, who admires the humanist statesman for his conscience, uses political arguments to defend him. Is there a contradiction here in More or only in those who seek to interpret him?

When Thomas was summoned to Court, he had no good reason for not accepting the call. A suitable and honorable field of action had been found for a wealthy bourgeois lawyer who was also a member of Parliament and local council official, and it was natural to obey both the King and the Lord Chancellor, Cardinal Wolsey. More was allowed his opinions, which on several occasions differed from those of his superiors. He also expressed them, sometimes in a partly coded manner, as in his *Utopia*, or in private, in correspondence or conversation, or partly even in public and, in a certain manner, officially. Perhaps he should have done that more often and forcefully, but he was a cautious and equable man (though not timid or indifferent). But he distinguished

---

23. Bremond, 132.
24. Chambers, 292.

between opinions as such and what, for reasons of faith or conscience, he held to be certainties, something altogether different.

He had his own views on the Chancellor's foreign policy, wars, and financial problems relating to taxation or commerce, and mostly he rejected Wolsey's measures because he considered them harmful to England. But Wolsey was in charge, and it was his opinions that counted, not More's. Such differences of opinion were not sufficient grounds for challenging the official line or resigning. More told himself that he did not have to account to God for England's policy, but only for the honest execution of his duties. The idea of an all-encompassing responsibility in the socio-political sphere rendering him liable for everything that happened, would have struck him as presumptuous and wrongheaded.

Where faith was concerned, it was quite different. People could hold differing views on political matters like alliances or taxation, but not on the doctrine of the Church and the faith that has been handed down. In More's view, that was not just an airing of opinions, but apostasy. God would forgive him for his mistakes as a politician and civil servant, but no king or chancellor could absolve him if, by obeying them, he betrayed his faith.

More probably should have distanced himself from Wolsey, accepted no benefits or favors, and perhaps looked more closely into his conscience. Perhaps he even did; but literary mockery was no answer to vices like Wolsey's. Moreover, he respected the Cardinal and for that reason acknowledged Wolsey's merits. There is no reason not to accept his sincerity in concluding a letter to the Cardinal: "I would be very blind, Your Lordship, if I did not acknowledge, and would be an unfortunate wretch if some day I were to forget, the great favor that you grant me, a benevolence I would never be able to repay except with humble prayers, in which I would beseech God to keep you in dignity and good health."[25]

But it was his friend Cuthbert Tunstall, not Wolsey, whom More immortalized in his epitaph. Tunstall was one of those cultured clerics versed in jurisprudence who, following a long tradition, served European princes as secretaries, counselors, and envoys until the early sixteenth century, when laymen increasingly began to occupy these positions. More's senior by four years, he had mastered Roman and canon law, theology, Greek, Hebrew, and mathematics at Oxford,

---

25. *Corr.*, 126; from Woodstock, September 26, 1523.

Cambridge, and Padua. No sooner had he returned from Italy, than, just before Henry acceded to the throne, he was appointed Chancellor to the Archbishopric of Canterbury by its Archbishop, Warham. On several occasions between 1515 and 1529, the King designated him his envoy. More probably knew Tunstall from his time at Oxford and had been a colleague in 1515 and 1516 in the Low Countries, as well as during the peace negotiations in Calais in 1529. He was one of More's most intimate friends, possibly closer to his heart than Erasmus.

Tunstall's ecclesiastical career kept pace with the royal esteem: in 1522 he was named Bishop of London, in 1530 of Durham. Although at first he spoke against Henry's ecclesiastical supremacy, in the end, much to his disgust, he resigned himself to accepting it. Personally honest and pious, a skilled diplomat, a humanist of fine spirit, he was one of those men of the Church who felt uneasy when faced with hard alternatives or extreme consequences and was not cut out to be a martyr. Although entirely orthodox, he avoided any kind of cruelty against Luther's followers and through his ingenuousness even helped them indirectly. Tyndale's translation of the New Testament was not authorized and was held to be heretical. When More asked an adherent of the new faith during an interrogation who was financing Tyndale and his foreign friends, he received the reply: "In truth it is the Bishop of London who has helped us. He has given us a very large sum of money for copies of the New Testament for burning. He has thus been our only support and comfort, and continues to be to this day." "Truly that is my opinion too," replied More, "and I said so to the Bishop when he started to buy them."[26]

Living through the beginning of Elizabeth I's reign, this affable pastor managed to save his head, though not his freedom or his position; for following the death of Queen Mary (1558), he failed to show himself sufficiently docile toward the new sovereign and the growing Protestantism, and so lost his episcopal see. He died, as Chambers puts it, under "light detention" at the age of eighty-five in 1559, almost a quarter of a century after More. As leading lights of the new scholarly studies, both had seemed to illuminate a new, humane century. Both had served the King, country, and Church. And both belonged to that long line, stretching through history, of nonviolent men of intellect who in diverse ways are entrapped by power struggles and fall victims to mindless violence.

---

26. Chambers, 260; quotes Edward Hall: *Chronicle*, Whibley edition, vol. 2, 162.

3.

More's brief chancellorship—it lasted only one and a half years—is of interest more because of him as a person than for the history of England, which he hardily influenced in the sense of shaping it politically and creatively. In that sense, it is misleading for Bremond to say More "acceded to power," since More never had any real power. Power was properly the King's, although at first tempered by Parliament and other considerations. Wolsey had wielded that power, and shown himself a pretentious wielder of it, yet the power never really was his either. Wolsey was no Richelieu; and his true successor in playing the game of politics was not More but Thomas Cromwell. Henry's reasons for entrusting the Seal of the State to More, while using Cromwell as a technocrat of power were patently obvious: initially, he needed an upright Chancellor, a strict lawyer, faithful to the Church, whose good character would make him a "front" for the King's designs: apart from the immediate objective of the "divorce," the creation of a modern, centralized form of government on Machiavellian lines.

More resigned in 1532, because, as the embodiment of old England and her judicial and ecclesiastical tradition, he no longer could continue along the King's path. But why did he not say no to an appointment which, even in 1529, was plainly going to involve him in an unresolvable conflict?

More believed in doing his professional duty to the full. The only absolutely unacceptable course of action was one that would place in jeopardy the eternal salvation of his immortal soul. Thomas was granted the grace of knowing when that point was reached, and he quit his King neither a moment too soon or a moment too late either—as was the case with his friend Tunstall. He separated himself from the "King's affair" precisely when loyalty and affection for Henry allowed him to do so, and loyalty to the Church and the Pope and love of Christ required it of him. Up to the very last moment, he still had hopes, though without being in the least naïve.

As a politician, of course, he was highly skeptical and entertained practically no hope that the King would change his mind. But as a Christian, he nurtured hope, and he remained hopeful right up to May 15, 1532, when the bishops capitulated and the King declared himself Head of the Church in England in place of the Pope. Thereafter his only remaining flicker of hope was for a future conversion in Henry or his successors, so that the spiritual harm to the English people might prove less devastating than the material destruction of the Catholic Church in England.

⊸&⊸&⊸&

More's time as Chancellor was dominated by struggles that raged around him, but of which he was neither the driving force nor the center. The quarrels with Luther, Tyndale, and the new doctrines had a place in his life extending beyond his period in office, but he never had the power to intervene in the conflict by political or state means, and his role was limited to pen and ink.[27] Only once, in fact, did the new Chancellor take the floor of Parliament in connection with fundamental political issues—at the very start, in connection with the parliamentary attack on the resigned Wolsey.

On October 18 the Grand Seal of State was taken from Wolsey; a month later, the King detained him "under his protection." That need not be understood ironically, since the toppled Cardinal truly needed protection against the Boleyn clan as the relatives of Anne Boleyn came to exert more and more influence at court and in the state. But the protection, while removing him effectively from private vengeance, put him at the mercy of royal spitefulness, always in the guise of lawful proceedings. Already, on November 30, the immense fortune he had accumulated had been confiscated by the Crown. Perhaps Wolsey hoped against hope that he could remain in the Archbishopric of York or at least be allowed to disappear quietly into some country retreat. In March 1530, after all, the Privy Council granted six thousand pounds for the removal of the ex-Chancellor to York, to which sum the King added one thousand pounds from his own coffers (replenished with confiscated funds!)

It is typical of the Tudors that acts of benevolence and disgrace followed one another uninterruptedly, a feature which helps give Henry VIII's reign the arbitrary and despotic character that became increasingly apparent from 1530 on. Wolsey scurries from place to place, staying only a short while in each, like an animal pursued and harassed; from his country house in Esher, near Hampton Court, to the farm in Richmond, from there toward Southwell, then to Scroby, and from there to Cawood, where he hopes to make final preparations for his

---

27. This statement does not contradict the fact that Thomas More, on taking the oath of office on October 26, 1529, in the Great Hall of Westminster, swore an oath, compulsory since March 1529, to act against heresy in the name of the King.

ultimate move to York. Here, on November 4, 1530, he is detained in the name of the King. That he may have tried to prepare his defense—or his flight?—and may therefore have contacted the King of France and the Emperor Charles V was sufficient grounds for a trial for high treason. But the governor of the Tower of London, arriving in Sheffield on November 22, found Wolsey gravely ill. Even so, he was transported as far as St. Mary's Abbey in Leicester, where he expired on the afternoon of November 29 after making his confession and receiving absolution and Extreme Unction. At daybreak he was buried in that same place.

As years earlier with the sudden fall of the Duke of Buckingham, so now More had an object lesson in the inconstancy of earthly glory. How must Wolsey, not long before the second man in England after the King, felt at having to address petitions to the Duke of Norfolk and even to his own creature, More? At having to rush from one temporary refuge to another? And at hearing what More had said of him in Parliament?

Known as the "Reformation Parliament," it was opened by Sir Thomas on November 3, 1529, met over eight sessions until April 1536, and ushered in a new political era for England, in which neither the resplendent Prince of the Church nor his successor, the modest layman, would have a part. In this Parliament medieval England came to an end, More's career was at its peak, his family's star reached its zenith—and laws were enacted that cost More his head and his family members their freedom, well-being, and homeland.[28]

In this Parliament, then, the new Chancellor weighed his predecessor in the balance and found him wanting. After applying the image of shepherd and flock to the King and his people, he said: "Thus, as you can see, in a large flock of sheep some animals, unfit or defective, are separated from the healthy sheep by the good shepherd, so the big ram that fell recently acted in a manner so perfidious, so corrupt and false before the King, that everybody must suppose from his conduct that he imagined the King was not intelligent enough to recognize his perfidy or would not notice his deceitful sleight of hand. But in that he was mistaken. His Majesty's eye was so sharp and penetrating that he saw through it all, and, knowing him inside out, everything became

---

28. Among the Commons were Thomas More's brother-in-law, John Rastell, his three sons-in-law, William Roper, Giles Heron, and William Dauncey; and Sir Alington, married for the first time to Lady Alice More's daughter. More's only son, John, could not be elected because he was still a minor. His father, John More, still living, would probably have been in the House of Lords, given that he sat on the King's Bench as a judge.

patently clear to him. He has been given a light punishment, which he deserved. In accordance with the King's wishes, the punishment's lightness must not be considered a precedent by other guilty parties."[29]

This speech has always caused problems for More's biographers. It is impossible to doubt its authenticity. So was this canonized saint of the Catholic Church kicking a man who was already down? Contemporary witnesses, biographers old and modern, and impartial historians who have said all there is to say almost always justified More. It is said that Sir Thomas acted leniently, considering the harm Wolsey had done England, the Church, the Queen, and Henry's soul; that reasons of state and loyalty to the King required showing the wrongdoing of his predecessor and highlighting the sovereign's power;[30] that the Chancellor spoke ex-officio, as the King's spokesman, reflecting the latter's opinion and not his own;[31] that he wanted to admonish Henry rather than severely reprimand Wolsey. "The age in which More lived was not very gentlemanly; More's good taste was not always infallible," Chambers writes.[32] All this is more or less plausible.

Still, there is something disagreeable about the incident. More was not free of faults, and saintliness does not mean being without sin.[33] And More's frailties cannot even easily be called sins: they have more to do with occasional excess in flattery in keeping with the style of the age, and with a certain lack of tact and, often, of kindly patience, particularly when faced with a lack of culture in people who were his intellectual inferiors.

More the lawyer came to the fore in More the Lord Chancellor, who was almost totally isolated from high politics, especially the "great matter" of the King's divorce. Now, though, the optimistic, cheerful young lawyer from Lincoln's Inn had become a judge of the realm, older and deeply troubled about the future. Much of his time was spent

---

29. Chambers, 290.

30. Ibid., 291.

31. *L'Univers*, 431, note 11. More, in Marc'hadour's opinion, spoke on behalf of the King in the same way that the King nowadays speaks in the name of the head of the government. Cf. also by E. E. Reynolds, *The Field Is Won: The Life and Death of Saint Thomas More* (London, 1968), 228ff. (referred to as Reynolds).

32. Chambers, 291.

33. Saintliness means "goodness," not lack of defects. According to Josef Pieper, to be good is the human, natural substratum of supernatural saintliness. In speaking of "goodness," one must differentiate between the generic saintliness of those who have been baptized, personal saintliness, manifest as an attempt by a living person to follow Jesus Christ, and the saintliness reserved to the judgment of the Church on a life already ended.

as Justice of the Peace for the realm. In the Star Chamber, he assayed the silver content of coins minted since July 1527. Measures against the dissemination of Protestant writings and interrogations and trials of heretics figure largely in his activities.

He felt exhausted and yearned to quit public life. Although the King kept his promise not to consult More again about the divorce, his refusal to cooperate was no secret. In defending the Queen's rights, as he felt duty and good manners required of him, he exposed himself to Henry's wrath. Furthermore, while the King insisted on the persecution of heresy, he also oppressed and extorted the clergy, and about this, too, the Chancellor's views were no secret. So, from the start of his chancellorship he foresaw its end, the only question being whether he would be allowed to resign gracefully or be put in chains immediately in the Tower of London.

There was danger on every side. During the Canterbury convocation, Bishop Fisher came out against royal supremacy over the Church in England, and a few days later an attempt was made to poison him in his Lambeth residence. More was at risk of being accused of treason if he neglected to act with maximum caution in his dealing with the imperial envoy. Charles V, after all, was a nephew of Queen Catherine, and Henry considered him his arch adversary, who was obstructing the annulment of the marriage. One of the duties of Ambassador Chapuys was to keep his sovereign informed about the situation in London and, therefore, about More. But the diplomatic pouch was not safe from spying eyes. On February 21, 1531, Chapuys reported that More was so bitter about the bishops' capitulation that he thought only of resigning. Seven weeks later, More was said to be complaining about the short-sightedness of princes who did not want to help the Emperor in his fight against the Turks.[34] Had those letters been intercepted and shown to Henry, they would have been sufficient to condemn the Lord Chancellor. In refusing to accept a personal letter from Charles V and asking Chapuys to dispense with a visit, he was only acting prudently.[35]

Thus did Sir Thomas manage his master stroke: to resign in good form, affably dismissed by the King amid laughter and apparently affectionate applause. It was the last small triumph of his political skills.

---

34. *L'Univers*, 453, 455.
35. Ibid., 455.

CHAPTER FOUR

The Heretics

"In all the successive posts he held of high office, and honors conferred on him, he conducted himself in such a way that his noble lord could object to nothing in his service. He was not hated by the nobility nor did the people find him objectionable. He was only a worry to thieves, murderers, and heretics."

1.

When Henry VIII claimed supremacy over the Church for himself, More regarded him as violating divine law in a specific, limited matter. His reaction suited this situation. Rather than refusing to carry out his duties as a subject or failing in personal loyalty to the King, he simply declined to assent to the particular act, invoking tradition, the Church in England, and the whole of European Christianity. That is, an authority that was intact and continuous, as opposed to royal authority, which at times in history had been abused.

The note of satisfaction in his epitaph with regard to his public reputation must be understood against this background. Not even the King criticized his official conduct. More did not die for serving badly but for refusing a particular service. He had no enemies among the great nobles of the country, and up to the point at which he composed his burial inscription had incurred no one's enmity.

But if no one feared him as a rival, it is another question whether he had friends among the Lords. Thomas Howard, Duke of Norfolk, a pragmatic and uncomplicated man who knew where his own interests lay, felt a certain rough camaraderie with him. Coming across More assisting at Mass wearing his robes of office—which he often did in his Chelsea parish—he demanded what the King would say about a Lord

Chancellor who did something so vulgar; More replied that the King would be pleased that his Chancellor served their Lord and everyone else's. When Norfolk later sat on the board of inquiry set up to resolve the "More case," he appeared to take personal offense at the "obstinacy" of an accused with whom he felt sympathy, and his somewhat forced anger made it easier to assent with a clear conscience to finding his old colleague guilty. Thomas's true friends were found among the prelates—Bishop Fisher and Bishop Tunstall—and they undoubtedly were included among the "nobility" as he used the word.

There are many testimonies to More's popularity: the large number of honorary appointments and positions of trust conferred on him by his fellow Londoners, especially his colleagues and the representatives of guilds and trade organizations; memorials including those of his adversaries, as in the account by Edward Halls; a rich trove of anecdotes; and particularly the Elizabethan drama *Sir Thomas More*, illustrating the esteem in which its hero was still held decades after his death.

In the last scene, the anonymous dramatist shows More on the way to his execution. A woman approaches and begs him to return important documents in his safekeeping, without which she faces ruin. More replies: "My old client, what are you doing here? Poor ingenuous creature! 'Tis true that I had those papers which are of great interest to you. But the King has taken the matter into his own hands and now owns everything I possessed. So, woman, put your complaints to him, for I cannot help you. Thou must bear with me."[1] The tone is patient, good-natured, and sad. He approaches the scaffold itself saying, "Thou must bear with me."

This scene is not invented. Hall's chronicle also includes it, though as an example of More's cynicism. In this version, Thomas says: "But, woman, have a little patience, for the King is so good to me that in less than half an hour he will relieve me of all business and will help you personally."[2] Hall failed to grasp that More was serious in speaking of Henry's kindness in bringing him closer to his goal by a relatively smooth shortcut. In the play, More's example elevates the poor woman above her self-concern: "I feel compassion for thee from the depth of my soul, noble Sir, who art the best friend of she whom they call unhappy and poor."[3]

---

1. Chambers, 290.
2. Ibid.
3. Ibid.

What actors were to speak years later from the stage in testimony
to Thomas's popularity, people sang in the streets when that "gentle
heart" still beat.

"When More some time had Chancellor been
No more suits did remain;
The like will never more be seen
Till More be there again."[4]

2.

The most difficult phrase in the epitaph is this: *furibus autem, homi-
cidis haereticisque molestus.* The meaning is roughly: "He was a worry to
thieves, murderers, and heretics." Erasmus advised Thomas to omit it,
and for some time now biographers have often overlooked this aspect
of the life of Thomas More, as if wishing not to call attention to matters that might make our kindly humanist appear politically incorrect
in these so-tolerant times. The problem has no entirely satisfactory
solution. More was a *"homo religiosus"* through and through, but his
religion was not limited to a private sphere of Mass, prayer, family life,
and charitable works. Religion permeated his whole life, including his
public life as judge, politician, statesman, and writer. The King and the
government regarded their defense of the Catholic faith as a political
matter, and by reason of office, More had to face up to the persecution
of heresy and heretics; and because of his writings, his public image,
and his own convictions, he felt obliged to take a clear stand in the
battle for the faith.

Erasmus, facing similar problems, was hardly pleased that his good
friend in London should explicitly defend the persecution of heretics,
which to Erasmus meant taking sides for political reasons. Nor was
he glad of the epitaph's listing of miscreants: thieves, murderers, heretics. To Thomas the connection was obvious: crimes against property,
against life, and against life eternal. In a letter to Erasmus, he explained
why he insisted in retaining the part that Erasmus criticized: "As regards
the reference to heretics in my burial inscription to the effect that heretics found me objectionable, I wrote it with feeling. I find this kind of
people so repugnant that I want, so long as they do not change their
opinion, to be as odious to them as I can possibly make myself. My

---

4. Reynolds, 234.

growing experience with them makes me shudder at the thought of how much the world will yet suffer because of them."[5]

For More, the basic ideas of Protestantism were so scandalous that its triumph would have been a catastrophe of great dimensions for humanity. He had no need of Luther or his follower Tyndale in order to comprehend the principles and fundamental ideas. After all, for more than a hundred and fifty years John Wycliffe and, later, the Lollard movement had pressed for England's separation from Rome and indeed from the Christian faith of the Fathers. Luther brought passionate demagogery and grandiloquence to the cause, but by the time he appeared on the scene, all essential elements of his doctrine had already been conceptualized and preached. Luther's contribution was simply to bring together all the theological theories and interpretations, all the anti-ecclesial and anticlerical resentments, that had been bubbling away in the politico-socio-economic melting pot of the times, and with that volatile mixture provoke a revolutionary explosion that we are accustomed to call the Protestant "Reformation."

⚓ ⚓ ⚓

To understand the situation in England, we need to go back to Wycliffe. He lived from 1320 to 1384, was professor of theology at Oxford, and subsequently parish priest in Lutterworth, where he died in peace, unpersecuted by either the state or the Church. His criticism of the papacy and England's willing submission to it flattered national sentiment, then on the rise. Above all, his criticism of the wealth of the Church pleased those who knew how to exploit desire that the Church live according to evangelical poverty in a way that served personal enrichment. Over the years, Wycliffe increasingly seemed to lose all sense of proportion and his own limitations and any capacity for self-restraint.

It is understandable, nevertheless, that he opposed the politicization of the papacy and the system of finance in operation in Avignon. But the issues of power, property, and, above all, law were much more complicated than the hot-tempered professor imagined. The practice of clerical poverty on the model of primitive Christianity is excellent when lived out; but as rhetoric only it bears witness to bitter resentment stoking a pre-revolutionary outlook. In Wycliffe's thinking and writing it eventually becomes impossible to distinguish honest and dishonest

---

5. *SL*, 46, 180; *Corr.*, 191.

motives, piety and the pursuit of prestige, ignorance of the world, and spoiling for a fight. He was like a man who sets out to clean a cathedral wall and ends by wanting to tear down the whole edifice, and put a small chapel in its place. But why a chapel? Can't people pray equally well under an open sky? And do we need prelates and popes? In fact, do we need even to invoke God? Isn't it enough to do good works? For how can anyone know God or even whether he exists?

Wycliffe anticipated it all. In 1366 he defended refusal to pay the English feudal tax to the Pope, and three years later the lien on church property to the Crown. This pleased the people. He could be sure of continuing popular sympathy by denouncing the degeneracy of the clergy and the materialism and secularization of the Church in general and, specifically, of the monasteries. These were real abuses, and Gregory IX's 1377 condemnation of theses from Wycliffe's text *De civili dominio* only increased his popularity.

But he did not stop at justified criticism. Instead he went on to urge the acceptance of Holy Scripture as the sole authority, the elimination of papal primacy, rejection of the power of priests to pardon sins, of auricular confession, of the Sacrament of Penance in general, an end to celibacy, to monasticism, to Transubstantiation and the Eucharist. The Church, he declared, is the invisible communion of those eternally predestined for glory; the pope is the anti-Christ. And just as Luther gave his people a translation of the Scriptures into their national language, Wycliffe published his New Testament in English in 1383.

Eventually the authorities managed to get the pre-revolution under control. But almost all of its ingredients came together less than a hundred and fifty years later in the wake of the triumphant revolution that began in Wittenberg. "As with every uprising," writes Reinhold Schneider, "so with Wycliffe, he set out in a bid to change a particular situation and ended up smashing the mold."[6]

3.

More knew perfectly well what it all meant: Wycliffism, to all intents and purposes defunct, was returning to life in the Lutheran movement, only now as an uprising across the whole of Europe that presented the appearance of social, spiritual, and national liberation. It was spread

---

6. *Das Inselreich. Gesetz und Grösse der britischen Macht* (Leipzig, 1936). Quoted from the Wiesbaden, 1955 edition, 220.

by pamphlets and books and in this way was greatly favored by the invention of printing. Merchants and traders, students, correspondence among intellectuals—all sped it forward. When by order of the King More published his *Responsio ad Lutherum* in 1523, England was still little influenced by the new doctrine, but in Germany it was spreading like wildfire. Froben, the publisher and printer, informed Luther early in 1519 that he had supplied France and Spain with six hundred copies of the 1518 edition of his works, while Erasmus congratulated Dr. Luther on the fact that the leading figures of the realm read his writings. Erasmus was right in saying Luther's books could be taken out of libraries but not out of people's minds.

Even so, the authorities tried to suppress the books. In Cambridge, the center of English Lutheranism, they were burned. And although Wolsey, to bring pressure to bear on Rome, declared that he had no power whatsoever to proceed against Luther's writings, he did prohibit their importation into England. After a sermon by Bishop Fisher, a book-burning ceremony was held to demonstrate the new alliance between England, the Emperor, and the Pope and make points against Francis I of France. Henry VIII encouraged his new friend Charles I to proceed against the "Lutheran pestilence" and wrote his own anti-Luther book. As we have seen, when Luther replied, Fisher and More were charged with preparing the response to "Luther's calumnies."

The differences between Catholic and Protestant doctrine can be summed up in the phrase "Scripture alone." For Luther and his followers, Holy Scripture, not the Church, is the final and supreme authority of Christianity.

John M. Headley, editor of the Yale Edition of More's *Responsio*, writes: "By scripture alone Luther understands a great deal more than might appear at first sight, but his opponents in 1523 were not aware of this fact. The best definition of 'ultimate authority,' in Luther's opinion, would be 'the word of God,' an expression by which he refers to the eternal divine proclamation of the Good News manifest in the historical liturgical forms of the Church and the Sacraments, but above all through the Scriptures, that is, the explanation of the doctrine of the faith and the understanding thereof. That is why justice is not done to Luther if his principle of authority is looked at solely within the limits of the expression 'scripture alone.'" [7] This, which sounds like a justification of Luther, in fact contains a harsh reproach. The quotation

---

7. Ibid., 732f.

necessarily leads to the conclusion that Luther, in theory, acknowledged Scripture and the Sacraments as being the word of God, and the Church's historical evolution, that is to say, the explanation of the doctrines of the faith and understanding thereof over time in history; but he did not recognize them in reality in the way that they had been handed down during a millennium and a half since the Resurrection of Jesus Christ. This would mean that "scripture" had not been understood straight down the line, according to God's will, or even that it had been intentionally misinterpreted. It follows, therefore, that the Church founded by Christ is capable of making mistakes and stumbling grievously and, consequently, that there was no firm and eternal guarantee of the authentic transmission of the truth.

It would also mean also that either the salvation of souls was not guaranteed within the Church, or that salvation would be attained by believing error faithfully and subjectively in objectively erroneous contents proclaimed by the "official" Church, i.e., the Pope and Councils. It also meant a great deal more: if with the passage of time false interpretations of the work and salvific will of Jesus had crept in and taken root, some overstated some less so, due to the increasing remoteness of time since His life on earth, it was necessary to go back to the point at which the distortions had started. But in attempting to do so, it was clear that if the "original Christian community" were taken as a basis for comparison, that precise moment in time did not exist, for in a given century a change could be registered; in another century a different change, and in a third century yet another change. Thus, the path of the Church for centuries could be subsumed under the headings: "correct" and "incorrect," "true" and "false" as it evolved through the various popes and councils, with changes that either have to be accepted or rejected. If that were true, the Holy Spirit would not have steered the whole Church, the Church visible, the body of Christ and European Christianity, but only a few believers. And then, after more than a thousand years of something "half right" and "half incorrect," God would have sent Dr. Luther to define what was "correct" and what "incorrect," to repair the Church, the community of Christ, just as he had willed and founded it, and as it had been in the beginning. "The Bible and tradition" were substituted by "the Bible and Luther," and "the Word of God" was replaced by "the Gospel plus the Word of Luther." The reformer himself was the witness to the tragedy of his own "exaggeration" (let us remember the imagery of what starts as the cleaning-up of a facade and ends up as a demolition job.) But neither is Scripture interpreted by itself then. From the "monopoly of interpretation" exercised by the pastorate of Peter and the Councils, it moved to arbitrariness on the part of the theologians. Zwingli, Knox, and Calvin understood the biblical message, including part of its fundamental points, in a manner different from Luther's and, therefore, taught a partially different faith, but with the same claims to authority which they would not accept in the "old Church," in Rome, in the Pope, and in the Bishops.

For Thomas More, the Love of God, which had saved man through the Word made Flesh, the Crucifixion, and the Resurrection of Jesus Christ, meant the absolute guarantee that man can find and reach God, and the implicit pledge of salvation. The bearer and seat of that authority is the historical Church, as he explains in the first book of his *Responsio*. The oral tradition already existed before the Gospels were written, something which did not happen immediately. The oral tradition, therefore, came first. God chose some witnesses who wrote down, under the inspiration of the Holy Spirit, the life of Christ. This was necessary because the day was approaching when there would be nobody alive of those who had had a personal relationship with one of the original witnesses. All this is so natural, even from a merely human perspective, that it must have been torture for Thomas to have to drive it home continually. Of course, not everything relating to the life of Christ on earth had been recorded: "If all were written down, the world itself, I suppose, would not hold all the books that would have had to be to written" (Jn 21:25). But it is absolutely certain that everything necessary for our salvation has been written down. But this does not mean that the existence of the Gospel texts and their canonical approval had put an end to the oral tradition or that only the written word was valid. It is a fact that canonical approval, the dogmatic doctrines of the Councils, including textual quality and translations (i.e., philological matters) did exist prior to, contemporaneously with, and after the writing as a historical and salvific process. For that reason, neither Scripture, tradition nor the magisterium are the true and definitive authority. That authority is the Holy Spirit, source of inspiration of all of them, who writes in every heart: *Saxeae tabulae protinus fractae sunt: ligneae duravere diu: in corde vero quod scripsit: duravit indelebile. In corde igitur, in ecclesia Christi, manet inscriptum verum evangelium Christi: quod ibi scriptum est ante libros evangelistarum omnium.* (Tablets of stone break immediately; those made of wood last a long time: what the Holy Spirit has truly written in men's hearts will never break. It is in the heart, the Church of Jesus Christ, that the true Gospel of Christ remains written down: that which was written before the books of all the Evangelists.)[8]

Basically, those arguing for and against Church reform were arguing over this question: what about the Church is divine and forever valid and what is solely human and temporal? This question in turn touched on the very substance of the Church: did Christ mean her to be an egalitarian body, without ministerial priesthood, hierarchy, or consecrated life? Were the ministerial priesthood, which separates some from the mass of believers by ordination, together with the episcopate comprised of successors of the apostles and the Petrine office as authentic representative of Christ on earth, merely historical accidents, offices of power, and theological departures from what Jesus Christ intended—in other words, mistakes? From this it was an easy step to indulgences, the veneration of saints and relics, pilgrimages, the treasury of priestly, monastic, and popular devotions, devotion to Mary, and even the sacraments.

The answers to these questions depend on whether divine legitimacy resides in Scripture alone or also in the oral tradition and historical development. And even if one's answer is "scripture alone," that also can lead to different results. Thus Headley: "The doctrine of the Trinity and the perpetual virginity of Mary are not established in Holy Scripture."[9] But others hold that they are. For Luther, not only were the cult of the saints, the papacy, and the vows of monks without meaning, but four, and later five, of the seven sacraments had no biblical basis; but More saw them as entirely well-founded there.[10] And here we reach a dead end, part of that Cross of Christ to which Christianity has been nailed from the start.

⚬❧⚬❧⚬❧

At the end of the first book of the first version of the *Responsio*, the so-called "Baravellus version," More notes the four assumptions that Luther would have to accept should he wish to continue calling himself a Catholic Christian: "1) A belief in Holy Scripture; 2) that there are things said, done, and taught by God which were not written down; 3) that being guided by the Holy Spirit, the Church is empowered to

---

8. *Responsio, CW* 5, 100.
9. *Responsio, CW* 5, 737.
10. Ibid., 739. More quotes Jn 20:30; 2 Thes 2:14; Heb 10:16; Jn 16:31; Lk 22:32; Mt 28:20.

draw a distinction between God's revelations and the traditions of men; 4) that concerning the interpretation of Holy Scripture, the judgment of the Fathers of the Church must be followed."[11] When More was writing those words, all of these expressions were understood in different ways, thus there was no way of resolving the fundamental disagreements.

The second book deals with secondary issues, such as the much-discussed question of whether communion should be given under both species or only the species of bread. But it also contains semi-hidden dynamite of a different kind.

The question was: How are law and conscience, law and salvation, related? Writing on the "Babylonian captivity" of the Church, Luther argued that knowledge of divine law made written laws unnecessary, even pernicious. In his view, Christian charity required no law.[12] Plainly the reformer failed to take sufficiently into consideration man's real nature and situation on earth, which, as with much else related to his eternal salvation, depends entirely on grace. His treatment is somewhat fragmented. Above all, any divine fusion of justice and love is ruled out. For people with an underdeveloped sense of fraternal charity and an inadequate sense of order, civil and ecclesiastical laws are necessary as protection against anarchy and despotism. Luther did not realize that the human system of laws is also an expression of the love of God, who knows what we need in this world to compensate for our frailty. Hence, as was evident even in his lifetime, Luther became a point of reference both for antinomian movements opposed to all authority and for tendencies in the direction of authoritarianism and state control.

As Luther's thinking evolved, he contributed to both the liberation and the suppression of anarchic forces. His doctrine, whether misinterpreted or not, encouraged subjects to rise against princes. But dismayed by the consequences, he then encouraged the princes to ruthlessly reimpose discipline and order. His relationship with politics, power, and the state was changeable, unbalanced, increasingly opportunistic, and at times naïve. The young Luther was a revolutionary religious not at all disturbed if his revolution extended to the secular sphere; but in his later years he transformed himself into a religious authority maintained by the secular power.

---

11. Ibid., 740.
12. *D. Martin Luthers Werke*, 58 Vols. (Weimar, 1883ff.), vol. 6, 554.

As a judge and a man of personal rectitude who respected people and had a natural sense of justice, Thomas More might well have been able to function with a Christian heart and conscience as his only criteria. But he saw in law in general, whether canon, Roman, or common law, an essential protection against arbitrariness, a framework of assistance to human frailty. He had no sympathy for justices of the peace who administered justice simply by what they read in the Bible or according to their own tastes or religious opinions. He wrote in his *Responsio*: "If you do away with the laws, and leave everything to the criterion of justices of the peace, either they will fail to command or condemn nothing, in which case they would be useless, or they will govern according to their particular bent or whim of the moment, and then the people will no longer be free, and will more likely than not find themselves worse off, having to obey not laws but caprices that change from day to day. And this would happen with the best of judges."[13]

When it came to demarcating areas of jurisdiction, More did not distinguish between "secular" and "religious." He thought it absurd to deny or prohibit the Church the right to have laws establishing order in her own sphere of life and worship. At that time, he had not turned his attention to the problem of authority within the Church, the primacy of the pope in particular.

It is difficult to understand the dispute over law between Luther and More. Headley comments: "Luther vehemently rejected the concept of legalism in theology."[14] What did this mean? Jesus did not annul "the law," but complied with it through the salvific work of Redemption; that is why the concept of "law" possesses in relation to salvation a new, deeper, and wider scope in the New Testament than in the Old. Was it then the dogmatizing of the essential elements of the faith that Luther rejected? Did he consider dogmas, such as the Incarnation and the Trinity constituting the basic principles of faith to be in effect "laws"? Or did he associate "law" only with an obsession with administrative or disciplinary justice?

Bearing in mind that the reformed creeds became dogmatized and "legalized" very soon—in part, during Luther's lifetime—we must conclude that the real issue about law was the authority to impose laws.

---

13. *Responsio*, *CW* 5, 276ff, 754.
14. Ibid., 758.

Without that, it would have been impossible in this world for a community, especially a religious community, to hold together. Thomas More was convinced that the successors of Peter and the apostles have power to legislate—have always had it, have it now, and will always have it; and that the Holy Spirit, the real legislator, works through them. And this, in his opinion, applies to dogmas and to laws that undergo change in the course of time. Luther, on the other hand, questioned not only the source of legislation but also the laws that up to then had been considered valid, the *leges credendi* and *leges orandi*. In impugning the credibility of popes and councils in matters of faith, he not only dealt a mighty blow to the edifice of the Western Church, with all its millennium and a half of antiquity, but also implicitly raised the question of whether an unerring faith could exist at all and, even supposing the Holy Spirit revealed himself, how the authenticity of such revelation could be verified.

In the final analysis, the issue was not defending Henry VIII or rebutting Luther or waging some battle of the day. The issue was the substance of the Church herself, and the task for More was to make her position clear. This is the aim of the second version of the *Responsio*, the so-called "Rosseus's version." The custom then was to cast a text in the form of an exchange of letters or an imaginary dialogue. Thus, in the case of Baravellus, More writes as a student in a Spanish university and the action takes place entirely in Spain. In Rosseus's case, the author presents as humanist, diplomat, and theologian, and every inch an Englishman who enjoys a good relationship with his sources of information on the continent. More naturally makes use of statements made by Luther himself, but he also uses opinions expressed about him and the reform movement, along with events in Germany. More was an extraordinarily well-informed man of his time, with a wealth of information at his disposal.

Luther's assault on the roots of the Church moved More to reflect deeply on what he, like countless other Christians, had up to then taken for granted, namely, the divine bedrock of papal authority. Not long before, he had advised the King to tone down passages on the primacy of the pope more prudently, and in the "Baravellus version" he even side-stepped the question; but now Luther compelled him to take an unequivocal stand, no less than a confession of faith.

Eschewing name-calling, More seriously challenges Luther on crucial points. He argues that the Church is the visible community of those who confess faith in Christ in a manner that has been handed down without interruption; the greater part of Christendom accepts the primacy of the pope; but if this "large number of people united in faith is not the Church, where then has she been during the time between the death of Christ and the birth of Luther?"[15] The Church is not joined to Rome, but to the pope, successor of Peter. "No matter how dispersed Christian communities may be, there will always be one visible Church"[16] whose head on earth is the pope. It was willed thus by Christ, Lord of ages and eternity. The pope is his vicar, the "chaplain of Christ." This is traditional doctrine as well as More's reading of Matthew's gospel: "And I tell you that you are Peter and upon this rock I shall build my Church, and the gates of hell will not prevail against her."[17] Once again More speaks, but in greater depth, of the correlation between "justice" and "charity" in the Church.

Then as now, misleading expressions like "institutional Church" and "official Church" and "visible Church" were opposed to no less misleading terms like "Church of love" and "Johannine Church." More emphasized that the Church needs law and authority precisely because she has her origin and existence in faith. Law and charity are not synonymous, but there is no Christian law apart from Christian charity.

More completed the Rosseus version of the *Responsio* at the end of 1523. Here he had expressed his definitive idea of the Church. Even here he expressly states that he does not mean to enter into a discussion about the power of the pope: "*Tacit interream de iure Pontificis.*"[18] But although someone misled by the abstract nature of the remarks about the primacy may consider them evasive, Thomas More shows himself here a realistic Christian speaking as befits his position, office, and knowledge—neither more nor less. He declared that he acknowledged Peter and the uninterrupted Petrine succession until the end of time, but he did not discuss the concrete form taken by that succession. The centuries-old argument about the relationship between popes and councils had not yet quieted down, and Thomas did not consider it up to him to settle it. He considered himself a lay person in both expertise and charism, and felt no compulsion to pronounce on every issue. Let

---

15. Ibid., 192, 763.
16. Ibid.
17. Mt 16:18.
18. Ibid., 608.

us remember that it was not until three centuries later, at the First Vatican Council, that the infallibility of the pope in matters of faith and morals was defined as dogma.

Up to this first active intervention of his in the great battle of his age, More had read practically nothing of Luther other than the Wittenberg theses. On the basis of these, he had formed a negative impression of the German reformer. But only when Henry VIII entered the arena did More feel obliged to examine Luther's writings more closely. After reading these along with reports about the effects they had produced, and doing his own research, his initial aversion became informed condemnation. The *Responsio* thus marked the beginning of a decade of anti-heretical journalism: *A Dialogue Concerning Heresies and Matters of Religion*, 1528 (published in 1529); *The Supplication of Souls*, 1529; *The Confutation of Tyndale's Answer*, 1532; *The Apology of Sir Thomas More*, 1533; *The Debellation of Salem and Byzance*, 1533.

It signals a great change in More that he wrote these controversial pieces in English. The academic disputant had become an impassioned controversialist seeking readers and results. He writes like a man personally offended. He speaks as an advocate for the souls in Purgatory, referring to the torment of that place of purification and the need for constant communication through prayer between those souls and the living. He emphasizes the reality of the communion of saints, and defends the Eucharist and the enduring Real Presence of Christ in the tabernacle. As far as he was concerned, Luther was responsible not only for major divergences in matters of faith, but also for painful secondary aberrations like the renunciation of celibacy, the rejection of the monastic life, disdain for chastity, asceticism, and devotion to the Virgin, and the decline, in the face of insults and brutality, of popular devotions like pilgrimages, the Rosary, and the cult of the saints. Sometimes indeed he failed to distinguish sufficiently between core problems and marginal issues, for he was grieved to see not only the assault on the faith of the Church but the contempt and ill treatment directed at devotion. To do justice to More and his *Responsio*, one must bear in mind that even though he wrote by order of the King, he himself was anguished at the collapse of the old and venerable order.

At that time, only those who shared Sir Thomas's love and pain were capable of understanding this. The very extensive work, written in Latin, seems to have found little resonance in England, even though Bishop Fisher in 1524 mentioned it in glowing terms in one of his London sermons. Few people knew of it besides those close to More, the King, and government circles. After its author's death, it was reviled and eventually forgotten in England. On the Continent, it earned the respect of Catholic apologists like Juan Luis Vives and Dr. Johann Eck. But the *Responsio* had no identifiable impact on the Reformation or the Counter-Reformation. True, when the Catholic Church, following the Council of Trent, launched its counterattack, More and his *Responsio ad Lutherum* received a renewed recognition, especially among cultured people, but this should not be overestimated. Only much later did More's "hour" arrive when he came to be esteemed for his books and his martyrdom, and especially for the consistency of his Christian life.[19]

4.

Luther's first supporter on English soil was William Tyndale. He was born in Gloucestershire around 1490 and by 1520 was working on the English translation of the Bible. Few denied that a translation of Scripture into the national tongue was necessary for the sake of effective pastoral work. But it had to be a translation commissioned by the Church, not the work of a private individual, much less one of Luther's devotees. Tyndale was accused of heresy, fled to the Continent, and in 1524 reached Wittenberg, where he soon became one of the reformer's associates. His translation of the New Testament was published in Cologne in 1525, and five years later the Pentateuch appeared in Marburg.[20] The official ban on the importation of books in English from the Continent was not working, and by 1526 Tyndale's translation and various heretical writings were everywhere circulating more or less furtively. Prohibitions were not enough; a comprehensive response was needed.

Organizing this intellectual and spiritual defense was entrusted to Thomas More, whose *Responsio* had shown him to be capable of mobilizing the intellectual resources and the printing presses. His old friend Cuthbert Tunstall, still Bishop of London and custodian of the Secret Seal of the State—which made him the second-ranking dignitary of the realm after Wolsey—in an official document charged More with the

---

19. Cf. the epilogue.

20. This translation, begun by Tyndale, was finished in 1537 by Coverdale and Rogers and revised by Archbishop Cranmer; but not until 1611, during the time of James I, was it published as an authorized version. Tyndale was apprehended by the Inquisition and put to death in 1536 near Brussels.

task of reading books by heretics in order to rebut them. "So that you may not have to go into battle like a blind man against his adversaries, I am sending you some examples of these wild and preposterous ideas composed in our very own language. The primary prerequisite of victory is to gain an exact knowledge of the enemy's plans. His strategy and objectives must be known, for if you accuse him of something he is not really saying, then all your efforts will have been in vain. I beseech God to aid you in carrying out this assignment, since you are also protecting the Church in a very special way."[21]

That same year, 1528, Thomas wrote *A Dialogue Concerning Heresies and Matters of Religion*, published in four volumes in London in June of 1529. It was the start of a series of treatises on controversial issues written by More in English. In the spring of 1531, Tyndale published his reply in Antwerp, a year later. More responded with the most extensive of his writings, *The Confutation of Tyndale's Answer* (its second part appeared in 1533, published like the first by John Rastell in London). Although this work did not appear until after More had retired from royal service, when he also composed his burial inscription, its conception, drafting, and printing for the most part took place while he still was Chancellor.

Almost ten years divided the *Responsio* and the *Confutation*. The issues dividing Western Christianity remained the same, but they had become defined. No longer were the questions whether priests should be allowed to marry, the value of the monastic life, the divine institution of the papacy, holy days, indulgences, and oral confession. Discussion of the role of the Virgin in salvation, the communion of saints, and Scripture vs. tradition had ceased. Now fundamentals were debated: the idea of God; the plan of salvation and redemption; predestination, choice, and grace; the relationship between grace and human freedom; and tied up inseparably with all this, the nature of the Church and the sacraments.

The international situation also had changed. The Protestants were advancing, the Catholics were in retreat. For although the Imperial Diet of the Holy Roman-Germanic Empire in Augsburg had issued a response to the *Confessio Augustana* of the Protestants and laws had been enacted protecting the ancient Church, many states of the Empire had already transferred their allegiance to the so-called "purified doctrine."

---

21. Blarer, 90; *Corr.*, 160. Letter dated February 7, 1528.

Sweden, Denmark, Norway, and the regions under Prussian military rule had followed suit. And Protestantism was putting down roots in France, the Low Countries, and England.

More's *Confutation* is a heroic and inspired defensive act: heroic because, although he was suffering mental and physical pain, it was written in a remarkably short period of time; inspired because it went far beyond theological accuracy and intellectual skill to touch readers' hearts. In his introduction to the Yale edition of the *Confutation*, Louis A. Schuster, comments that this "gigantic work," whose theme is "the destiny of the Catholic Church and her enemies," has no effect on a contemporary audience that, moved by a liberal culture, "faces" the world with brazen skepticism. The tone, often coarse and vengeful, is frightening, and "the best arguments lose their value in the face of the enormous and somber wall of modern atheism."[22] No doubt all this is true, but what is one to conclude from it?

Where genuine atheism rules, all religious and theological writings, including the Bible and the Koran, and not just More's books, are seen as irrelevant. But the strength of atheism is more apparent than real. Modern secularism's response to a personal God is not so much "no" but "who knows?" Conversion remains an option for individuals— indeed, for an entire age. And many Christians (their number may perhaps be growing) are not indifferent to the truths of faith. To such as these More still has much of importance to say.

Although More deals in the *Confutation* with the Church and her authority, as he also did in the *Responsio*, he probes more deeply here by including the question of God and his accessibility by man. Thomas Aquinas had proposed that human reason can know God's existence and some of his qualities, whereas followers of Duns Scotus emphasized the limits of our understanding so as to discourage exaggerating man's capacity to comprehend the divine. Instead, they taught, we must approach him who is Love through love. Both strains of thought are present in the *Confutation*. More knew that no one can grasp the reality of God through his intellect. The Christian must humbly accept the fact that he can understand only what God wills to reveal through the Church, whereas Tyndale, distrusting what is

---

22. *CW*, vol. 8, *The Confutation of Tyndale's Answer*, Parts I–III, edited by Louis A. Schuster, Richard C. Marius, James Lusardi, Richard J. Schoeck (New Haven-London, 1973) (quoted as: *Confutation*), 1271.

perceptible to the senses, scoffs at ritual and believes the sacraments' effect is purely spiritual.

In this context, More stresses that God, with our nature in mind, joined his deepest mysteries of grace to matter. Jesus, God incarnate, performed his miracles in a visible, tangible manner. Thus, for More, the puritanical spirituality of Tyndale and the reformers was pure arrogance. He writes: "Tyndale seeks to understand God's mysteries.[23] But no man has the right to understand the "reasons" for the works and ways of God. Moreover, the very fact of wanting to is blasphemy and stupidity. God could have saved man in a way other than through the Incarnation, the Cross, and the Resurrection, but he has willed to save us in this specific way."[24]

More berated Tyndale and Luther for relying on a subjective interpretation of Holy Scripture instead of the Deposit of Faith handed down through the ages. They dismissed more than a millennium of Church history as a time of error that only Lutheranism and the reestablishment of the true Church would end. To More, this was equivalent to dismissing all of Christianity from Chalcedon in 451 A.D. to the events at Wittenberg in 1517.[25] It implied the existence of an invisible Church within the erring "official Church," and it was to this invisible true Church that those saved by their pure and simple faith had belonged, while the Holy Spirit led a kind of catacomb existence.[26]

For more than ten years the expression "the true Church" had featured prominently in discussions. What did it mean? With all her faults and frailties and the sins of her members, the Church had existed in uninterrupted continuity from the first Pentecost down to the present day. More regarded as absurd the claim that the true Church had only emerged into the light of history through the efforts of Luther and his partisans. But the strain of having to continually repeat the same arguments was very real. When the modernizers called Scripture

---

23. *Confutation, CW* 8, 79ff; 1272–77.

24. Ibid., 464.

25. The Council of Chalcedon (A.D. 451) declared the Church's faith in the one Lord Jesus Christ, perfect in his divinity and humanity, of the same nature as the Father as regards divinity and of a nature same as ours as regards humanity, begotten by God the Father before time began and born of Virgin Mary, Mother of God (*theotokos*). Cf. R. Kottje, B. Moeller (eds.), *Ökumenische Kirchengeschichte*, vol. 1 (Mainz, 1970), 182.

26. *Confutation, CW* 8, 108; 679.

fundamental, More would say that not Scripture but the people of God came first. "Christ did not leave us a book, but a people—the Church—from whom Scripture emerged."[27] Furthermore, he says, "The authority of the Church remains the only means of being sure what belongs to Scripture and what does not. Without the Church's interpretation nobody would know what Scripture means, for not only must it be taken as the word of God but it also must be understood properly."[28] Christ's promise to be with us until the end of time did not apply to a book but to a Church.

More strongly than in the *Responsio*, the author here insists on the "corporeal nature" of the Church and the "material character" of the sacraments. He also sought to demonstrate from the Bible the institution of the five sacraments denied by Tyndale: Penance, Confirmation, Extreme Unction, Matrimony, and Holy Orders.[29]

But the central issue of the treatise concerns redemption as such, including choice, collaboration, faith, and works. More insists that the cause of the conflict between the Church of Rome and the modernizers turns on how one understands Church.[30] She is not an invisible community of those predestined for salvation, but a community founded by Jesus Christ that from the start includes wicked and unworthy members, even some damned, for among those called by the Lord was Judas Iscariot, "the son of perdition."[31]

Time and time again, More refuted the doctrine of the reformers on predestination as he understood it, for, as Richard Marius says, he "made it even more cruel and horrible than it already was."[32] Tyndale had not said, as More believed, that of two people who both wanted to please God in the same way, one could be arbitrarily chosen and the other rejected, but only that the fact that someone sincerely wanted to serve God was proof enough that he was chosen. Yet the question remains: Are some predestined from eternity to make a sincere effort to find and serve God or must a man collaborate in his own salvation? More vehemently denied that salvation is not linked to collaboration;

---

27. Ibid., 1287.
28. Ibid., 677.
29. Ibid., 688f.
30. Ibid., 761.
31. Ibid., 499.
32. Ibid., 1319ff.

that someone can know whether he is among the chosen or the rejected; that salvation is absolutely certain for anyone, and that a Christian can never lose grace. More understood that hair-splitting about "choice" and "predestination" leads nowhere. But as a lawyer skilled in spotting discrepancies, he points out the need to distinguish between predestination and divine foreknowledge. His argument is based on the fifth book of Boethius's *De Consolatione Philosophiae*, which notes that human free will is not cancelled by divine foresight. The fact that God may know in advance which option he is going to choose does not influence that man's choice.[33]

Naturally, he never doubted that divine goodness which passes all human understanding, but neither did he doubt its mysterious relationship to justice. God is a loving Father and also Lord and King. The words of the Letter to the Hebrews (10:31) remain perfectly valid: "It is a dreadful thing to fall into the hands of the living God." Nobody can claim to have done so many good works that God is obliged to grant him eternal salvation, says More, for in working well one has only done one's duty, and not acquired a right.[34] Because "if we act wrongfully after having acted rightfully we are no longer sons of God, no matter what dear little darlings we may have been before that."[35] This sounds harsh, but what More means is that grave sin is voluntary and conscious separation from God; and, unrepented of, the end of such separation is damnation.

Where the question of free will and grace is concerned, it is doubtful whether those who disagree can be reconciled by logical argumentation. Luther, in his *De Servo Arbitrio* and Erasmus in his *De Libero Arbitrio* (1524) had influence on each other. although neither is short of passages from Scripture to prove his point. It is time wasted. More in his *Confutation* does not refer to Erasmus, but he does not go beyond what Erasmus had said, except perhaps by adding certain graphic expressions. "It is very true" he writes, "that no one can believe without grace and God's help, but . . . if nothing in man enables him to add something, acting in conjunction with God, then Our Lord would not call on men and admonish them to believe, and would not reject those who fail to do so."[36]

---

33. Ibid., 1331.
34. Ibid., 426.
35. Ibid., 757.
36. Ibid., 503f; 1321.

In Holy Scripture nonbelief is stigmatized as a rejection of God's gift, an act incurring guilt. If the gift of faith is accepted, however, it finds expression in good works. Whether such works are necessary for salvation aroused strong feelings in the time of Luther and More; but to us, the question seems ingenuous. Is a tree only roots or is it branches and leaves, too? The roots give life, but a living tree sprouts branches and leaves and brings forth fruit.

Lastly, a Christian's responsibility for his own salvation carries with it responsibility for his brothers and sisters and the whole world. In their own way, monks, hermits, and members of contemplative orders also serve the world. But the world needs those who work in it: it needs Christians who pray through their work. One of the strangest contradictions following the Protestant break with Rome is that it should have been the Protestants who developed a work ethic that, exaggerated at times to the point of idolatry, placed its stamp on the modern era; while the Catholics, whose "justification through deeds" Luther so hated, often saw work more as a consequence of original sin than a way of sanctifying themselves.

Both Thomas More and the reformers placed a high value on work and social responsibility, while disagreeing profoundly about what this entails. In the *Responsio*, More rejected Luther's view that a Christian requires no laws other than the Gospel. He returned to this idea in the *Confutation*, relating it to the questions of free choice.[37] While regarding human nature as less corrupt than Luther and the reformers supposed, he was reluctant to place too heavy a burden on it. While people very often want what is good, he held, they are weak and need a framework of laws and institutions to protect them.

More saw that only a few short steps separate faith in predestination from the subjective conviction that one is oneself among the chosen ones. From that it is only another short step to autocracy, considered to be a sacred duty. The Geneva Republic and Cromwell's Puritan Commonwealth are the result. One of More's main aims in all his controversial writings, as Marius says, was to defend the reality of the Church against reformers "searching for a different kind of Church: predestined, small, and invisible to all except God."[38]

---

37. Cf. in this respect and for what follows: ibid., 1329f.
38. Ibid., 1334f.

5.

In More's day, Church and state formed one unit representing the two parts of man's ordered existence. Notwithstanding more than half a millennium of controversy between religious and earthly power, between emperor and pope, between the various kingdoms and the Holy See, unity in the faith and a common struggle against deviations were considered natural. This situation prevailed in England even under King Henry VIII, at least while More was in his service. Thus he could write in his *Confutation*: "Due to my position and because of the oath I have sworn, I feel duty-bound in a special way, together with all those who serve the jurisprudence of the realm, to cure this ill [heresy] not only with good arguments but also with the backing of official decrees and statutes. And, should it be confirmed that the ill is incurable, we are prepared to amputate the damaged part for the sake of the health of the whole to prevent the rest being infected."[39]

From 1535 onwards, when the defacing of Thomas More's image in his own country began, among the posthumous criticisms heard was that accusing him of cruelty toward "reformed Christians." The first thing to say about this is as Lord Chancellor, neither Wolsey nor More had the right to condemn and execute heretics. Trials for heresy came exclusively within the competence of bishops and ecclesiastical tribunals. If a "hardened heretic" was condemned to death—something that happened less frequently than was subsequently claimed in the heat of religious controversy—it was the state judiciary that did so, and the condemned could save himself up to the very last moment by renouncing heresy.

In his *Apology* of 1533, More recounts that, having taken a child from a Protestant family into his home, he once had the child beaten with a stick for spreading heresy among the other children of the household. In the same work he mentions having had "an imbecile heretic" flogged, not for heresy but for molesting women during Holy Mass.[40] More himself notes a case of character assassination: A Cambridge bookseller, jailed in Chelsea for four or five days, claimed that he was tied to a tree in More's garden and beaten, and that the Chancellor robbed him of a purse containing five marks. Two other claims blaming More for unlawful arrest turned out to be unsubstantiated and were rejected, though this did not keep them from being repeated.

---

39. Ibid., 28; *Works*, 351.
40. Chambers, 333; *Apology*, in *Works*, ch. 36, 901.

In sum, there is no reason to doubt More's statement: "Among all the heretics ever to be handed into my safe custody (and perhaps not so safe, for Georg Konstantin slipped through my fingers), there is not one to have received a single blow, or even a light tap on his forehead on orders from me."[41]

From 1519 to 1531 not a single sentence of death for heresy was imposed in the London diocese. Only after February 1531, when the English clergy caved in to the King and accepted him as Head of the Church "insofar as it may be compatible with the law of Christ," were the bonfires relit to provide a show of orthodoxy. At the time, More had no power that made him a threat to heretics; the newly installed Bishop of London, Stokesley, Tunstall's successor, was responsible for the three burnings that took place during the last six months of More's Chancellorship. There are no bloodstains on his hands.

So what did Bremond mean in speaking of "bloodstains on Thomas More's ermine"?[42] In fact, he is referring to More's Christian charity. To understand that, we have to understand something about the controversies of that day. Thanks to printing, they took place in a veritable whirlwind of publicity. Polemics were not confined to intellectual circles. Leaflets and pamphlets were distributed by roving scholars and preachers who read them aloud and added their own comments. Ideas were spread in the marketplace, in inns and taverns, at gatherings and parties, within the family, among friends and neighbors.

Moreover, many of the matters in dispute were visibly lived out. Monks and nuns left their monasteries and convents, gadded about, got married. Princes embraced the new faith while confiscating church and monastic property. Peasants found in the Gospels liberation from oppression and a new special order in human society. Thus the stage was set for the German peasant wars with their horrific atrocities on both sides. Ordinary Christians were not qualified to join in doctrinal debates, but they found it easier to understand the idea that Christ is *not* really present in the Eucharist than the idea that he is. And saving money on Masses for the dead because they are of no practical use is somehow more agreeable than creating charitable foundations to benefit them.

As for the physical side of the great intellectual and spiritual struggle of his time, More considered it his duty to resist heresy. Lending a secular

---

41. Chambers, 334; *Works*, ibid.
42. Bremond, 145.

arm to the harassed Church seemed to him desirable. A year before being appointed Lord Chancellor, he wrote Johannes Cochlaeus,[43] "Surveying the present situation, the fast-spreading decadence and its advance from one day to the next, I believe that in the near future someone will come forward to disown Christ. And should such an insensitive buffoon emerge he will not lack sympathizers, given the present crazy state of the masses."[44]

More considered the repression and punishment of heresy to be the duty of the state; but the Church had a moral responsibility, however. As he makes the adversary say in the *Dialogue Concerning Heresies*: "In effect, it is the bishop who puts the heretic to death the moment he hands him over to the civil tribunals."[45] More saw nothing wrong in this. And he leaves no doubt that he also approved of the more extreme consequences: "If a man is so deeply rooted in evil that not even the appropriate legal action can restrain the daring, overweening arrogance, and the obstinacy of his poisoned heart not prevent him from spreading his rebellious errors, I prefer that such a man were gone in good time."[46]

Here are Bremond's "bloodstains on Thomas More's ermine." But his views must be seen in the context of his times, of which, great and good though he was, he was a product. In those days thieves were hanged, and to him destroying a crucifix was worse than theft and desecrating the consecrated Host worse than murder. There was no religious tolerance then. Simon Fish, of whom we shall speak later, demanded that "clerics, especially monks, should be flogged, paraded naked tied to a cart through the city, and then make them marry."[47] Lastly, one must bear in mind that the Lutheran revolt was happening at a time when Europe and Christianity were menaced by the Turks, who in 1529 were at the gates of Vienna. This was a huge act of treason in More's eyes, and he trembled at the reformer's saying that he preferred to see Germany Turkish rather than Catholic.

---

43. Johannes Cochlaeus (1479–1552), was a highly educated, versatile, and very productive humanist, a Catholic theologian and (after 1519) a priest. Besides his topographical description of Germany (*Brevis Germaniae Descriptio*), he became famous for his radical opposition to Luther and the Protestant Reformation. He was court chaplain to the Duke of Saxony (1528) and, until the advent of Protestantism in Saxony, canon in Meissen and later in Breslau.

44. *SL*, 41; *Corr.*, 162.

45. *Works*, 211; Chambers, 340.

46. Quoted by Bremond, 144.

47. *Works*, 307; Bremond, 146; Chambers, 320.

Thomas felt no guilt in signing the death sentences in the instances mentioned, and Bremond reasonably asks whether a government official incurs guilt in this way.[48] There is ample evidence that More did his utmost to prevent this extreme measure; that he conducted the interrogations in an indulgent, caring, and sincere attempt to convert the heretic; and that he sent the condemned who did not renounce heresy back to the appropriate bishops to save them from burning, in the knowledge that the bishops could keep heretics in prison.[49]

Above all, he sought conversion. "If people only knew what proofs of indulgence and compassion I have given," he said, "I swear that nobody would contradict me on this score."[50]

---

48. Bremond, 149.
49. Ibid., 148.
50. Ibid.

CHAPTER FIVE

A Father and His Children

"His father, Sir John More, was appointed Judge of the Royal Court by the King; he was an open, kindly, upright, pious, compassionate, honest and sincere man. Even at a venerable age he kept himself very fit for a person of his years. After seeing his son appointed Lord Chancellor of England, he felt his life on earth had come to an end and with joy passed on to the heavenly life.[1] When the father was alive, the son was always measured against him, being called 'young More.' And now he felt the loss of his father, and seeing the four children and the eleven grandchildren he had engendered, he began to feel that he was getting old."

1.

Thomas used the burial inscription to dedicate a eulogy to his father. Much love and veneration inform these lines, along with jovial, mischievous humor. It is not difficult to imagine the bond between father and son: loving, caring, full of mutual respect and good humor, without sentimentality, rather dry.

The elder More was one of the most senior and highly respected judges in the land, and no doubt at home the two discussed current legal cases and political events. There also are records of judicial and administrative activities in common. Thus, in the years 1514 and 1529, we find the two Mores on commissions for the construction of canals, once in London (together with John Roper), then in Middlesex;[2] and in 1518 the three were mentioned as Justices of the Peace in the county of

---

1. Cf. *SL* 46, 182.
2. *L'Univers*, 203; 417.

Kent.[3] The date of John More's elevation to knighthood, mentioned in the epitaph, is unknown. It appears that he was proposed, at the age of seventy-two, for the King's Bench (Supreme Royal Courts) after having sat, six years previously, as judge in the Court of Common Pleas, a high civil tribunal. Sir John was a judge who followed a strict routine, more dispassionate than his son, more "ordinary," so to speak, in everything he did, but above all more moderate in matters of religion. He would probably not have mounted the steps to the scaffold for its sake, but would have opted for an "arrangement." He was a pious man; a saint he was not.

On the sheet of good quality paper bearing the 1527 pencil drawing by Holbein[4] one sees a gentleman, elderly but robust, remarkably unwrinkled, gazing into space, with a somewhat disagreeable area around the mouth. With consummate artistry, Holbein succeeded in capturing what indeed was old in and around the eyes of that man, in his mid-sixties. Beneath somewhat heavy eyelids, his eyes have a fixed, cold look, whereas his son's expression is sad and mild. Sir John is said to have likened the choice of a wife to putting one's hand in a sack full of snakes and eels, seven snakes to one eel. Yet, he was not put off. When he married the fourth time he was close to seventy; the third stepmother survived not only him but Thomas, who under his father's will of 1527 received next to nothing after Sir John's death in 1530. The son did not take it badly. "It would be difficult to find people who got on as well with their mothers as he did with his stepmothers," writes Erasmus.[5] More's attitude never changed. It expressed an inner nobility that moved the Lord Chancellor, already over fifty, to kneel before his father for his blessing.

<h2 style="text-align:center">2.</h2>

Nothing is more appealing and revealing about Thomas More as a family man and about his household than Eramus's letter to Hutten, which has already been mentioned several times. Nor is there any testimony more profound than More's own letters to his wife and children especially.

---

3. Ibid., 269.

4. This is one of the drawings from the first journey to England, among them are the portraits of the More family; cf. Ulrich Christoffel, *Hans Holbein the Younger* (Berlin, 1950), 34ff.

5. Cf. note 16 in the same chapter. Letter to Hutten dated July 23, 1519.

Of the four children from his first marriage (there were no children from his marriage to Lady Alice), Margaret, born in 1505, was closest to him. On one occasion she fell gravely ill, probably with typhus, and fell into a coma-like sleep. Doctors and relatives gave up hope. More, praying on his knees, recalled a certain medication and mentioned it to the doctors. Ashamed not to have thought of it themselves, they administered it to her while she slept. Margaret awoke, made a full recovery, and "everyone was convinced that it was due entirely to her father's fervent prayer."[6] More later said that if she had died, he would have withdrawn completely from the world. He dearly loved his other children—Elizabeth, Cicely, and John—but he loved Margaret best and showed it. His prison correspondence with her lets us to peer into Thomas's heart.

Margaret was extraordinarily gifted and had an excellent education. Erasmus dedicated a short tract to her and allowed her to translate his *Treatise on the Our Father*. More was very proud of his cultured daughter. Once he showed one of her letters to the Bishop of Exeter, "a very cultured man and of very good reputation." More went on: "When he finished reading it he declared that such a letter . . . but why don't I join my opinion to his? He admired your brilliant Latin and all your wisdom, but he also praised your expressions of filial love for me. On hearing such eulogy, I also showed him your exercise on rhetoric. He also read the poems."[7] Evidently the proud father carried with him the writings of his favorite daughter.

On another occasion, a year later, More received and read a letter from his daughter while Reginald Pole was visiting him.[8] The young and noble gentleman was impressed at such culture and wisdom. More writes: "My dearest Margaret, you know very well that your name will never be very well-known, even if you continue to cultivate your knowledge and merits. You have such great love for your husband and for me that we suffice entirely as your audience. For our part, we pray for you,

---

6. Chambers, 219.

7. Blarer, 63f. John Vosey (1465–1534) was Bishop of Exeter since 1519. On Margaret Roper, cf. E. E. Reynolds, *Margaret Roper* (London, 1962).

8. Reginald Pole (1500–1558) was a cousin of Henry VIII. In 1529/30 he tried to obtain an opinion from the Sorbonne in Paris favorable to the King in the question of the divorce. In 1534, he was made a cardinal. In a tract in defense of the unity of the Church, addressed to King Henry and published in Rome 1538, he refused to accept the royal supremacy and was exiled. He worked as a member of the commission for reform in Rome, and in 1545/46 was papal envoy to the Council of Trent. Under the Catholic Mary I, in 1553, he was envoy to England and in 1555 was installed as Archbishop of Canterbury.

that the imminent childbirth will be easy and joyous. May God and the ever-blessed Virgin Mary grant that you give birth easily and trouble-free; you will present us with a descendant whom we hope will be in everything, except gender, like his/her mother."[9]

Realizing the injustice of these last words, typical of the prejudice of those times, he adds: "I know a woman who, because of being a woman, will never attain the celebrity she truly deserves. Through her special endeavors in the sciences, and the virtues of a good mother, she attempts to correct such a disadvantage. I much prefer, of course, such a woman to three lads. Farewell, my dearest daughter."[10]

To be sure, among the higher nobility there were important and influential women and queens, such as Isabel of Castile or later in England, Mary I and Elizabeth I, and Mary Stuart in Scotland. In the religious sphere there were always great saints, abbesses, and nuns. But these were the exception. Women generally had no role outside the family circle. Yet More's daughters, Margaret, Elizabeth, and Cicely, like their brother John, learned Latin and Greek, and were taught theology, philosophy, logic, mathematics, and astronomy. Writing to his friend Guillaume Bude (Budaeus) in 1521, Erasmus confessed that he formerly had believed "that the sciences are harmful to the innocence and good name of a young girl, but More has dragged me out of that error."[11]

Thomas was not a champion of feminine emancipation, as we understand it now, that is, a functional equality between man and woman in society. But to exclude a woman from learning and culture simply for being a woman seemed to him stupid, unfair, and sinful. To his children's tutor, William Gonell, he wrote: "I do not have to tell you that both men and women can be successful in the sciences, for they speak the common language of men. Both were endowed by nature with the understanding that differentiates them from animals. Both man and woman have the same right to study, given that they have the understanding to do so. Some people say that the intelligence of women is limited, that they can only create trivial things and can never pursue the sciences properly. It is not surprising that, given such words, women should feel inhibited. If all that were true, it would be even more necessary that women should receive good training in literature

9. Blarer, 65f.

10. Ibid., 66.

11. Ibid., 55.

and in all the sciences, so that nature's deficiency can be repaired. Cultured persons and saints long ago shared the same opinion as I."[12]

More took the long view of education. He wrote:

> My dear Gonell, pride is a malady that is difficult to root out and so, from a tender age, efforts have to made to prevent it emerging too much. This malady is so obstinate for various reasons. We hardly come into the world when it is implanted in our sensitive infantile hearts, and later it is cultivated by teachers and encouraged by our parents. By then nobody wants to exhibit goodness without immediately wanting praise as a reward. And if one gets used to being praised by the masses, that is, by those who do not matter, in the end one feels ashamed to be counted among the upright. I want to keep my children away from such a malady at all costs. You, my dear Gonell, my wife and all my friends, must explain to them how subject to reproach and unworthy is such ephemeral glory. . . . There is nothing better than that humble modesty that Christ repeatedly bids us. Act with prudent charitableness: instruct them in virtue, guarding against censuring vice, for it is with love that you will achieve more than with sternness. Let those who would act rightly read the writings of the Church Fathers, who never showed anger. Their saintliness, which moves us to obedience, exhorts us to imitate them.[13]

This important letter carries the footnote "Written at court, on the eve of Pentecost." One can almost see the writer, separated from his family by professional duties, loving his children and concerned for both their temporal welfare and their eternal salvation.

Erasmus considers it noteworthy that in More's family there were never any "scenes or beatings." Thomas himself reminds his children that when he had to chastise them, he did so with peacock feathers. Such respect for the dignity of the child was unusual in those times, but it signaled no lack of authority and discipline. He expected, without excuse, a letter a day from each, in Latin, and he offered this advice: "Always write after you have thought about it, and with care, without worrying whether the subject is serious or not. There is no harm in writing it out first in English, and afterwards transcribe it with greater ease into Latin. . . . I want to urge you to look at everything in detail

12. Ibid., 57.
13. Ibid., 58.

before making a fair copy. If you consider that the overall standard is good then see to the phrases and look at their construction one by one. . . . When you have corrected them all, copy out the whole letter once again and read it once more, because it can easily happen that errors which have already been put right are often reproduced."[14]

⁓⚬⚭⚬⁓

John, born in 1509, had difficulties keeping up with his elder sisters, and especially the clever Margaret. With delicacy, Thomas helps him put away any feeling of inferiority. He says in a letter to the youngsters: "If I really want to be sincere, I have to acknowledge that John's letter is the one which has made me happiest. In the first place he is the one who writes most in detail, and also seems to make a greater effort than the others. He relates the events of the day in a lively fashion. He also marshals his thoughts in a very logical way and, besides, he knows how to joke. . . . He likes to cheer up his father with his tomfoolery but is careful not to show disrespect."[15]

But still Margaret was the favorite. It would be hard to find a comparable friendship between father and daughter in either history or literature. As eldest daughter she holds a place of special trust, and is something of an assistant in the education of the younger siblings. When at the age of thirteen Margaret asked him for money, her father replied: "You ask your father for money with far too much timidity and moderation, my dear Margaret, if you know that I am always happy to be able to give. Now I send you only the desired amount; in truth, I should like to add something more; but by giving again I shall once more delight in the joy of giving. I enjoy being asked, and it flatters me somewhat, that my daughter should ask me; her virtue and wisdom make me love her in a special way. The sooner you spend this money well, as you always do, the sooner you will ask me again, and the greater will be my pleasure."[16]

Not only More's children but the many other youngsters who lived in the house attended classes. Among them was Margaret Giggs (Gyge), Margaret More's foster-sister, to whom Thomas showed much of the love he showed his eldest daughter. She married John Clement, who

---

14. Ibid., 62f. (letter dated September 3, 1522, from Court).

15. Ibid., 62.

16. Ibid., 61 (1518).

also belonged to the Thomas More family circle and who, as a young man, accompanied Thomas on his journey to Flanders in 1515. Also forming part of the "school" were Alice Middleton, a daughter of Lady Alice's first marriage, who later was wife of Sir Giles Alington; Margaret à Barrow, future wife of Sir Thomas Elyot, of whom Holbein in 1532 did a marvelous portrait; and Anne Cresacre, More's ward and later daughter-in-law.

"Greetings from Thomas More to all the school"—so begins a letter dated March 23, 1521, written at Court.

> Athough I love each one of you with a special name, so as not to leave anyone out I do not love you more under any other name than "scholar." Your eagerness to learn unites me to you almost more than family ties. If I did not love you so much I would envy you on account of the good luck of having so many and such excellent teachers. But I think you no longer need Professor Nikolaus [Kratzer], because you have learned everything he had to teach you about astronomy. . . . So, forward with this new and admirable science whereby you reach the stars! But while you observe these with enthusiasm, bear in mind that this sacred time of Lent reminds you—and the beautiful poem of Boethius resonates in your ears—to raise your spirits up to heaven so that the soul does not lower its gaze to the ground, as animals do, as you walk upright. Farewell, my loved ones.[17]

This typically amiable letter combines in a few phrases traits of the essential Thomas More: seriousness brimming over with humor and banter that knows exactly how to win over children together with a well-balanced hierarchy of values, even in the smallest matters: science, learning, astronomy, gazing up at the starry skies—that is all well and good, but far more important is lifting one's heart to God.

More's household is a miniature world. The sciences are practiced, meals are eaten, study, work, and prayers take place. So do weddings. John Harris, the private secretary, marries Dorothy Colly, lady's maid to his daughter Margaret; son John takes as wife Anne Cresacre, More's ward. Holbein drew them together in 1527, when John was eighteen

---

17. More refers to the following poem, contained in the Fifth Book of *De consolatione philosophiae*: "Man alone can proudly raise his brow, / with body erect, despising the world. / If you are not beside yourself, wretch, look upon that image:/ You who haughtily look up to heaven and raise your brow, / lift also your spirit to the Most High, / that the spirit may not be vanquished and the body be raised higher still."

and Anne fifteen, and the two were already sweethearts. Their grandson, Cresacre More, wrote a biography of his great-grandfather.

More's younger daughters, Elizabeth, nineteen years of age, and Cicely, a year younger, were both married on September 29, 1525, Elizabeth to the courtier, William Dauncey, and Cicely to Giles Heron, son of Sir John Heron, treasurer to the Royal Household. Son-in-law Giles also was a one-time pupil. Looking at all these interrelationships in the More household, one spontaneously thinks of the word "clan."

Margaret's husband, William Roper, had also lived for three years in the house. He came from an excellent family of lawyers and was about twenty-three when he married. The date was July 2, 1521. She was not yet seventeen. Shortly afterwards, Thomas wrote to the young wife:

> I was glad that you have decided to take up philosophy with such diligence, so as to positively make up in the future for what you feel you may have lost through neglect in the past. Darling Margaret, I have never seen you be negligent. And your extraordinary culture in every field shows how well you have come along. . . . I seriously hope that you will devote the rest of your life to medical science and spiritual literature, so that you will be well prepared to meet all eventualities in life, a sound spirit in a healthy body; and I know that you have already laid the foundations for these studies, and that there will always be possibilities open for continuing to build upon this edifice. But I tend to think that you can still devote a few years of your flowering youth, for your own profit, to the human sciences and the so-called "liberal arts". . . . So, farewell, my most beloved daughter, and please give my greetings to my dear son, your husband. I am very happy that he has taken up the same studies as you. I always follow the custom of advising you to submit yourself in everything to your husband, but in this instance, on the contrary, I grant you complete freedom to get ahead of him in the knowledge of the celestial system.[18]

"The celestial system": that is to say, the Christian faith. In More's eyes, dark clouds hovered over this marriage, for Roper was a follower of Luther's doctrine. And not just a follower, as Harpsfield relates: "Master Roper was not content to keep his new-found faith to himself but positively aspired to propagate it. He thought himself well-placed to

---

18. *SL*, 31, 147ff.; *Corr.*, 106.

do so, even from the pulpit of St. Paul's church. Indeed, he longed to encourage and spread Luther's new doctrine and so happy was he in his own role that he aspired to nothing more ardently than to get on to a pulpit. To realize this daft desire, he would gladly have parted with a considerable portion of his land."[19]

Roper was intelligent, studious, generous, and, above all, sincere, but he was also headstrong, even obstinate, and of a violent temperament. If his mind was made up about something, nothing could dissuade him. Having heard about Luther and the Reformation from German merchants living in London, he became convinced that faith was the only justification and good works were useless to attain salvation.

More lodged an official complaint against the merchants for having propagated heretical doctrines. Cardinal Wolsey also invited Roper to attend an interrogation, together with some other Englishmen and some Germans. But while the others were pilloried, Roper was let off with a mere "friendly warning" out of consideration for his father-in-law. Still, nothing could change the young man's mind. Talking and reasoning achieved nothing whatsoever. "Meg," Thomas told his daughter, "I have been patient with your husband for a very long time. I have spoken and discussed religious matters with him, and have always given him fatherly advice, as far as my weak energies have allowed me. But I do not see that all of that can drag him away from his ideas; and so, I do not want to continue quarreling and arguing any longer, but simply leave him to his fate, and return once again to God for a while and pray for him."[20]

More's sons-in-law, Roper and Giles Heron, behaved in a manner reminiscent of Nicodemus, Joseph of Arimathea, and others of Jesus' followers who proclaimed their discipleship during the time of persecution following his death. Indeed, Heron, a very difficult young man while his father-in-law lived, followed him to his death five years later. He was executed in 1540, a victim of false testimony, like Sir Thomas. William Roper returned to the Catholic Church before 1533. He passionately defended the traditional faith and, continuing More's charitable work, made generous donations, particularly to the asylum for the poor in Chelsea that More had founded. He aided harassed Catholics, showing prudence, fortitude, and much personal bravery while

19. Cf. note 17 in the chapter "Statesman and writer," Harpsfield, 64.
20. Ibid., 87.

concerning himself with his brethren in the faith who had fallen into misery or were in prison. In 1542 he himself spent some time in prison. During the reign of Elizabeth I he was brought before the courts for giving assistance to fugitive Catholics. On the whole, it ended well, and he was even allowed to practice his profession as a lawyer. He died in 1578,[21] almost eighty, outliving his wife by thirty-four years.

She had remained a fearless and loving wife, very much influenced by her father. When the King's messengers arrived to search the house after More's execution and her husband's arrest, they were surprised to find a calm and collected woman instructing her children. With the same coolness she rescued her father's decapitated head and notes, and obtained permission to keep them "for her consolation." She died at Christmas in 1544, at the age of thirty-nine, three years before her brother John, who, having stood in Margaret's shadow while she lived, ensured, with his nine children, the More family's continuance.

3.

No one in More's family, whether related by blood or not, was disloyal during the times of persecution or gravest personal danger—and from 1534 onwards—there were many such moments for three decades. No one avoided Sir Thomas or disowned him. This is something quite remarkable and testifies in his favor even more eloquently than all the memories and anecdotes that have come down to us while adding to the credibility of the numerous oral and written accounts of his personality and life. Possibly details have been embellished, but the overall picture is undoubtedly true.

The many individual elements of that picture come together in his family life. Situated first at Bucklersbury and then, after 1524, in Chelsea, this was a home full of life and warmth, in touch with the great world thanks to More and kept orderly by Lady Alice. Erasmus, a guest during a long and intense stretch of time, is once again an exceptional witness. Erasmus tells Hutten:

> As to his figure and measurements he is neither thin nor strikingly small. Overall, the harmony of all the parts is such that all the proper standards are met. The color of the skin is white, the face tends towards a clear shine rather than to paleness, although at the same

---

21. Reynolds, 387ff.

time this is very far from reddish, with a hint, if at all, of a pale rose
tint. His fair hair has a dark touch or, if you prefer, is of a dark hue
that tends towards blonde. The beard is sparse; the eyes bluish grey
and spattered with tiny specks, which usually indicate an extremely
sympathetic nature. Among the British it is considered attractive,
whereas here we are attracted more by dark looks. It is said that no
particular type of eyes is less disturbed by vices.

The expression befits his nature. He is always pleasant, given to
laughter and, to be frank, he is made more for practical jokes than for
seriousness and formality, yet very far from lacking wit or being above
a bit of buffoonery. The right shoulder seems a little higher than the
left, especially when walking. This is not from birth but from habit,
for many such things often stick with us. There is nothing in the
rest of his figure that draws our attention. Only the hands, compared
with the remainder of his appearance, are somewhat like those of a
peasant. The charm he had in his youth can still be glimpsed: I have
known this man since he was twenty-three years old; he is now not
much more than forty.[22]

Erasmus describes More's health as good, but suggests that his
constitution is not basically robust. "His voice is not powerful, or
excessively soft, but such that it enters the ear easily. It is not sono-
rous or smooth, but simply that of a 'speaker,' for he does not seem
endowed by nature to sing, even though he delights in all kinds of
music. His speech is admirably clear and articulated. It does not rush
or falter mid-way."[23]

Moderation, modesty, even austerity, typify More's personal conduct, whether in regard to the pleasures of the table or fashion.

I have never known a person less particular at the moment of choos-
ing what to eat. Up to the age of adolescence he only liked water to
drink, but so as to put them at their ease, he would trick his guests
by drinking very watered-down beer and frequently plain water,
from a tin beaker. He would taste wine sometimes in little sips, so
as not to give the impression that he was rejecting it altogether, and
also to accustom himself to the social imperatives, for there it is
customary for people to invite each other to drink out of the same

---

22. Eckert, vol. 2, 441.
23. Ibid., 442.

glass. He prefers eating beef, salted fish or heavy leavened bread, rather than those foods which are commonly found in tasty dishes, but otherwise he is not averse to the innocent pleasures of the flesh. More than anything he has always liked dairy products and fruit of all kinds. Egg dishes he considers among the delicacies. He is quite happy with simple attire, he never wears silk, purple or gold chains, except when he has no choice. It is marvelous to be able to say how little ceremonial matters to him, when the vast majority of people put so much store by it when they think about gracious manners. He does not demand it from anybody, and is not afraid of putting it on for others, at meetings and social gatherings; and when he wants to make use of it he is totally in control. But it strikes him as effeminate and unworthy of a man to waste a great deal of time on such silliness.[24]

If one were to translate this into religious terms, one might say that More lived asceticism in a natural and unobtrusive manner. His spirit of poverty was not such as to embarrass others, but to encourage them quietly and, if possible without being noticed, in the imitation of Christ. But that did not rule out cheerful social occasions and attendance at theatrical events. To the great of the world he showed the honor due them, without being stiff or servile ("without timidity," Erasmus says).

Erasmus, with his great gift for friendship, stresses the same trait in More.

He seems to have been born, created, for friendship. He is its most sincere servant, lives by it, and is not afraid either to have many friends, being always open to seal the alliance of friendship. He is not particular in his choice of friends, whilst at the same time being the one who pays the greatest attention to encouraging it, and also is most constant in his allegiance to it. When he comes across someone whose faults he cannot mend, he lets go the acquaintance when occasion presents itself, dissolving rather than breaking it off. He so enjoys relationships . . . that in them he sees the greatest satisfaction in life. He feels a deep antipathy for ball games, dice, cards, and other games with which the majority of the nobility usually disguise their utter boredom. Just as there is hardly anyone who cares less about

---

24. Ibid.

his own gain, so is there nobody more diligent in fostering all the advantages that friendship brings. But why so many words? Whoever wishes to have a perfect example of true friendship will not find any better than in More.[25]

In the family portrait by Holbein one sees the low comedian of the household, Henry Patenson, who saw to the coarser side of humor that the ups and downs of everyday life in a large household required. In this, Thomas was a man of his time who saw nothing demeaning in the role of the buffoon, and found entertainment in the odd and abnormal. Erasmus relates: "His greatest amusement was provided by observing the shapes, features, and perception of different living beings. Hence, there was almost no kind of bird that he did not keep under his roof, nor any other animal, usually rare, such as a monkey, ferret, weasel, etc. If he comes across any creature that is exotic or interesting in any way, he usually buys it eagerly. His house is filled with things of this sort, so that at every step those entering it come across something to attract their eyes."[26] But the real pleasure of the owner of such curiosities, the letter writer adds, lay in the admiration and enjoyment of his visitors.

Erasmus called the house in Chelsea "a Platonic academy based on Christian principles," while Chambers spoke of "patriarchal monastic Utopias."[27] The descriptions blend the Christian and the humanistic. As has been suggested, the best synthesis of both may be captured by speaking of a deliberate imitation of Christ—of the living out of love of God and love of neighbor.

Something like that was strikingly noticeable throughout the More household. "More was in the habit of praying whenever he was at home or if he happened to be staying at a place where there was a woman in labor."[28] He gave alms constantly, without inquiring into the claim on his assistance made by the particular seeker of alms. "He used to visit the most isolated places at night, through the darkest streets, to seek out and help the poor who were too ashamed to beg openly. During the day he would visit families in need and help them not with trifling hand-outs, as often happens, but giving away small sums of money. If their

---

25. Ibid., 443.
26. Ibid.
27. Chambers, 213; Letter from Bishop Faber, of Vienna, 1532.
28. Bremond, 107; quote is from Thomas Stapleton, 1535–1598.

wretchedness was great he would from time to time give one or more gold coins."[29] But he did not stop there: humble people need personal esteem. "He would often invite the farm laborers from all around to a meal and receive them cheerfully and amiably. . . . No week went by without his finding some ailing person to be given care and assistance. He rented a large house in Chelsea where he took in a number of elderly people and sick women, paying for their upkeep out of his own pocket. In his absence, the running of this 'House of Divine Providence' was left in the hands of Margaret Roper."[30]

More's own domestic community had certain rules. Dice and card games were prohibited, as were "amorous relationships." The sleeping quarters of male and female servants were in separate buildings and, except for grave necessity, it was strictly forbidden for those of one sex to set foot in the others' building. Studies, music, and gardening shaped the way of life, together with Holy Mass—an obligation on Sundays and holy days—prayers, reading and meditation on the gospels, and vespers, led by More whenever he could be present. On important feasts, the household celebrated a vigil and midnight office. On working days, a member of the family (almost always Margaret Giggs) read from the gospels at morning prayer or at meals, which were eaten in common. On Good Friday, all attended the reading of the Passion, at which More's secretary, John Harris, commonly officiated.

About six hundred feet from the main building toward the river, More built a kind of intellectual-religious center consisting of a chapel, library, and a gallery.[31] Every Friday that he could be in Chelsea he spent reading, writing, and praying in this "New Building." He rose at two in the morning and devoted himself to work and prayer until Mass at seven a.m. Stapleton reports that he always ended his morning and evening prayers with the seven penitential psalms, the introductory psalms, the *Beati Immaculati*[32] psalm, and the Litany of Loreto. Before retiring, he would summon the family to his study, recite night prayers with them, and afterwards, praying aloud by himself, add *Miserere mei Deus* (Psalm 61), *Ad te, Domine, levavi* (Psalm 24) and *Deus misereatur*

---

29. Ibid., 108.

30. Ibid.

31. Cf. plan of Chelsea in Reynolds, 180.

32. The seven penitential psalms: 6, 31, 37, 50, 101, 129, 142: Ps. 118, *Beati Immaculati* (Blessed are those whose way is blameless . . .).

nostri (Psalm 66), followed by the *Salve* and the *De Profundis* (Psalm 129) for the dead.[33]

At Mass, More's bass voice accompanied the chanting of the priest. He also carried the cross in processions. When he became Lord Chancellor, he was invited to ride horseback in processions because of his elevated position. "In no way do I want to follow on horseback my divine Lord, who goes on foot," he replied.[34] Just as Thomas followed his Lord on foot to prison and death, so did his children and those who lived under his roof, on the way to the Tower, the scaffold, or exile. He told them in advance how it would be: "We cannot expect to get to heaven on soft feather beds as and when we choose. This is not the way. Our Lord went through much pain and suffering, and the servant must not expect to find himself in a more privileged position than his Master."[35] There was no special merit in being honest and upright in times when these qualities are highly prized. "But if you get to live in times when nobody gives you good advice or sets a good example, in which you see virtue punished and vice rewarded, if then you remain firm and continue to be faithful to God, I swear on my life, that you will be judged just, even if you were only half just."[36]

4.

Two outstanding visual chroniclers, Lukas Cranach the Elder (1472–1553) and Hans Holbein the Younger (1498–1543) have left painted records of this era. Their portraits—Cranach's of Luther, Holbein's of More—have been likened to spiritual photographs in which the monk from Wittenberg and his Prince Elector from Saxony, and More and the court of Henry VIII come alive for us.

Holbein arrived in Chelsea in November 1526, recommended to More by his friend Erasmus. He was hoping to exchange the narrow world of Basle for the wider vistas of so culturally ambitious a country as England. The young man of twenty-eight was already held in high esteem. Born in Augsburg in 1498, that is, twenty years younger than his host, he had worked as an apprentice under his father, Hans Holbein the Elder, and then gone to Basle. In 1516/17 he traveled in northern

---

33. Bremond, 112.
34. Ibid.
35. Roper, 26f; Chambers, 227.
36. Ibid.

Italy, and in 1524 in France, thus viewing renaissance art in its most important centers. In Basle, he got to know the typographer and editor Froben, the local humanists, and especially Erasmus, whom he painted several times and whose book *In Praise of Folly* he illustrated. Besides several works on religious themes, it was above all his wood engravings of the Dance of Death, executed around 1525 that brought him fame as an artist of the first rank.

Thus he had begun to enjoy access to prominent personages in England even before his second visit in 1532, which led to his permanent residence until his death in 1543. For a few months in 1527, Holbein lived in Chelsea as part of More's household. It would be gratifying to know the subject of evening discussions around the fireplace between More, almost fifty years old and an active adversary of the new doctrine, and this young and genial German. Although it appears that Holbein was not a fanatical Lutheran but one of a more relaxed sort, he undoubtedly leaned more toward the Reformation than toward the old Church of Rome. But be that as it may, More was the first Englishman to give a commission to Holbein, and he paved the painter's way into society and to the King himself. Henry used to visit More, almost always unannounced, and it is possible that Holbein's portraits in the Chelsea gallery caught the royal eye and the painter was presented to him. It is said that when More offered him as a gift the portraits the King had admired, Henry replied: "Now that I have the artist, I have no need of the portraits!"

Holbein first drew and painted Thomas More in 1527. The sketches are at Windsor Castle and the portrait is in the Frick Collection in New York. Sir Thomas is seen standing, resting his right forearm on a console in a relaxed pose. With a dark green curtain behind him, he is dressed in official ceremonial robes of dark red velvet, his coat trimmed with fur, and wears a judge's cap and a gold chain from which the five-leaved rose emblem hangs. Contrasting with the insignia of high office is the air of melancholic solitude that surrounds him.

If we compare the drawing with the portrait, we observe that in the former the nose appears a little flatter and fleshier, whereas in the latter it is somewhat thinner and delicate, giving a more noble impression. The shape of the mouth, with its lower lip lightly sculpted, is pleasant—quite different from the drawing, where it is precisely the mouth that creates a more forced expression. More's sense of humor, impishness, wit, and sarcasm are perceptible in both likenesses. In both, too, the gaze, serious and concentrated, seems directed to infinity. The longer one looks at this face, the more tranquil one feels, as, taking the hint from More, one gazes calmly into one's own soul.

Along with More, John and his sweetheart Anne Cresacre, Elizabeth, Cicely, Margaret, and Lady Alice were drawn or painted by Holbein. It is not certain whether the portraits of the last two women are originals or copies.[37] The drawings of the first four, which are at Windsor Castle, are a high point of European graphic art at the beginning of the Modern Era.

As for the famous portrait of the More family, the original, painted in oil, was lost, but the Art Museum in Basle has a study in pen and India ink, which Holbein took to Erasmus when he returned from England. The group looks at ease and alive. This is not a scene depicting statue-like figures, but a glimpse of everyday life, an informal gathering at the end of the day's work. Sir Thomas, although in the middle of the group, seems surrounded by a zone of inner silence. What might he have been thinking? Perhaps that his fatherly role as educator and teacher, having been performed to the best of his ability, had now come to an end. "Young More" was no longer himself but his twenty-three-year-old son. Between John the elder and John the younger, the past and the future, Thomas suddenly found himself in the present, standing alone.

---

37. Reynolds, 10.

CHAPTER SIX

Farewell and Parting

More expected neither miracles nor respect after quitting public office. Certainly the religious schism would not disappear suddenly, England would not revert to the Catholic faith, the King's divorce would prevail, and Henry would marry Anne Boleyn. Better therefore to pray for the strength to persevere during the persecution to come than call on God to turn aside sufferings that evidently were part of his salvific plan. Of course, this did not mean doing nothing. From a lengthy letter to Erasmus explaining his resignation dated June 14, 1532, it appears that along with preparing himself for death, he meant to continue the struggle against heresy.

In this letter he speaks first of his health: "I admit that I did not imagine my retirement would be like this; it was my wish to spend my final years full of life and energy and free from physical illness (insofar as can be expected of old age.) This may have been wishful thinking on my part and entirely inappropriate. . . ."[1]

No doubt, his physicians had advised him to resign. "Clearly I would have to resign if I did not want to carry out my duties incompetently, and I understood that to do my job properly would mean ruining my health altogether. I would probably succumb to my illness, and be unable to continue as Lord Chancellor. So, as I did not want to lose life and position at one fell blow, I tendered my resignation."[2]

Of his plans for his closing years, he says: "I want to use all my energies to protect those who renege on their faith not on their own initiative but because they are taken in by the wiles of astute orators."[3]

---

1. Blarer, 86.
2. Ibid., 86 f.
3. Ibid, 90.

In the two years he was able to enjoy freedom, he devoted himself to this end, but without success.

Ten years earlier, in 1522, he had opened his treatise on *The Four Last Things* with shattering, grotesque, chilling pages on death. "So many torches, so many candles, so many black robes, so many funeral processions, and all the time laughing beneath their black habits: a sumptuous funeral at long last! As if the deceased could from a window observe his own cortege and see with what honors he is being carried to the church."[4] This preoccupation with appearances at such a time struck More as ridiculous and incomprehensible, just like most people's obliviousness to the transient, fleeting nature of life. He wrote: "Certainly, the greatest king may attempt to dispel the uncomfortable vision of death as he strolls leisurely or rides on horseback flanked by an impressive escort, but even so he knows that he cannot escape from it. The sentence has already been passed. Unless he is a fool, he will not be able to live without fear. Tomorrow, today even, the cruel executioner will come: death, which from the moment he was born has been stalking, watching, and lying in wait for him."[5] There is, however, a huge difference between the literary conventions of meditating on death and waiting for death "consumed with love." More prayed: "O God, grant me the ardent desire to be near you; not to be free from the miseries of this sad world, not to escape from the flames of Purgatory or Hell, not even to attain and enjoy Heavenly bliss, nor for my own profit, but simply and solely for the love of you."[6]

Thomas's controversial treatises of 1532/33 were not written with literary relish or intellectual fire but with pain, fear, and a sense of isolation: pain because they were necessary, fear of future developments, and isolation because his writings could no longer alter the paths being taken by the King, the country, and history. More realized that what he was doing might cost him dearly. Very gradually at first, then more rapidly, and intensely, he grew in the awareness that suffering accompanies love. To share in the agony of Christ is the dread and the hope of every Christian. In the end, Thomas was able to embrace the joy of the Cross, and, filled with inner peace in the Tower of London, he trod the road to the scaffold like a bridegroom filled with anticipation.

---

4. T. E. Bridgett, *Life and Writings of Sir Thomas More* (London, 1891), 1892 edition revised with vol. 2: *The Wisdom and Wit of Blessed Thomas More*, ibid., 72.

5. Ibid.

6. *CW*, vol. 13: *Treatise on the Passion; Treatise on the Blessed Body; Instructions and Prayers*, edited by Garry E. Haupt (New Haven-London, 1976), 230. Cf. Bremond, 184.

CHAPTER SEVEN

The Two Women

The postscript to More's epitaph is as follows:

❧ ❧ ❧

Here lies my beloved wife Jane. I, Thomas More, desire that this tomb should receive me and Alice as well. The first of the two ladies, my wife in the days of my youth, made me the father of a son and three daughters; the other loved her stepchildren, something unusual in a stepmother, with an intensity rare even in a mother for her own children. The one ended her life by my side, the other continues to share it with me, and in such a way that I am not able to judge whether I loved the first one more or loved the second more. How happy the three of us would have been together had destiny and morality allowed it! I pray, therefore, that the grave, like heaven, will reunite us. Death will thus afford us what life could not.

❧ ❧ ❧

1.

For the young More, deciding not to embrace the clerical state was the equivalent to deciding to marry. "He contracted marriage," Erasmus writes, "with a young and somewhat uneducated woman, of noble lineage, who had always lived with her parents and brothers and sisters in the country, and he did it with the idea of educating her in his way." More, however, was no Pygmalion. Thanks to Roper, we know more details of his marriage. Invited by John Colt to his Netherhall estate in Essex, Thomas found himself among seventeen brothers and sisters from two marriages. Three of the daughters were of marriageable age, and their "honorable conduct and virtuous upbringing managed to elicit his affection for them."[1] More fell in love with the second one, but realizing that "it would mean much pain for the eldest, and a degree of shame too, if her younger sister were preferred for marriage . . . he inclined for the eldest of them, since he felt a certain compassion for her, and soon after he got married."[2]

This was conventional behavior in these times. For the orderly transfer of dowry, daughters married in order of seniority, with the eldest usually first.

Not only among royal dynasties and the nobility, but also in the social class to which More belonged, many marriages were entered into for specific reasons of class rather than subjective inclination. There is no evidence that there were more unhappy marriages then than now.

Among the many reasons for marrying, "compassion" was by no means the worst, and, often love soon followed. This marriage of Thomas More and Jane Colt, ten years younger than himself, was a happy one. Even twenty years later, he calls her his *cara uxorcula* ("his beloved little wife"), remembering, probably with some emotion, a brief happiness that lasted only six-and-a-half years.

It is not difficult to believe that when Erasmus speaks, in his *Colloquia Familiaria* ("Confidential Conversations"), about the critical phase in the marriage of a young married couple, he is referring to the More's, with whom he frequently stayed during his second visit to England in 1505/1506. In the account,[3] cast in the form of a dialogue between two married ladies, the woman Eulalia says: "I know a noble person, cultured and particularly capable in all the facets of human relationships. He married a young woman aged seventeen, who had always lived with her parents in the country. He wanted an ordinary woman whom he could mold more easily to his own way of life. He started by giving her lessons in poetry and music, to get her used little by little to repeat what she heard in sermons, and to teach her such other things as later on might prove useful to her."[4]

Here we see More as a pedagogue perhaps too little conscious that, in marriage, success in pedagogy goes hand in hand with love. The

---

1. Mentioned in Chambers, 107.

2. Ibid.

3. "The Domestic Dragon, or: On Marriage" (*Uxor sive coniugium*), in Erasmus von Rotterdam: *Augsgewählte Schriften*, 8 volumes, Latin-German, published by Werner Welzig (Darmstadt, 1967), (referred to as *ES*), vol. 6, *Coloquio familiaria*.

4. Ibid., 159ff.

pupil-wife, according to Erasmus, "never stopped crying, threw herself to the ground and banged her head against the floor as if wanting to kill herself." Evidently, the husband can think of nothing except to take his homesick wife to visit her parents in the country. There he confides in his father-in-law, who advises him, according to the wisdom of the time, to give the young woman a good hiding. "I am aware of my rights, sir," the son-in-law replies, "but I prefer her to be cured by your own skill or authority, before resorting to extreme measures."[5]

Erasmus goes on to relate how the latter, feigning anger, makes his daughter see reason, presumably by means that would make a modern psychologist's hair stand on end. The story has a happy ending: "The young woman, following the conversation with her father, returned to the bedroom and there she found her husband all by himself. She threw herself at his feet and said: 'Dear husband, not until now did I understand you or myself. You will see how I shall be different in future. Forget everything that has gone before up to this moment.' After hearing these words, the husband took her to him with a kiss, promising her everything if she kept to her promise. " So she did, and we may suppose that the husband for his part became more restrained in his pedagogic zeal and more reasonable in his thinking. . . . Jane died in the summer of 1511, at the age of approximately twenty-five, leaving the young More a widower with four children between the ages of six and two. Erasmus comments: "He had practically succeeded in so molding her that he would have wished to spend his entire life with her."[6]

2.

Only four or perhaps six weeks later, Thomas married again. Even for those times and even for a man in urgent need of a mother for his children, this was unusual haste. Erasmus's third visit to England coincided with this event, and we rely on his version.

> A few months after having buried his wife, Thomas married a widow, more due to worry about his family than desire, since she was neither a beauty nor a young thing, as he himself would jest. But she proved an energetic and active mother to the family. Despite everything,

---

5. In the Latin text: *Tum gener, novi, inquit, ius meum; sed malim eam tua vel arte vel auctoritati sanari quam ad hoc extremum remedium venire. ES*, 160.

6. Eckert, vol. 2, 447.

he behaved towards her in as affectionate and pleasant a manner as if she were a young woman of the most striking beauty. Hardly any husband succeeds, by being bossy or inflexible, in achieving the same degree of docility from his wife as he did with praise and lightheartedness. . . . He has already managed to get that wife, who is approaching old age and has a none too even a temperament and is also materially acquisitive, to learn to play the zither, the lute, and the flute, and every day to grant her husband the practice time that he demands of her.[7]

More himself contributed to our contradictory and on the whole not very attractive image of his second wife. For instance, on December 15, 1517, he writes to Erasmus: "In reply to your wish to receive a long letter, my wife commands me to send you a million greetings. She wants to live for a long time so that she can keep lecturing me even longer." This may be a joke, possibly even of her own making, but many brushstrokes in a similar vein have created a picture of her similar to that of Xanthippe, wife of Socrates.

Harpsfield, More's biographer, makes no effort to disguise his antipathy towards Lady Alice, and highlights those traits—quarrelsome character, readiness to contradict: "When this woman saw that Sir Thomas not only stopped working to get ahead in life but also took on the tribulations that prison meant, she began to get cross with him and asked him: 'Why don't you do what everybody else does? Do you just want to sit by the fireplace drawing shapes on the ashes, like children do? I know what I would do if I were a man!' 'What would you do, woman?' asked the husband. 'I tell you truly that I would join the strongest side! My mother always used to say that it was better to govern than to be governed; I would not be so foolish as to let myself be governed if I were able to do so myself.' 'Now you have spoken the truth,' retorted her husband, 'because I have never seen you disposed to let yourself be governed.'"[8]

One day, relates the same author, Lady Alice, returning from confession, said, "Cheer up! I have ceased being wicked for today, but tomorrow I will start again."[9] But here Harpsfield misses the point: this is banter, though it is true that in More's case even banter could quickly

---

7. Ibid.
8. Bremond, 93f.
9. Ibid.

turn serious. In any event, this husband often played the same game, as in an incident related by Bremond: "Once when he saw the trouble she went to in combing her hair backwards so as to make her forehead seem higher and her figure half as ample, he said to her, believing that she was inclined to being vain and coquettish: 'God does you an injustice, dear wife, by sparing you hell, for to be sure you have paid good money for it.'"[10]

A so-called biography by a pseudonymous Ro. Ba. tells a story that shows More, with an entirely docile wife, exercising the judgment of Solomon.[11]

> Sir Thomas's second wife loved little lap dogs, and it so happened that she was given one which had been stolen from a poor beggar woman. The beggar spotted her pet dog in the arms of a servant and claimed it back. This was refused and there ensued a lively altercation. Eventually, the incident was reported to Sir Thomas, who called for his wife and the beggar woman to come before him, and spoke to them in the following fashion: "Wife, you go and stand at the top end of the room, since you are of noble stock; and you, neighbor, stand at the lower end. No injustice will be done to you." He then went and stood between them, holding the dog in his arms and said: "Are you in agreement that I should decide the dispute between you over this dog?" They replied in the affirmative. "In that case let each of you call the dog by its name, and the one the dog goes to shall be the owner." As the dog did go to the beggar, they gave it to her. Sir Thomas then gave the beggar a French crown coin and asked her to let his wife have the dog. The poor woman felt herself so well repaid with his kind words and alms that she gladly left the dog with Lady Alice.[12]

Apart from More himself and Erasmus, Roper is the most important source of information about More if only because he lived for sixteen years in his father-in-law's house. The documentary value of his biography is limited by the fact that it was not put together until some twenty years after More's death and was not published until 1626 in St. Omer. The author himself comments on the "many details" that have been "wiped from my memory through negligence and due to the long period

---

10. Ibid.

11. Chambers, 38ff. *The Life and Death of Sir Thomas More*, published in 1599 under the pseudonym, unexplained, of Ro. Ba., edited by E. V. Hitchcock, P. H. Hallett, and A. W. Reed (London, 1950), (EETS, OS 222); Cf. other early biographies *L'Univers*, 555ff.

12. Cf. Wordsworth: *Ecclesiastical Biography*, vol. 2, 202f.; Chambers, 327f.

of time which elapsed since then."[13] Uncertainty also surrounds passages in which Roper relates events he knows of only from hearsay, particularly concerning More's time in prison, such as the well-known conversation between Thomas and Alice in the Tower of London. Lady Alice presumably reported the conversation, and, given her state of mind, may not have recalled it accurately. At the same time, however, Roper knew both well enough to produce a credible reconstruction of that conversation in a dungeon that corresponds to what we know of them.

It appears that the wife was granted permission to visit the husband after he had been imprisoned for some time. "Without beating about the bush, she greeted him with the following words:[14]

> 'My God, Master More!... I am surprised to see you, whom until now I had held to be wise, turned into a nitwit, stuck in this cramped, dirty prison; that you should be happy to be locked up with mice and rats, whereas you could be at liberty and enjoying the King's mercy and counsel. It would suffice if you were willing to do like all the bishops and most cultured men in the country have done! In Chelsea you have a beautiful house, your own study, garden, and your own orchard, and all the other comforts, where you could be happy in the company of your wife, your children, and your servants. I am astonished at why, for the love of God, you so stupidly choose to remain in this place.'"

To this More replied with a smile:

> "But, my good woman, for God's sake, I beg you to tell me one thing only ... is this dwelling-place not as near to Heaven as mine is?" to which she, who was not at all pleased to hear those words, only replied in her usual rough and ready manner: "Tilly vally, tilly vally" [which meant something akin to "silly nonsense" or "rubbish"]. "What do you say, madam Alice" he remarked "is it not so?" "*Bone Deus, bone Deus,* husband, is there no end to all this?" "Woman, if that were so, I do not see any reason to feel happy about my beautiful house and everything that goes with it; for if I were to return to it seven years after I am buried, I were sure to find someone else living there who would turn me out saying that I had no business there. So you see, what reason is there for me to have feelings for a house that can so soon forget its master?"

---

13. Chambers, 20.
14. Roper, 82ff.; Chambers, 20.

Roper did not need to invent much, for Thomas himself fed him ideas. In one of his writings from the Tower, he recounts how:

> . . . a very important lady, who for humanitarian reasons visits a poor prisoner whom she found in a cell which, truth to speak, was well enough appointed; at least it was sufficiently solid. The walls and floor the prisoner had lined with straw matting, so that in that sense at least she did not have to worry about his health and should feel relieved. But among the other painful things she suffered on his account, she very much lamented one of them, namely that the door of his cell was bolted at night by the jailer . . . "In the name of God," she said, "if my door were closed in this fashion I would be unable to breathe." When she said this, the prisoner had to laugh to himself. He could not laugh out loud because he was a little intimidated by her, and also because it was to her kindness that he largely owed his subsistence in that place. But inwardly he could not contain his laughter because he knew for a fact that every night she bolted her chamber from the inside, and likewise the door and windows, and never opened them throughout the night.[15]

More himself shaped the image of his second wife for posterity. It is two-sided: one side the mocking image of an anglicized wife of Socrates; the other, sketched with humor, respect, and, basically, love, that of a good woman who did her duty as a mother, housekeeper, and manager of the household "school." More's responsibilities took him away from the family often; but he could have peace of mind because of Lady Alice. Whatever their marriage lacked, there was no absence of mutual respect and a clearly defined sharing of duties.

Thomas More truly and sincerely loved both of his wives, each in the way most fitting and appropriate according to her age, circumstances, and character as well as his own. In his two marriages, to Jane Colt and Alice Middleton, More experienced the growth and maturation that normally occurs in just one.

---

15. *Works*, 1247; Chambers, 22f.

PART TWO

The Testimony

Nothing ever happens that is against God's will. The fate he has prepared for me can only be the best no matter how hard it may appear by human standards.

—THOMAS MORE TO HIS DAUGHTER MARGARET,
FROM THE TOWER OF LONDON, 1534.

Everybody knows perfectly well that there are matters in which one is allowed to have one's own opinion, despite not being in agreement with the crowd, without jeopardizing the salvation of his soul.

—THOMAS MORE TO DR. NICHOLAS WILSON,
FROM THE TOWER OF LONDON, 1534.

CHAPTER EIGHT

The World of Erasmus

1.

Erasmus was born in Goud, the Netherlands, probably on October 27, 1469, the same year as Machiavelli. He was the son of a parish priest, in whose house he lived until 1478.[1] He later attended the school of the Brothers of Common Life in Deventer and then in Hertongenbosch. Here the lad was given a religious upbringing that later proved resistant to the intellectual temptations and storms of his later life. The Brothers of Common Life were the best-known representatives of *devotio moderna*, a religious reform movement that began around the beginning of the fourteenth century. Jan van Ruysbrock (1293–1381) of Brabant, also known as Dr. Extaticus, summed it up like this: "Work and contemplation—both well-ordered in a person—that is the pious life, the saintly life." On this foundation, Geert Groote (1340–1384) of Overyssel near Utrecht, built the edifice of the *devotio moderna* that was to bring so many graces to the Church.

Like many pious Christians, the Brothers of Common Life disapproved of the abuses then existing in the world, society, and especially the Church. But their response was more temperate than that of the reformers, for they recognized evils and injustice as fruits of original sin. God, the Church, and the world, they held, need not so much reformers as Christians who follow Christ.

This religious and spiritual attitude marked not only Erasmus of Rotterdam, but such other key personalities of that era as Charles V and Pope Adrian VI. Besides Erasmus, the *devotio moderna* movement produced Nicholas of Cusa, Thomas à Kempis, and Adrian

---

1. His father was ordained a priest after Erasmus was born.

of Utrecht (spiritual mentor of the young Charles of Burgundy, the future Emperor).[2]

Following the death of his parents, his tutors induced Erasmus, then fourteen, to enter the Augustinian monastery in Steyn, close to Goud. Although in later life he sought to remain objective and balanced in judgment, on one matter he was never able entirely to overcome his bitterness—namely the state of monasticism and religious life—and he never tired of saying he had taken his vows under duress. Yet in the early days in Steyn he apparently felt at ease making friendships, studying the classical writers, writing poems, and composing his early works, *De contemptu mundi* (On contempt for the world) and the first versions of his *Antibarbari*.[3] In 1492 the Bishop of Utrecht ordained him a priest. A year later, in 1493, Erasmus left his monastery and became secretary to the Bishop of Cambrai. Thereafter he traveled with the bishop, met many people, and continued to write. Undoubtedly, he lived a somewhat worldly life, despite which he enjoyed theology, was given permission to study it, and was even given a scholarship.

From 1495 until 1499 he studied in Paris. Initially he lived in the College de Montaigu, later in a private home. It was then that he began to distance himself from the clerical-monastic state, though only many years later, in 1517, was he formally laicized. The awarding of his bachelor's degree in theology from the Sorbonne in 1498 also marked his abandonment of the subject. Abandoned by his episcopal benefactor, he took on pupils in order to support himself in Paris and taught them literary composition. Among these was the young William Blount, Lord Mountjoy, who invited his teacher to England in June 1499. This first

---

2. Thomas Hemerken, called "à Kempis," (1379–1471), an Augustinian canon, lived in the Low Countries and as a spiritual writer has had enormous impact on the Christian world through his *Imitation of Christ* (*De Imitatione Christi*). Nicholas of Cusa (or Cusano; originally Chryfftz or Krebs) lived from 1401 to 1464. He was the most important philosopher and theologian during the transition from the Middle Ages to modern times, a cardinal after 1448. He strove for that Catholic reform that was not achieved until a hundred years later. [Karl Jaspers, *Nikolaus Cusanus* (Munich, 1964); E. Meuthen, *Nickolaus von Kues* (1964); *Nicolo Cusano e gli inizi del mondo moderno* (Florence, 1970).] Adrian Florisz of Utrecht (1459–1523), before becoming the teacher of Charles of Burgundy, future Emperor Charles V, in 1507, was a renowned theologian and important university professor at Louvain. He became Bishop of Tortosa in 1516 and a cardinal in 1517, acting as co-regent, with Cardinal Ximenez de Cisneros (d. 1517), for the young King Charles, and after 1520 as his representative in Spain. In 1522 he was elected, surprisingly and *in absentia*, successor to Pope Leo X. This ascetic, severe, and pious pope brought to a close the Renaissance period of the papacy and, as an uncompromising enemy of Luther, must be considered precursor of the Catholic reformation.

3. Eckert, vol. 1, 54ff.; George Faludy, *Erasmus von Rotterdam* (Frankfurt, 1973), 50ff.

of Erasmus's four visits lasted until January, 1500, and ended in discord when customs officials, acting by order of Henry VII, confiscated practically all of his belongings, including his money. His English friends understandably had their hands full soothing his feelings.

His friendship with More started with this first sojourn in England and was to last until Thomas's death. Their mutual affection was inseparably bound up with the fundamental issues of their day. Both were interested in problems of faith, knowledge, and science—of God, man, and the world.[4] Between them there existed no clearly perceptible differences.

Erasmus's most significant encounter in England during that first trip was with John Colet. Three years older than the Dutchman, Colet had been young More's teacher. His studies in Italy and France had made him a highly cultured man. As Dean of St. Paul's in London, he created a great stir with sermons, explaining the Gospels according to St. Paul. Colet sought to return to Scripture and the Fathers of the Church, while pruning the excesses of medieval commentary. In this he had a profound influence on Erasmus and Thomas.

A letter from Erasmus to Colet in October 1499 reflects the self-image of these humanists as sincere, pious modernizers of religion.

> If you say that this generation of young theologians, grown old in mere nuances and sophisticated discourse, displeases you, dear Colet, then we think alike. Theology, queen of all the sciences, adorned and decorated with the eloquence of the elders, is spoilt by their charlatanism and their foul saliva. Therefore, you see the sovereign of yesteryear, full of majesty, now practically naked, defenseless and reduced to rags. Moreover, people, who because of their intellectual sclerosis are useless at almost any science, are milling around to study theology, the first among all the sciences. You, my dear Colet, have started the battle in order, as far as it lies within your power, to give back to the old and true theology its ancient splendor and dignity. You have thereby taken on a task which, God knows well, is in many ways beautiful and very profitable for theology, and this is in the interests of all students, above all of this flourishing University of Oxford.[5]

---

4. Cf. in this respect E. E. Reynolds, *Thomas More and Erasmus* (London, 1965).
5. Köhler, 38ff.

Brash and aggressive as this missive may be, it makes a sound point. Part of the run up to the Protestant Reformation was a vigorous throwing open of windows to let fresh air into a musty, shuttered room. The circle of friends to which Colet and Erasmus belonged included, beside More (by far the youngest), William Grocyn, who since 1491 had taught Greek at Oxford; Thomas Linacre, who also taught there and founded chairs of Medicine at Oxford and Cambridge, and was appointed in 1508 Doctor of the King's Chamber; and William Lily, head of St. Paul's School in London. All but More were clerics who had lived and studied in Italy and brought back with them the Renaissance spirit that encouraged a philologically conscious acquisition of knowledge. These men constituted something like a brotherhood of culture sharing mutual admiration, self-confidence, and profound disdain for "barbarians."

Although Erasmus's relationship with Colet had some of that occasional touchiness typical between intellectuals of the same age, his friendship with More, nine years younger, was above all based on mutual affection. It developed during Erasmus's second visit to England (1505–1506), culminated during the third (1509–1514), and thereafter—especially in the fourteen years from 1521 until More's death, during which the friends did not see each other again—became something of an institution. There was no visible parting of the ways, but their vocations diverged, Erasmus remaining a peace-loving intellectual, pious in his ways, who meditated, spoke, and wrote about God, while Thomas's love of God reached such heights that he accepted the dungeon and the scaffold almost joyfully.

But that lay in the future. In these early years what occupied the friends was their struggle for the renewal of the sciences and classical culture. Revitalizing the Church, the humanists agreed, would come about through the publication of the purified texts of Scripture and the Fathers. Opposed to them were those who feared that textual criticism might get out of hand and provoke a general questioning, skepticism, and distrust of the faith. More, Erasmus, and their friends fought against such "ignorant people," "the enemies of progress." Thomas wrote to Colet: "Just as the Greeks came out of the Trojan horse to destroy the barbarian city of Troy so, they believe, from your school will likewise come out those who will show up and destroy their ignorance."[6]

---

6. SL, 3, p.6; *Corr.*, 8, London, March 1512.

While such people undoubtedly sensed a real danger, humanists such as Colet, Erasmus, and More had no intention of doing away with the verities of the faith or casting doubt on the role of the Church. "I cannot put into words, dearest Colet," Erasmus writes in December 1504 from Paris, "how much Holy Scripture attracts every fiber of my being, and how repugnant I find everything that drives me away or keeps me apart from her. I want with all my heart to devote myself to Holy Scripture and dedicate my entire life to her."[7] The contemporaneous writing of *Enchiridion Militis Christiani* (The Christian Soldier's Handbook) shows the sincerity of these words. In the same letter Erasmus says: "I have not written it to show how clever I am, but to remedy the error of those who still see the essentials of religion in ceremonies and physical rituals more or less Judaic in character. At the same they astonishingly ignore piety. I have attempted to present some kind of theory of piety, in a manner similar to those books which show the exact internal relationship between the sciences."[8]

For More, this compendium of secular devotion, with its lastingly beautiful "Twenty rules of the Christian soldier,"[9] was simply what he believed in and lived by. The twenty-first rule is this: "Remember the fleeting nature of life, and also bear in mind how sad and fleeting is your present existence. On all sides it sees itself threatened by perfidious death, that comes upon those who do not expect it. Immense is the danger of prolonging life (in sin), for no one is sure of his life not even for one moment."

The spirit and letter of this "Brief manual" are present throughout More's work, from his *The Four Last Things* to his writings in the Tower of London. In this sense, Erasmus was a powerful influence on the young More. The difference between them was their difference in living the imitation of Christ.

Erasmus's second visit to England lasted from January 1505 until July 1506. During this time he stayed almost continuously in Colet's house or at Bucklersbury, where he saw the married life of the young Mores, worked on translating Euripides, and disputed with his host over

---

7. Köhler, 46; 79f.

8. Ibid.; Eckert, vol. 1, 108. With his collection *Lucubrantiunculae Aliquot* ("Small elucubrations") published in 1503 in Antwerp by Dirk Martens, Erasmus also published, for the first time, his *Enchiridion Militis Christiani*. The book was translated into English in 1518, into Czech in 1519, and into German in 1520 (Eckert, vol. 1, 105).

9. *ES* I, 148–350 (*Regulae quaedam generales veri Christianismi*) (Some general rules of true Christianity).

Lucan's dialogues. When Henry VIII's Physician of the Royal Chamber, Giovanni Battista Boerio, sought a private companion-tutor for his children on a journey to Italy, Erasmus took the post, which allowed him to stay in Italy for three years. There he obtained a doctorate in theology and visited Bologna and Florence, while avoiding the regions where the various campaigns of the bellicose Pope Julius II were under way. He got to know Aldo Manucio, the best-known typographer of those times, Aleander, subsequently papal envoy and Luther's adversary, the future Cardinal Pietro Bembo, and the celebrated humanist Johannes Lascaris. With his pupil Alexander Stuart, illegitimate son of King James IV of Scotland, he traveled to Padua, Ferrara, and Siena. After four months in Rome, where he established contacts in the papal court, he visited Naples then returned overland to England, passing through Bologna, Constance, Strasbourg, and Antwerp. He arrived in England in September 1509, and remained there for five years, except for a brief stay in Paris during 1511.

Unlike this scholar free of professional constraints and family obligations, More had to apply his energies as undersheriff of London to trivial legal matters and disputes, and be a writer only in his spare time, this is probably what most differentiates them. Both were extraordinarily hard workers, but where Erasmus's many publications make up a more or less integrated body of work, More's have something of the character of occasional pieces.

Erasmus gave theological lectures in Cambridge (*De Ratione Studii*), composed for his friend Colet a tract on teaching (*De Copia Verborum*), and anonymously produced a scathing satire, whose authorship he always prudently denied, against the warlike Pope Julius (*Julius Exclusus e Coeli*). Especially, during his stay in More's house, he wrote the dialogue *Moriae Encomium*, whose title alludes to his friend's name. Its Latin title is *Laus Stultiae*—in English, *In Praise of Folly*. It became one of his most popular works.

Writing in the guise of "Lady Idiocy," Erasmus here criticizes his time and place, employing a literary convention known since the early Middle Ages that acquired its definitive form in *The Ship of Fools* by Sebastian Brant, published in 1494. By the end of the sixteenth century *In Praise of Folly* had been reprinted seventy times; in the seventeenth century, another forty, and in the eighteenth century, over sixty more. Appropriately in a work dedicated to More, it is an apparently comic-grotesque, yet in reality profoundly wise, treatment of the concept of "folly." At the end, says Eckert, "Erasmus unveils the deepest dimension which the word 'folly' embraces. He speaks of the folly of the Cross as the apostle of the gentiles, Saint Paul, taught us to understand it. And, hence, that the Christian has to be educated to understand that folly."[10]

Erasmus's creative explosion between 1509 and 1516 was just the beginning. Next came his works against war (*Dulce Bellum lnexpertis*) and on education (*Institutio Principis Christiani*) dedicated to King Carlos I of Spain, the future Emperor Charles V, then sixteen years old, then the Greek edition of the New Testament. As for Thomas More in this period, only two documents can be ascribed to him: the celebrated letter from Bruges to Martin van Dorp dated October 21, 1515, and his *Utopia*, published in the autumn of 1516 in Louvain. Both reflect the person and work of his Dutch friend. In the *Letter to Dorp* he defends him against attacks; while the *Utopia* is More's version of the kind of social critique presented by *In Praise of Folly*. However much one may admire *Utopia*, the *Letter to Dorp* is probably the more important key to comprehending a humanism that wishes to remain Christian, as well as to understanding the downfall of More, humanist civil servant, and the victory of More, humanist saint.

2.

Marin van Dorp (1485–1525) hailed from the southern part of Holland. Having studied classical languages and liberal arts at the University of Louvain, he became professor of Latin there in 1504. Already in 1503 the writing of this eighteen-year-old had drawn Erasmus's attention. At the age of twenty, he started his theological studies. During the following ten years, and probably under the influence of the Louvain theologians, he veered toward a strict conservatism. Nevertheless, it came as a great surprise when his lengthy letter criticizing Erasmus became public knowledge. He had sent copies to various people but not to the person criticized, and Erasmus did not see it until May 1515. Dorp claimed to speak on behalf of the faculty of theology at Louvain, which had greeted *In Praise of Folly* with great reservation. Contending that Erasmus had damaged the authority of the theologians in the public eye, he declared that a systematic philological criticism of the sacred texts undermined the authority of

---

10. Eckert, vol. 1, 136.

the Church and of Scripture itself. Although the new edition of the letters of St. Jerome was praiseworthy, he added, the Greek version of the New Testament, whose clear purpose was to correct the Latin Vulgate,[11] had firmly to be rejected, since doubts surrounding that translation of the Bible, in use for the past millennium, would eventually undermine the faith.

Erasmus answered courteously and ably, with a short version sent to Dorp and a much longer one intended for publication. Regarding *In Praise of Folly* he was moderate: "Frankly speaking, I almost regret publishing *In Praise of Folly*. The little book has made me very famous or, if you like, sadly celebrated. In publishing all my books, my sole purpose always has been to do good through my diligence; and if that was not possible, I sought at least not to cause any damage."[12]

He asserted that he meant to criticize theologians only when they engaged in sterile, subtle debates instead of studying biblical languages and the writings of the Holy Fathers. *On the Novum Instrumentum*, on the other hand, he stood firm, defending the right and necessity of the renewal of the Greek text. Dorp, who meantime had been appointed professor of theology at Louvain and enjoyed his colleagues' support, replied on August 27, 1515, in a much harsher tone. While maintaining that he was only quoting the opinion of others and was basically a defender of Erasmus, he generally denied the need to know Greek in order to study Holy Scripture and emphasized the fundamental and permanent superiority of the Latin Vulgate as opposed to the original Greek texts.

In June 1515, when More, serving as member of a legation to Flanders, met Erasmus in Bruges, the friends had the opportunity to compare notes and discuss the attack. The long letter,[13] written on October 21, when Erasmus had already returned to Basle, is almost the length of a small book. While More's eloquent defense of Erasmus expresses his personal feelings, in this matter, the two friends spoke with one voice.

---

11. *Vulgate*: the Latin translation of the Bible, produced by St. Jerome (345–420) at the request of Pope Damasus (366–384). This version had been in use throughout the Roman Church for about 600 years; in 1546, the Council of Trent declared it "authentic." *Septuagint*: the oldest translation of the Old Testament into Greek, produced during the times of Ptolemy II (308–246 B.C.); on the history of the *Septuagint* see J. Jellicoe, *The Septuaginta and Modern Study* (Oxford, 1968).

12. Köhler, 125–131, from Antwerp, June, 1515.

13. *SL*, 4; 8–64.

It is important to understand just what lay at the heart of this controversy, which often was concealed by personal differences and incidentals. Erasmus and the humanists reproached the academicians for stagnant speculations and ever-growing and impenetrable layers of interpretation and analogy that threatened to smother the light of faith. They sought to return to sources and saw the study of languages, especially Greek, as necessary to this end. In effect, philology was being enthroned as natural sciences were later to be. At first, there was not the slightest hint that a religious conflict could result.

On the side opposed were the theologians of late scholasticism, for example, Adrian of Utrecht, the future Pope Adrian VI (1459–1523). Many religious, especially Dominicans and Franciscans, were not interested in whether the views of the humanists had any merit but only in what all this might lead to. What would happen if the people came to see their bishops, clergy, and religious as superstitious charlatans, especially considering that they already had to put up with scandals of clerical greed, lust, covetousness, and laziness? Would faith not be undermined if a version of Scripture held to be valid up to then were now set aside in favor of a purified text—especially if this were done by specialists whose knowledge of Greek placed them beyond review and challenge by anyone else? Would this not be to create an authority separate from and superior to the hierarchy?

These were and are serious questions to be taken seriously. So what did Thomas More in fact understand as progress? In the first place, it was the elimination of linguistic sophisms, pseudodialectics, and imaginary problems. He believed that all this clouded people's vision of the essentials both in religion and science. In his letter to Dorp, he points out again and again that in his *In Praise of Folly* Erasmus intended only to criticize such excesses. "Everything that is written down," says More, "can be interpreted badly—including what Martin Dorp wrote; but every author deserves the benefit of the doubt at the start."

More then moves on to what in his opinion is the crux of the matter: the wretched training of many theologians and of clerics in general. The defense of Erasmus now becomes an attack. Those who assail Erasmus for his knowledge of Greek and his desire for better scriptural texts often have no knowledge whatsoever of Holy Scripture in any version.

In his letter indicting Erasmus, Dorp had written: "Do not think, Erasmus, that a man who understands the Bible word for word is a perfect theologian, and neither is he who can draw moral interpretations from it. There are many things which are much more difficult to understand, and of greater practical value to Christianity. . . . When should a repentant sinner receive absolution and when should it be withheld? Innumerable problems of this kind could be listed. If I am not mistaken, a large section of the Bible can be learned by heart effortlessly quicker than it takes to solve a single one of such problems."

Hoping to demolish Dorp with his own words, More cites these remarks as if they were proposing a substitute for deep knowledge of the Bible. But the sense of the passage is only that, generally, biblical knowledge is not enough for doing pastoral work. Here we have a dialogue of the deaf. The humanists demand that appropriate respect be shown due to Holy Scripture, including seeking the most accurate text, though without dismissing the unwritten sources of Christian faith found in tradition and liturgical celebrations. Many late scholastics failed to grasp the idea of renewing faith by means of Scripture, considering it useless by comparison with practical pastoral work; yet it goes without saying that they acknowledge the importance of the Bible. In sum, the "progressive" humanists had no intention of doing away with the sacraments, any more than the "conservative" scholars with Holy Scripture. Yet precisely these were the reproaches they leveled at one another.

When More, in his letters to Dorp and, subsequently, to "a monk" rails against the improper use of the Bible, in no way does he mean to suggest that knowledge of Scripture should be spread independently of the magisterium of the Church. In mocking the ignorance of the clergy who based their opinions solely on commentaries without having read the Bible, he is not accusing all clerics of being uneducated or ignorant of the Bible. He merely distinguished between faithful clerics who know Scripture and are obedient to it, and ignorant storytellers. But finally all were part of the Church; while the difference between heresy and orthodoxy was not that between knowledge and ignorance, but that separating arrogance and humility, insurrection and obedience. "My dear Dorp," he wrote, "I am convinced . . . that we have been given in abundance all that is necessary for our salvation: on the one hand, through Holy Scripture, then through the Fathers of the Church, and finally through her sacred decrees." It was a confession in favor of the Church that More would repeat years later in his *Responsio* and his *Confutatio*.

In his view, purifying the biblical text is always necessary, but it is licit only if carried on with ecclesiastical approval. In every case, the Church has the last word. Here he is speaking specifically of the Greek edition of the New Testament, the *Novum Instrumentum* of Erasmus. Dorp's misgivings about the consequences of such textual revision are groundless, he insists. More did not change from being a "progressive" humanist to being a timidly conservative late scholastic. He was and remained a Christian and a humanist throughout his life.

In the final pages of his letter, Thomas takes up Dorp's condemnation of *In Praise of Folly*. The same question is at issue as in the debate surrounding the *Novum Instrumentum*. In attacking Erasmus, Dorp has used a specific and limited work to draw general conclusions about the intentions behind it and about its effects. By now there is a hint of weariness in his defense of his friend.

More uses restrained language when engaged in scholarly dispute, but he can become exercised on the subject of theologians, clergy, and monks and their failings. At times his anger is excessive and he treats lack of education as if it were in itself a vice. Of this too we have an instance showing a rough, sarcastic More, full of scorn and intent on annihilating his adversary. This is *The Letter to a Monk*, and it makes uncomfortable reading.[14]

The monk, as we know, was John Batmanson. More apparently had known him in his youth. Born in 1488, a deacon since 1510, he was a self-taught man. In 1523 he was elected prior of Hunton and in 1529, of the Carthusian convent in London, where he died in 1531.[15] He wrote a book entitled *Contra Annotationes Erasmi Roterodami* attacking the *Novum Instrumentum*, Erasmus's New Testament in Greek, and in particular its notes.

Just as Batmanson had a right to express doubts about Erasmus's edition and to state his objections, so More had a right to demolish the doubts and the objections. But he did this in a disproportionate and not very attractive manner, with long-winded explanations and a frequently haughty and disdainful tone in regard to a young religious and his manuscript.

The epistle, probably written in July 1519 and printed in August 1520, begins: "Letter from the celebrated gentleman Thomas More, in which he rejects the irascible and upbraiding accusations of a certain monk whose stupidity is as monumental as his arrogance." More's argument moves along the same lines as in his reply to Dorp, but now he

---

14. *SL*, 26; *Corr.*, 83, This is the complete text, from which *SL* (pp. 114–144) covers the second part only.

15. *SL*, 114. Cf. *The Religious Orders in England* (Cambridge, 1959), vol. 3, 469.

writes with much greater impatience. To Batmanson's reasonable concern that a multitude of biblical translations, constantly argued over
and in competition with one another would create doubts in readers'
minds, Thomas replies: "It is a sound objection in the case of an utterly
stupid reader, devoid of sense or reason. But if he is intelligent, it would
be even easier—as Augustine says—to recognize the true sense of the
different versions." More would have many opportunities in the future
to realize that this was false.

To the monk's charge that Erasmus was in sympathy with Luther,
More reacts furiously, yet at the same time such an idea was by no
means preposterous. A torrent of irate and furious words is unleashed
against the erring monk, and not only him but "present-day monks"
as a group. "Written texts tell of times when there were monks withdrawn from the world who did not permit themselves to read letters
from their own friends even. They did not want to cast a backward
glance at the Sodom they had left behind. But today's monks, from
what I can observe, read heretical and apostate books, and big tomes
full of nonsense."

He invokes all the authorities who have spoken well of Erasmus
and, in particular, his edition of the New Testament. "Has not the Pope
himself [Leo X, 1513–1521] twice paid explicit homage to what you
now condemn? What the head of the Christian world honors with his
support do you now, miserable little monk, uneducated and unknown,
wish to scorn with your murmuring tongue through the hole in the
door of your cell?"

This was, as far as I know, the only time when More set aside all
restraint in berating someone in many ways weaker than himself. One
senses a deep, long rankling at last rising to the surface: the wrath of a
layman in the face of monastic pride grounded in the belief that the
monk in principle was the better Christian, the one closer to God and
more sure of his salvation. A very raw, hidden, and personal wound in
More plainly had been touched.

There was another reason as well. The Carthusian had accused
Erasmus and, through him, all his humanist friends of heresy resem-
bling Luther's. Was it not the grain of truth in this that irritated More?
His own words here—about Marian devotion, the monastic life, faith
and works, grace and free will—could easily have come from Luther's
pen and easily have been interpreted in a Lutheran sense; the differences
now so clear to us were not so clear then.

The monk, in his criticism of Erasmus, had articulated a half-truth, while missing the service rendered by the Rotterdam humanist in purifying the sources of the faith and by all the humanists in integrating classical antiquity into Christian thought. But More's defense is no less a half-truth. He brilliantly defends Erasmus, humanism, and humanists against narrow-minded charges of being unorthodox and vehemently stigmatizes the pitiful state of the clergy and religious. But he was deaf to the justified and understandable concerns of those he opposed. In replying to Dorp and Batmanson, he saw perversion of the faith by superstition as the real threat to the Church and humanism as its authentic remedy. That the remedy could become the malady had only begun to be suspected. When, much later, More saw the other half of the truth, he completed the picture by his orthodox defense of the faith in his major controversial writings.

3.

People who know little about Thomas More often know only that he wrote a book called *Utopia* and that he was beheaded. Philologists, historians, and specialists in the history of economics and sociology have obvious reasons for being interested in a document that provides so much information about the English language and literary style at the beginning of the sixteenth century, about More the humanist writer, and about the ethos of Henry VIII's England. There are ideological reasons as well. With the dawning of the age of great social schemes and radical proposals for changing the world, it is natural that there should be heightened interest in men and books that presumably had already undertaken this task: Bacon's *Nova Atlantis*,[16] Campanella's *The City of the Sun*,[17] More's *Utopia*.

---

16. Francis Bacon (1561–1626), was a nephew of the important Elizabethan statesman Burleigh, and a figure of very dubious character. His *Essays* or *Counsels, civil and moral* (1625), develop forms of life "beyond good and evil." His last work, *Nova Atlantis*, a description of an "ideal philosophical state," was never completed.

17. Tomasso Campanella (1568–1639), was a Dominican, imprisoned for twenty-seven years in Naples for his opposition to Spanish rule. His tract, *Citta del Sole*, 1602, was written in prison. In it he develops a collectivist Christian state ruled over by sacerdotal philosophers under an ideal pope. The life in the State of the Sun is regulated by a totalitarian regime, including even the time for having children. In a way, the reductions (mission settlements) of the Jesuits in Paraguay, between 1589 and 1768, can be seen as an attempt to make real that vision.

There was undoubtedly dissatisfaction in the England of the Tudors between 1500 and 1515. There was also an awareness of not being able to change things for the better. More's book may be a protest, but the protest is put in a playful way, and this aspect of it is frequently overlooked. German intellectuals especially, from Kautsky[18] to the present day, have outdone themselves with terribly serious interpretations that take no account of the author's humor. In fairness, though, it must be said that this brand of humor is not ours, and often it is quite incomprehensible to us. There is no laughing now at the totalitarian state of Utopia any more than at Orwell's *1984*. But to More and his readers it was laughable indeed. The second volume of *Utopia* was written first, in 1515. It contains the "Speech by Raphael Hythlodaeus on The Best State of a Republic," and includes the material that was to cause such headaches to later interpreters. In 1516 More wrote a prologue to this second part that later became the first volume. The first edition was published in the autumn of 1516 in Louvain.[19]

⚓ ⚓ ⚓

These days anybody can pick up a paperback edition of this most famous of More's writings, and it has been written about time and again, so I make only a few remarks. *Utopia*, it must be emphasized, is a tale, a fable, not a personal manifesto. It considers the times, the rulers, and the Christianity of its day through a work of the imagination in a somewhat didactic tone. Furthermore, it is a highly readable book, intended for the enjoyment of a refined society. More no doubt would have found amusing the question of whether he considered the state of King Utopus desirable and would have liked to build it himself.

Thomas put his tale into the mouth of a traveler, Raphael Hythlodaeus, and invented not only an alphabet and language, but also every detail of the geography, clothes, customs, and traditions of the island "Utopia." Thus he became the inventor of a totally enclosed world,

18. *Thomas More und die Utopia* (Stuttgart, 1888). Seventh edition, Bonn-Bad Godesberg, 1974.

19. *Utopia*, written in Latin, had its last printing during More's lifetime in November 1518 in Basle. It was subsequently translated into all the important languages. Cf. for the older edition Victor Michels and Theobald Ziegler: *Thomas Morus, Utopia* (*Lateinische Literaturdenkmaler des 15. und 16. Jahrhunderts* (Berlin, 1895); *The Utopia of Sir Thomas More*, edited by J. H. Lupton (Oxford, 1895). The most important edition of today: *CW*, vol. 4, edited by E. Surtz, S. J., and J. H. Hexter (New Haven-London, 1965).

similar to that of his countryman Tolkien[20] four hundred years later. In this way he gave free rein to his playful inclinations. The island's capital—"Amautorum"—is a kind of fantasy London. The state is a modern version of Sparta. His well-ordered day, balancing leisure and hard work, is a critique of the very long working hours of his times, which he considers a price paid for the leisure of so many. Among the leisured classes he explicitly names "priests" and so-called pious "religious." What a numerous and lazy lot they are! Add to them the rich, especially large landowners, plus their servants, all that armed hooligan filth! And then all the able-bodied beggars of sound mind: "You will certainly find that all that is necessary for daily use by man is based on the labor of fewer people than you might imagine."[21] Not surprisingly, More has been considered a predecessor of "scientific socialism." Just as for what he says about such matters as colonies, alliances, treaties, he has been viewed as a founder of British imperialism. Those who think this way are quite right. But there is nothing surprising in that, given that the number of theoretical structures in any society is fairly limited.

From the outset, the paragraphs on the religion of the Utopians have troubled interpreters. Having invented a world, More could not ignore religious ideas. In theory, he could have invented a version of pure Christianity for his Utopians. But by making Utopia a non-Christian state, the author can exercise his imagination to criticize the shortcomings of Christians.

The contradictions in *Utopia* have always been a challenge: noble humanity, religious tolerance, high moral standards, material justice, on the one hand; and on the other, war crimes, state control, lack of personal privacy. At times there are no visible differences between the Utopian states More approves of and those he looks at askance. A further difficulty concerns the discrepancies between the state principles of Utopia as Hythlodaeus describes them and those which the author subsequently describes. But are the problems really so large? Consider More's account of the Utopian priesthood in which he says those priests, "who were not women themselves took the most noble women as wives."[22] This is not a bit of advocacy on More's part but simply a literary invention for the "land of nowhere." And it is logical: in the Catholic Church, the priesthood is reserved for men, because the priest

---

20. J. R. R. Tokien, *The Lord of the Rings*, 3 vols., Allen and Unwin, 1954–1955.
21. *Utopia*, 51.
22. Ibid., 104f.

represents Christ; but where this is not so, as in Utopia, women can be admitted to the priestly calling.

Another example is communism. Hythlodaeus observes that the Utopians "had received news of the name, doctrine, nature, and miracles of Jesus Christ" and were very receptive. It was very important to them to learn "that Christ had validated the communal way of life of his disciples, something quite normal even today among genuine Christians."[23] This simply says that Christian fraternity, even in material things, is regarded sympathetically by the Utopians because they already practice a form of non-Christian communism.

A third example is tolerance. Hythlodaeus tells the story of a fanatical Christian, a "neo-Christian," who was arrested in Utopia: "He got so carried away that he soon raised our confession above all others, damning them unremittingly, calling them profane and denigrating their confessors as infamous blasphemers, deserving of the fires of hell."[24] He was exiled, not so much for his offenses against religion but for "scandalizing and agitating the people." As we have seen, More was to find this scandalizing and agitating a real offense but he was also to go much further, fighting the new, Protestant faith with every means at his disposal. Had he undergone a conversion, from a liberal and tolerant man in his mid-thirties to a somber fanatic in his fifties? The answer requires a closer look at this matter.

King Utopus had conquered the islanders because they had fallen out among themselves over religion. After his victory, he decided: "Let all follow the religion of their choice; it is also lawful that they should attempt to convert others to their religion, provided only they present their beliefs amicably, without presumption, and basing them on rational arguments, without violently denigrating other points of view. If, despite all exhortations, they do not succeed in convincing others, violence must not be resorted to and insults will have to be repressed. Whosoever acts with excessive violence in this matter will be punishable with exile and slavery."[25] More sticks to his basic concept of building a state and a society upon the idea of a rational religion. In such a situation, the fundamental equality of the various products of reason is an acceptable principle, and the only acceptable intolerance is not to tolerate intolerance itself.

23. Ibid., 98.
24. Ibid., 99.
25. Ibid., 99f.

Once again, More proceeds logically. Where a religion exists that is not of human making but divinely revealed, one no longer has the option of holding religious opinions but a duty to believe. There is a huge gap separating faith and opinion, and God cannot want human veneration in any way other than through Christ in whom all salvation lies.

In this non-Christian world of More's imagining, Hythlodaeus says of his Utopians: "that nearly all of them are convinced that eternal happiness awaits mankind. They feel saddened, therefore, when they fall ill but never when death strikes, unless they see the moribund letting go of life terror-stricken and putting up a resistance. They believe that it will not be pleasing to God to see the arrival of a man who does not answer his call cheerfully."[26] They speak of the community of spirit that exists between the living and the dead, the prayerful entreaty for the souls of the departed, praise of the Creator at the sight of nature, and hard physical work as a means of showing love for God. In short, this non-Christian world of Utopia is a pre-Christian world wanting only a focal point of reference to give it Christian meaning.

The contradictory character of More's Utopia is a mark of its quality, a guaranteed seal of the author's veracity. The man who wrote this book deserves our trust because he gave it a title to remind us that the ills of this world must be overcome in this world; immigration to the country of King Utopus is not a possibility.

The Latin work whose full title in that language is *De optimo republicae statu deque nova insula Utopia* (Concerning the Ideal State and the New Island of Utopia) had six printings on the Continent before it was published in England. It was translated into German and Italian before it was published in English in 1551. Nevertheless, knowledge of the book spread like wildfire among the English intelligentsia. In November 1516 More thanked Tunstall for his praise: "I cannot tell you how pleased I am that your opinion has been so positive. You have almost convinced me that you are telling me what you really think. I know that you are far from all simulation and that I am not of sufficient importance for you to feel you owe me adulation; and I am too fond of you to deserve to be mocked. . . . On the other hand, if your affection for me should have blinded you in your perusal, I am no less pleased, for such affection must have been very great indeed to have deprived a Tunstall of discernment."[27]

---

26. Ibid., 101.
27. *SL*, 10; *Corr.*, 28; from London, 1516.

4.

Where More invented a rational religion for his Utopian society, Erasmus counseled religious understanding in contemporary society, and at times fought bravely and decisively for it. He believed that consensus could be achieved through respectful argument and knowledge of the issues, provided everyone showed good will and reasonableness. Believing no conflict to be unavoidable, he never really took sides, something for which he is commonly praised these days.

Following his last visit to England in the spring of 1517, Erasmus was soon drawn into the maelstrom at the beginning of the Lutheran revolution and debated the theses of Luther with the theologians of the University of Louvain. On the whole, he welcomed what the German friar had done, but he also voiced certain objections. In June of 1521 he wrote to Melancthon: "I support Luther as far as I am able despite the fact that my affairs are associated with his everywhere. In England they were going to burn his books. I am sure that I prevented that by the letter I wrote to Wolsey, Cardinal of York; all who love Luther well—and practically all of them are good people—would have preferred him to write in a more courteous and restrained way. I can see that the affair is going to end in upheaval. I pray that it will be to Christ's honor. 'Obstacles indeed there must be but alas for the man who provides them' (Mt 18:7), but I do not want to be their cause. The activities of Luther's opponents are diabolical, whose sole aim is to suppress Christ and be in command in the name of Christ."[28]

The opposing sides naturally wished to enlist the authority and pen of Erasmus. But for the rest of his life that erudite person, so little belligerently inclined, devoted his energies to remaining apart from—or above—the fray. He and his friends did not need Luther to tell them that much needed reforming in the Church, having often given voice to their own criticisms. Now the reformers could claim that those criticisms justified what they were doing, while many humanists took a favorable view of Luther as someone who would put an end to many scandals in the Church. There is no saying how far Erasmus really followed Luther in matters of theology. But this man who detested quarrels and conflicts and preached tolerance showed a certain intellectual courage, falling out with his friend Hutten in 1523 and in 1524 completely breaking with Luther.

---

28. Köhler, 271f.

This was not just because of profound differences in the understanding of "free will"; Luther simply got on his nerves. In 1527, Erasmus turned against the Inquisition and, in 1528 against the "neo-pagan rhetorical deterioration of contemporary humanists."[29] Later he tried unsuccessfully to steer the council of the city of Basle in the direction of religious tolerance. But when the followers of Zwingli used violence in taking over the city, he finally left in April 1529 and went to Freiburg in Breisgau in southern Germany, where he remained for six years. In the summer of 1535 he returned to Basle. It was there that he died on July 12, 1536, almost a year to the day after Thomas More.

Self-regard prevented him from understanding how people could misinterpret or even ignore his advice. Shattered by the news of what had happened to More and Fisher, he voiced his opinion that the two martyrs should not have stood against the storm, though he would have been glad if Henry VIII had behaved with more moderation. With this, along with remembrance of Fisher in the prologue to his last work, *Ecclesiastes*, he was content. There was no cry of indignation against Henry. Erasmus at sixty-six took satisfaction from the hostility toward him on both sides of the religious divide, seeing it as confirmation of his superior wisdom.

Thomas More, who knew Erasmus well, recognized that his friend's intellectual audacity did not always go hand in hand with physical bravery. In a letter of December 1526 noting Erasmus's delay in producing another volume in an ongoing controversy with Luther, More acknowledged that there might be good reasons for it; but then he added to his friend: "But if the delay has occurred—as some reports claim—because you have been intimidated, have lost all interest in this work and feel discouraged, then I feel extremely concerned and unable to contain my sorrow. You, my dear Erasmus, have fought many battles and many perils and performed Herculean tasks. You have spent the best years of your life burning the midnight oil until you dropped, for the good of everybody. May God not permit that now, at your age, you allow yourself to be influenced so pitiably, preferring instead to abandon God's cause rather than lose an argument. I have not the slightest doubt that you will continue to show your intellectual mettle to the last breath. . . ."[30]

More always defended his friend against the accusation of having been the real intellectual instigator of the Lutheran revolution. And with

---

29. Faludy, 265.
30. Ibid.

good reason, for if the cause of the schism is to be found in humanist learning, the study of Scripture, and the longing for reform, More was an instigator too. In fact, however, Erasmus and More were alike in their loyalty to the faith of the Church. But while the country of nowhere existed for More only as the product of his pen—which he soon abandoned to work, fight, suffer, and die in his own real country—Erasmus lived his entire life in a kind of Utopia: not the island of King Utopus, but a supranational cultural realm whose inhabitants shed more ink than blood while thinking of themselves as the supreme world authority. Erasmus took part in theological controversies as a distinguished scholar and publicist. Thomas was led by friendship with Christ to give his life like a soldier defending his general.

CHAPTER NINE

The Souls in Purgatory

1.

Germain Marc'hadour, in the prologue to his edition of More's tract *The Humble Supplication of Souls*,[1] notes that the author chose the dialogue form for all his works in the culminating phase of his literary career, including *Utopia*, the *Dialogue Against Heresies*,[2] and the *Consolation in Suffering*.[3] As Marc'hadour notes, this was the form best suited to the Socratic method. But More could not always find time to write carefully. *The Humble Supplication* is a case in point in which he had to rush to repel an assault on the Church's doctrine on Purgatory.

By now, in 1529, More was a man of fifty, opposing those of a younger generation, among them his own son-in-law Roper, who seek a new religion, a new society, a different way of life. His allies are those monks he had so often and harshly pilloried. It was not the hour of champions of traditional truths but of Luther, Tyndale, Zwingli, and

---

1. *Saint Thomas More, Lettre a Dorp.—La Supplication des âmes*. Textes traduits et presentes par German Marc'hadour. En introduction: *Thomas More vu par Erasme* (Namur, 1962), referred to below as *Supplication* MH. Between 1557 and 1950 *The Supplication of Souls* was not published even once. In that year, Sister Mary Thecla edited the work according to modern orthography (Maryland, 1950). Soon after, the first critical edition by Germain Marc'hadour was published as Volume 7 of the Yale Edition. As mentioned in the epilogue, I have been unable to consult the original version or a modern English version. Despite certain reservations in principle, I have relied on the French translation.

2. *A Dialogue concerning Heresies and Matters of Religion*, the first of More's controversial writings in English, was published in 1529 by Rastell. In this connection, Marc'hadour says of it: "Carefully expounded, full of highly amusing anecdotes, often surprisingly animated, dazzlingly good-humoured. Self-assured with the commonsense and steadfast faith of the English people." This text is intended for the Yale Edition, edited by T. T. C. Lawler, R. Marius, G. Marc'hadour, as Volume 6 of *CW*.

3. Quoted by Bremond, 124f; also: Thomas More: *Trost in Leid Ein Dialog*. Ausgewählt, übersetzt und eingeleitet von Martha Freundlieb (Munich, 1951), 228.

their followers. For many years of isolation were to precede More's final solitude in the Tower of London, years of gradual confinement, internal at first and, from 1532, also external, within the day-to-day world around him.

Though older and more mature, he was essentially unchanged. There is no contradiction between his letters to Dorp and Batmanson and his defense of the souls in Purgatory. He had always sought to join the new secular learning to the tradition of the faith, to combine a questioning spirit interested in this world with piety that looks to life eternal. Now it was all coming apart, and the separation of the two spheres was the deepest source of his suffering. He had always defended whatever was in the greatest jeopardy, and by 1529 that no longer included the humanists but the priesthood, especially the monks who were now under pressure from fanatical innovators.

More wrote the *Supplication* in haste, and Rastell published it in London, probably in September of 1529, a few weeks before the author's appointment as Lord Chancellor. He wrote in English so that everyone might read and understand. The result was an argumentative text, the most impassioned to flow from his pen, which can still move the reader who does not close his mind to it.

During this decade two currents had come together that gravely imperiled the old Church. One was a diffuse and very widespread enthusiasm for the gospels, understood as the keys to primitive Christianity. The other was material envy of the clergy, especially the higher echelons of the priesthood. The Mass, the sacraments, the doctrine of indulgences and Purgatory were unavoidably involved, since from the early Middle Ages donations and legacies to the Church and monasteries usually had stipulated the offering of Masses and prayers for the dead. Mass stipends of this sort were one of the most important sources of income for the local clergy.

In the years leading up to the emergence of Protestantism, attitudes in a large segment of the population, especially the more educated and well off, were poisoned by the mixing of pastoral ministry and Mass stipends. The explosion was triggered by Richard Hunne, a wealthy London draper well known for acts of charity.[4] When his

---

4. Cf. Richard J. Schoeck, *Common Law and Canon Law in their relation to Thomas More*, in "St. Thomas More: Action and Contemplation. Proceedings of the Symposium held at St. John's University," October 9–10, 1970. Published by R. S. Sylvester (New Haven-London, 1972), in a chapter entitled "The Case of Richard Hunne," 23–42.

infant son died in 1511 at five months, Hunne refused to pay the usual "mortuary" fee for the tiny baptismal dress or shroud. "The baby," he said, "owned nothing, and neither did he owe anything." The parish priest took Hunne to court, an ecclesiastical tribunal presided over by the cleric William Horsey, and the decision went against Hunne. His "obdurate arrogance" during the proceedings caused him to be suspected of heresy, for which in 1514 he was hauled before the London episcopal tribunal. On December 5, 1514, he was found hanged in his cell. An immediate inquiry showed that he had been strangled, on Horsey's orders. The Bishop of London petitioned Wolsey to bring the suspect before a royal tribunal, since the anticlericalism of London juries made a fair trial doubtful. Horsey was set free, paid a fine, left London, received various prebends, and died in 1541 in Exeter as a canon. Hunne was posthumously declared an unrepentant heretic; his body was burned on December 20, 1514, in Smithfield.

Apart from the human aspects of the case, many of them quite shameful, the affair involved some very complicated judicial issues in common and canon law. Should the pros and cons of Hunne's refusal to pay fees to the parish priest have been heard before an ecclesiastical or civil tribunal? Before which should a clergyman accused of a crime appear? Implicated in the affair of Richard Hunne were the contentious relations between church and state, clergy and people, and the aspirations of the Crown to be independent of the Church. Thus, the Hunne case, beyond being a sad and sordid incident of a private nature, raised questions that were debated in an atmosphere of tension. The Parliament of 1515 sided with Hunne's widow and children and opposed the confiscation of their property, but the complex dispute remained a kind of fuse carrying a spark that decades later was to touch off an explosion.

The split from Rome, especially the loss of respect and affection, along with obedience, continued to grow regardless of official policy. Schoeck rightly claims that the Reformation in England began in 1515 in connection with the legal scandal just described, and the Wolsey era only marked a pause.[5] More followed the Hunne incident at close hand as barrister, undersheriff, and member of Parliament, and his brother-in-law John Rastell became the legal guardian of the two daughters of the unhappy draper. The case etched itself so vividly in More's memory

---

5. Ibid.

that fifteen years later he devoted a lengthy chapter to it in the *Dialogue Concerning Heresies* and also addressed it in detail in the *Supplication of Souls*. Convinced of Hunne's heresy, of his suicide—in fact, it was never really established whether it was murder or suicide—and of Horsey's innocence, he defended the persecution of heretics under the current legislation and did not accept Parliament's competence in canon law litigation not because of conservative obduracy but because of the application of the parable of taxes to royal policy.

2.

Toward the end of 1528, a fourteen-page pamphlet called *A Supplication for Beggars* was published on the Continent. This anonymous work had been translated often, reprinted hundreds of times, and distributed widely. More considered it so dangerous that he devoted to it a treatise ten times as long. A certain Simon Fish was identified as author of the satire; he had studied law in London and later, on the Continent, became a follower of Tyndale.[6] Under the guise of a "petition" in favor of London's beggars, he advised the King that he should confiscate all the assets of the clergy and force priests and monks to marry. Thus, at a stroke, all the ills of the realm would be solved: begging, depopulation, injustice, and exploitation. The doctrine of Purgatory was pivotal inasmuch as celebrating Mass and saying prayers for the holy souls were among the most important duties of priests and religious.

Fish's argument against Purgatory is not theological but populist. If donations to help the souls in Purgatory are abolished, the dead will suffer no harm, precisely because praying and offering Mass for them are a waste of time. His pamphlet was popular because it did not enter into difficult questions of faith, but appealed to low instincts: There is nothing you can do for the dead, so do not let lying priests take your money—take theirs instead.

Fish based his case firmly on Reformation theology. There were serious differences among the innovators on matters of faith, especially the doctrine of the sacraments and the Eucharist (in 1529, Luther and Zwingli fell out definitively over the question of Christ's real presence in the Eucharist), but they were of one mind in denying Purgatory. From the Protestant point of view this denial was perfectly logical, for if faith without works was what justified, works were surely of no

---

6. *Supplication* MH, 132ff.

use to the souls of the dead. Moreover, as Marc'hadour[7] points out, what use was Purgatory, a place of purification, if there were only two kinds of people: those predestined to be saved and those predestined to condemnation?

More felt more hurt and personally challenged by these theses than by almost any other religious controversies of his time. Issues like free will or ecclesial authority or Scripture and tradition he could discuss dispassionately, but that was not possible for him in anything having to do with the dead and our relationship with them. To rob them of our prayers and the sacrifice of the Mass was, in More's opinion, like denying food and drink to neighbors, family, and friends. Purgatory seems on the face of it a relatively minor part of the doctrinal edifice of Christian faith. But from More's viewpoint it is comprehensive and involves the Church as Mystical Body of Christ, the communion of saints, and the reality of eternal life in God. From this perspective, Purgatory is not punishment but preparation. More could not see it any other way, and he found it equally incomprehensible that the living should be indifferent to the fate of the dead.

The *Supplication of Souls*, written in English, is meant to be listened to and understood by all. It is an impassioned, didactic, and prayerful discourse aimed at family, friends, and companions at work. Although More emphasizes that the place and state of purification originate in and lead to the love of God, Purgatory, as he conceives it, is a place of horror as befits the author's late-medieval imagination.[8] Although the imagery need not be taken literally, it is surely closer to the facts than our contemporary imaginings, at once ingenuous and audacious, regarding God, the devil, heaven, hell, and Purgatory, for More bases himself on the Old and New Testaments, and the magisterium of the Church.

The work is in two books of almost equal length. In the first, More demolishes Fish's text in language marked by deep anger; in the second, he attempts to prove the existence of Purgatory from reason, Scripture, and tradition, in the process rejecting and rebutting Luther's deviations from Catholic doctrine. Speaking in the name of the dead, the

---

7. Ibid, 134.

8. *The Treatise on Purgatory*, by St. Catherine Adorna of Genoa, had been published in 1510. Cf. L. Sertorius, *Katharina von Genoa* (Munchen, 1939); Jacob Bergmann: *Lduterung hier oder in Jenseits* (Regensburg, 1958); Wilhelm Schamoni, *Daswahre Gesicht der Heiligen* (Wurzburg-Hildesheim-New York, 1966), fifth edition, 142.

text addresses the living: "If you would have the goodness to read these pages at your leisure, for your love of us poor souls in torment, you will find therein a preventive remedy against the fatal poison of those broadcasters of pestilence who seek to make you believe that there is no such place of purification."[9]

More denounces Fish's tract as "indignation dressed up as advice, haughty arrogance dissimulated as humility. Pretending to help the poor he [Fish] hides the devilish intent to damage at one fell swoop both the poor and the rich, priests, and religious and laity, the King, the high and mighty and the little people, the living and the dead."[10] It is not the souls in Purgatory who are the most affected—God in his mercy would look after them even if they were forgotten on earth[11]—but people who, separating themselves from the ties between heaven and earth, invite future misery for themselves and all of society.

Seeking to reawaken awareness of the truth of the traditional doctrine on Purgatory, More takes three realities as his points of departure: "The immortality of the soul, which no sensible person can doubt, justice, and the goodness of God. From these facts alone it follows that Purgatory is a necessity. Given that God in his justice lets no sin go unpunished, but in his mercy, after conversion and repentance of the sinner, does not punish any fault with condemnation, it follows that punishment would have to be 'temporary' [i.e., limited]."[12]

If a man dies before the requirements of justice and love have been sufficiently met, penance must continue after death. "Some may perhaps look to God's infinite mercy and reassure themselves that, given the sinner's conversion, not only are all sins forgiven but also all punishment rescinded. . . . Those who say this thinking to praise God's mercy not only do so at the expense of his justice but also impair the sovereign notion we must form of his bounty. . . . People would then say: we do not have to suffer for our sins, however grave, numerous, and persistent they may be; so long as we have been baptized and have the faith, we need but a brief moment to return to God for all sins and punishments to be forgotten. All we need do is say, "Sorry," just as a woman who steps on the hem of another's dress might say."

---

9. Ibid., 140.

10. Ibid., 143.

11. Ibid., 141.

12. Ibid., 212–215.

Thomas in no way denies that a final "sorry" spoken by a contrite heart could gain it salvation. But just here is where purification begins. Even in this life images of "fire" and "burning" arise spontaneously for a Christian. Hence the prayer: *Ure igne Sancti Spiritus renes nostros et cor nostrum, Domine* (Cleanse, with fire of the Holy Spirit, our heart and affections, Lord).

After setting out the Christian logic of his argument, More enumerates the biblical proofs for the existence of Purgatory,[13] culminating in the celebrated passage from the first letter to the Corinthians:

> You are a field of God's tilling, an edifice of God's design; we merely his assistants. With what grace God has bestowed on me, I have laid a foundation as a careful architect should; it is left for someone else to build on it, but whosoever builds on it must be careful how he builds and mindful of what doctrine he teaches, for no one can lay a foundation other than that which has been laid already, I mean Jesus Christ. And on this foundation different men will build in gold, silver, precious stones, wood, hay, or waste matter, and each man's handiwork will be plainly seen. The day of the Lord will show it up, for that day is to reveal it by fire, and fire will test the quality of each man's workmanship. If the edifice that one has built remains standing without being consumed, he will get his reward; if the work of another is consumed in flames, he will be the loser and yet he himself will be saved, though only as men are saved when they pass through fire.[14]

Of this More remarks: "The dead man who enters the hereafter with work comparable to a house made of wood, hay, or waste matter will not get through the purifying flames as intact as the one whose work is made entirely of a pure material or one that has been purified by penitence before his death. But fire cannot damage pure gold."[15]

And he adds: "Here, for example, is a man who prays, but without paying due attention, allowing his thoughts to wander. He gives alms, does good works, but there are vain thoughts and longing for praise which interpose themselves."[16] What can be more natural than that the fire of divine love should perfect such an individual?

---

13. *Supplication* MH, 11 ("Ils son disposés en un savant crescendo.")

14. 1 Cor 3: 9–15.

15. *Supplication* MH, 226ff.

16. Ibid.

The words of the Gospel suggest as much to a pious and objective spirit. What Christ says about sins that will be pardoned neither in this world nor the next[17] implies, according to More, that there are other sins that will indeed be forgiven in the next world, that is, posthumously. Purgatory is the place in which man, after death, can have venial sins and the punishment for them and for mortal sins wiped away.

3.

In writing the *Supplication of Souls* More had two intentions: to refute heretical deviations from traditional doctrine and to move the hearts of men. The book reflects his consternation at the unfettered increase in rationalist thinking. He finds inexplicable this craze for doubt. It is not the interpretation of this or that biblical passage that determines the truths of faith, but the doctrine of the Church founded on the inspiration of the Holy Spirit. Even Scripture cannot withstand cold cynicism. "With such an attitude," says More, "hell, heaven, and Purgatory can all be equally denied. And even if someone were to return from the dead to tell us about the 'other side,' it would all be pointless since nobody would believe him."

Closely connected with the doctrine of Purgatory is the doctrine on indulgences. The abuse of indulgences had created a festering indignation that contributed to the radical Protestant revolution. Both doctrines are rooted in the idea that it is possible to obtain remission from sins by the infinite value of the Holy Sacrifice of the Mass and the loving prayers of Christians in this world and the saints in the next. One of the central mysteries of Christianity, the basis of redemption, is the principle of substitution. Just as Christ atoned for our sins by standing in and dying for us, so can Christians stand in for one another and for their brothers and sisters in Purgatory. It was hardly this doctrine that pious people found repugnant but its being linked to money. More seeks to emphasize the theological correctness of the traditional doctrine, without mentioning the abuses and while railing against demagogical misrepresentations and distortions.[18]

Thomas places in the mouths of the souls in Purgatory the argument that in the absence of a transference of merit between human

---

17. The passage Mt 12:32 reads as follows: "Whosoever says a word again the Son of Man, it shall be forgiven. But whosoever speaks against the Holy Spirit it shall not be forgiven neither in this world nor the next."

18. Ibid., 240f.

creatures, "all the merits of the painful passion of Christ would be lost to humankind. . . . [But] if God through human entreaty releases a man on earth from light punishment and bearable imprisonment, do you not think that he will allow himself to be moved more by the humble and fervent supplications of others [the living] when it is a question of showing his mercy to those who suffer in the flames of Purgatory?"

Finally, nonetheless, the author cannot avoid speaking of the "source of scandal," money. It is a true lawyer's plea. Priests do not offer the Sacrifice of the Mass and pray for the dead for money and stipends, since this is the quintessential purpose of the priesthood. Nor do the faithful pay them for doing these things, which lie completely beyond payment, but only give alms that contribute to the upkeep of priests. Say the souls in Purgatory:

> We are those in most need and, as men cannot see us, only a deep faith can move them to help us. They give to others who suffer poverty simply because they are good at heart, out of natural commiseration, or simply to silence their irksome begging. But who would give a few coins for us poor souls of the departed, whose plight is invisible, whose calls cannot reach any human ear that does not believe that we live forever or that we suffer a punishment, or who do not expect their actions to get their reward in heaven? This blend of faith and hope, together with an efficacious and generous charity, turns such alms into one of the most sublime things that exist on this earth.[19]

It is a cruel Purgatory that More describes, something very close to hell, and he appeals for a natural thoughtfulness, as between brothers and sisters.

> Remember the bond that unites us [implore the souls in Purgatory], remember the loving words you have spoken, the promises you have given. If there remains in your hearts the slightest residue of your former sympathy, the barest vestige of affection, if you do not deny all the blood-ties or loyalty towards friends of yesteryear, if you still retain the merest spark of love, some feelings of pity, do not allow a bunch of hotheads and fanatics who engage in battle against the priesthood, the religious life and your faith, to extinguish in your hearts pious petitions for your family, concern for your past friends

---

19. Ibid., 245.

and the memory of the faithful departed. Remember our thirst when you sit waiting for a drink, our hunger when you are eating, our feverish insomnia when you lie down to go to sleep, the shooting pains we feel while you are amusing yourselves, the fire that consumes us when you are happily enjoying life. And so, may God grant that your children will remember you and preserve you from these flames. . . . For our part, we shall do our utmost to help you so that we may be united with you in the hereafter.[20]

Reading with a sense both of history and of religion, we must distinguish More's horrific description of Purgatory and bitter and scornful polemics from his call to show the same solidarity with the dead as with the living—in other words, to take the communion of saints seriously. Here after all is a trustworthy friend.

---

20. Ibid., 274.

CHAPTER TEN

Corpus Christi

1.

Driving Simon Fish's treatise against Purgatory were above all the author's anger toward the clergy and religious orders. Basically, it was not theology and truths of the faith that concerned him, so much as social change and especially the redistribution of wealth, of which he felt the Church had far too much. And on this point he could count on the protection of the state—for Henry VIII, like the German princes, was not slow to realize that whatever was taken from the Church would find its way into his own coffers. Thus it is hardly surprising to find Fish returning to England in 1530 with a safe-conduct from the King; he died of the Plague in 1531, reconciled, as More tells us in his *Apology*, to the "Church of old" that he had so persistently attacked.

Unlike Fish, John Frith launched an attack on the heart of Catholic faith on a matter that did not translate into increased power or wealth for the King, and thereby lost his life. Frith was a young priest who had gone over to the new doctrine, helped Tyndale with the translation of the Bible, served a long time in prison, and finally managed to flee to the Continent, where he joined the German Protestants. In 1532 he returned to his native England on a visit, was arrested, and was sent to the Tower of London while More was chancellor. There he composed a document denying Eucharistic doctrine. More's reply, the long *Letter to John Frith*,[1] is dated December 7, 1532. Although printed by Rastell, it was at first not put on sale, perhaps because More wanted to avoid giving greater publicity to a heretical work, and was only offered to the public a year later.

---

1. Blarer, 92–117.

In April 1533, More took up the pen again as defender of the Eucharist in response to a paper published in Antwerp, *The Supper of the Lord* by George Joye, which likewise denied the doctrine of Christ's Real Presence in the tabernacle. More's *The Answer to the Poisoned Book Named 'The Supper of The Lord,'* went on sale, together with the letter to Frith, at the end of December. By then, Frith had died at the stake in Smithfield on July 4, as an "obstinate heretic." Before he died, he wrote a reply and a pamphlet against More. Smuggled out of jail, these documents reached the Continent and were printed there. Thus More's impassioned rebuttal of Frith's views on the Eucharistic doctrine was published simultaneously with an equally impassioned refutation of the rebuttal by an adversary who by then was dead.

Going much further than Luther, Frith had denied any real presence of Christ in the Eucharistic bread and wine, whether a permanent, substantial transformation or, as Luther believed, a temporary yet real presence; for Frith, this was only a remembrance, a commemorative meal. Noting that Christ uses many metaphors in Scripture, he argued that "This is my body, this is my blood," was no less metaphorical. "Neither bread nor blood are present in the Sacrament. The bread and wine are only, for us and for the disciples, a remembrance of him who parted from us. . . . It's the same as a betrothed who has to go off to a distant country and, before he departs, gives a ring to his sweetheart as a token of his fidelity."

"I am not offended in any way by the comparisons," More replied, "neither do I wish to criticize the examples given by Frith, when used in their proper context. The analogy of the token ring that the betrothed gives to his sweetheart on his departure seems a good one to me, because I too look on the Most Holy Sacrament of the Altar as a reminder and remembrance of Christ. But I go further and declare that the gift is the body of Christ." Frith, he added, was like someone who gave a young woman on behalf of her beloved a beautiful ring with a valuable ruby "but deceives her saying that the ring is only made of copper or brass." To understand Scripture properly, the sacred authority of the Church is indispensable. "Think what might happen if every Christian were to interpret Holy Scripture simply to suit himself; then each one would believe his own interpretation, and thereby could come into absolute conflict with the Holy Fathers and Doctors of the Church. Neither would I have any difficulty in inventing fifteen new sects with as many

proofs taken from Scripture as the theologians of the new current thinking do with their heresy."

But Thomas does not merely leave it at that. He recalls that the
Church has always taken into consideration not just the literal sense of
Christ's sayings but also the circumstances in which they were spoken.

> When Christ spoke of the Sacrament of the Altar, the effect on those
> who heard him was completely different from that of the parables.
> In them we can see his intention that his words not be construed as
> symbolic. None of his listeners found it strange when he compared
> himself with a gate or a vine. Why? Because they knew perfectly
> that he did not really think he was a gate or a vine. But when he
> announced to his disciples that his flesh would be their food and his
> blood their drink, and that no one who did not eat his flesh and
> drink his blood could be redeemed, their surprise was great. Why?
> Because in his words and the manner in which they were spoken
> they could see that he really meant his flesh and his blood. . . . The
> miracle seemed to them so great, so enormous, that they asked how
> that could possibly be. Does this not prove that the disciples took
> these words not as a parable but were trying to comprehend how
> Christ would really give them his flesh and his blood?

Thomas was horrified that more and more Christians no longer believed
in Transubstantiation and Christ's Real Presence in the sacrament. And
still more inconceivable was the arrogant indifference with which this
question was addressed.

More ends his letter with a sincere prayer for John Frith, and
anyone who fails to understand its sincerity understands nothing
of More. The prayer is this: "I ask God to extirpate all poisonous
heresies from the heart of this mistaken person and make him his
faithful servant."

When Thomas wrote that, the time for the assassination, torture,
and burning at the stake of staunch defenders of every confession was
already at hand. The Carthusian monks of London, Fisher, More,
Cranmer, Tyndale, Barnes, and Frith all died for their faith, and from
their ashes or dismembered bodies there was no telling if they died
for believing or disbelieving in the papacy, personal confession, or the
Sacrament of the Altar. And their salvation? Perhaps that had less to do
with the issue for which each of them died than with the presence or
absence of love in the depths of his soul.

2.

This high-water era of literary controversy reached flood stage in England in 1532/33. Aware of the encroaching darkness, More sensed that there was now little he could achieve. Yet he went on writing night and day out of personal fidelity to his Lord.

It is hard to keep one's bearings among the religious controversial writings of that day.[2] *A Disputation of Purgatory*, also by John Frith, was published in London toward the end of 1532 in response to treatises by John Fisher, John Rastell, and Thomas More defending the doctrine of Purgatory. As we know, in that same year the first three books of the *Confutation* appeared, as did *A Treatise Concerning the Division between Spirituality and Temporality* by a lawyer named Christopher Saint-Germain. Early 1533 brought George Joye's tract attacking the Eucharist, *The Lord's Supper*, which was followed a few days later by More's *Apology*. Of its fifty chapters, twenty-six were devoted to refuting the treatise by Saint-Germain, who replied in September with *Salem and Byzance*. In October Thomas countered with his *Debellation of Salem and Byzance*, and in early December he completed his response to Joye's denial of the Eucharist, *The Answer to the Poisoned Book Named the Supper of the Lord*.[3] The year also saw part two of the *Confutatio* (an answer, let us not forget, to Tyndale's reply to More's *Dialogue Concerning Heresies*); Frith's answer, already mentioned to the letter from the ex-Chancellor; and an anonymous satire, *The Image of Hypocrisy*, directed at a "gentleman quibbler who has written an *Apology*, a *Dialogue*, a *Supplication*, a *Debellation* and even a *Utopia*."

That More wrote so much does not mean he enjoyed it as, years earlier, he enjoyed writing lengthy letters as a controversial humanist or his *Utopia*. "I would prefer," he said, "that others take on the work of dealing with the issues that I write about. It would suit me to put such problems to one side."[4] He was a lawyer, and a man of the establishment, self-taught as a theologian and always aware that he was only an amateur. Yet he considered his efforts altogether necessary. Not only professional defenders of the faith, theologians and priests, but also the laity had to be involved. And if the cause already was lost, due to

---

2. Cf. for what follows: *L'Univers*, 473–487.

3. Ibid., 485. The work was featured in the 1557 edition: "The Answer to the Fyrst parte of the poysoned booke which a namelesss heretyke hath named the Souper of the Lorde."

4. *Works*, 845; Vázquez de Prada, 371.

the spirit of the times, he had never been one to undertake only those causes that promised success.

Sometimes he piled up too much detail, repeated himself, showed impatience. Not literary honors but the salvation of souls was his aim. Yet even so his language in attacking opponents is colorful and filled with original images and dramatic comparisons. The steps in the breakdown of religious unity in Europe were for him blows dealt to the body of Christ, hammer blows of the Crucifixion.

During 1533, feeling more and more harassed and downcast, the retired Chancellor wrote page after page as if racing against an ever-lengthening shadow. Meanwhile his financial situation went from bad to worse. One day the bishops of Durham (his old friend Tunstall), Bath, and Exeter visited him in Chelsea to present on behalf of the English clergy five thousand pounds contributed by the various dioceses in recognition of his service to the Church. Though genuinely moved, Thomas thanked them, but firmly declined, saying: "Gentlemen, rather than I or any of mine accept even one cent of it, I would prefer that all that sum be cast into the Thames. . . . Neither for that donation nor a multiple of it would I have gone without sleep on so many nights as I have done. [But] I would not get cross at all if I had sacrificed the night's rest and seen how they burn all my books and destroy all my work, if thereby at least the heresies were extinguished."[5]

Thus More prudently forestalled any suggestion of being bought by the Establishment. And so it was not only in the two precarious years following his retirement but throughout his decades-long service in administration and the law: all attempts to show More guilty before the King of bribery by clumsily falsifying his statements failed.

Henry VIII and his Privy Council sought to affirm their undeviating Catholic orthodoxy and tried to assert that the argument surrounding the divorce, the conflict with the pope, and the submission of the English clergy to the power of the state was unrelated to Protestantism and sympathy with the reformers. Whoever declared the new interpretations of the faith mistaken, it was said, was automatically defending the Church of old. But it was impossible by 1533/34 to be orthodox in England without becoming entangled in the spider's web of ecclesiastical policy pursued by the King. When therefore a printer's delay caused his response to *The Supper of the Lord* by Joye to come out in

---

5. Ibid., 373; Roper, 46ff.

January 1534 instead of December 1533, it was construed as an indirect criticism of the Nine Articles, a brief résumé of official positions on the King's new marriage, the Church, and the position of the Bishop of Rome. To be sure, More's treatise concerned the Eucharist, but it also contained statements about the Church that seemed like a refutation of the Articles. More had to write Thomas Cromwell, defending himself against allegations that he had attacked the official policy.

But he knew he was being hemmed in. These days a man could lose his head for one ill-considered word, and there was no shortage of topics that could produce that result: Henry's remarriage, the legitimate Queen Catherine, the illegitimate Anne Boleyn, the child Elizabeth, born in 1533, the rift with Rome. Thomas thus formulated a maxim to which he held steadfastly to the end: "As long as I live, may the Most High also grant me the grace to freely profess the truth always and everywhere, and to keep my conscience clear as my duty before my God and King, as a poor man but honorable lover of the truth. But if a book with whose contents I cannot declare myself in agreement is published in the name of the King or on behalf of his venerable Council, even so I would not forget to render homage to the King and show respect to his Council. It would never occur to me, therefore, to compose a reply to such a book or suggest the idea of doing so to another person."[6] In other words: he speaks as God requires and remains silent where God permits. Of all imaginable attitudes this was the least acceptable to the King.

3.

The idea and the reality of the Body of Christ are fundamental to understanding Thomas More—his sacramental life and prayers, his writings, and his martyrdom. His great works—the *Responsio ad Lutherum* and *Confutation of Tyndale's Answer*—in the final analysis turn on the Mystical Body of Christ, the Church. The letter against John Frith and the short fragment supposedly written shortly before entering the Tower of London (*A Treatise to Receive the Blessed Body of our Lord, Sacramentally and Virtually*) both[7] were dedicated to the Eucharistic Body of the Lord. Finally, the prisoner, fixing his eyes on Jesus Christ and his earthly body

---

6. Blarer, 120.
7. For the genesis of this fragment, cf. Louis L. Martz, "Thomas More, the Tower Works," in *St. Thomas More: Action and Contemplation*.

capable of suffering, gave expression in his treatise on the Passion to his loving acceptance of his own cross as the Cross of Christ—that is, a participation in the redemptive sufferings of Christ for men's offenses against God. Written in Latin, as he faced death, this unfinished work is entitled *De Tristitia, Tedio, Pavore et Oratione Christi ante Captionem Eius*.[8] It repeats the theme of a meditation in English begun before his imprisonment. Between the English and Latin versions, Thomas wrote the *Dialogue of Comfort*. It is not only the most important of the works written in the Tower but one of the most significant overall; we shall consider it below.

Thus all of More's last works revolve round the Body of the Lord, and fuse compassionate love and astonishingly humble love, experienced in properly receiving Holy Communion. "If we could truly imagine that the precious Body of the Lord enters our depraved and poor hovel . . . how we would scrub the floor so that not the slightest stain or trace of sin remained! And when he arrived, we would let him speak and with the disciples of Emmaus we would say to him: 'Lord, stay with us, because it is getting late and the end of the day is nigh.' "[9]

More distinguishes among sacramental, spiritual, and real reception of Communion. In his view, receiving the Eucharist sacramentally simply means receiving the Body and Blood of Christ in its substance, but not spiritually in the soul: in other words, receiving unworthily, either with "the intention of committing a mortal sin again, or without contrition for mortal sins already committed." Someone who takes Communion in this way is not a living member of the Mystical Body of Christ.[10] Receiving spiritually means that, although the Eucharist is not received in the sacramental form of bread and wine, there is a true spiritual union. "This is valid," More writes, "for those who lead a clean life and piously attend Mass. . . . They are more strongly united with Christ in the spirit and become living members of the spiritual community of the saints."[11] And finally, as the extract from *A Treatise to Receive the Blessed Body of Our Lord* begins: "The Christian who loves yearns to receive really, that is, sacramentally and spiritually both at the same time, the Body of the Lord."[12]

---

8. Cf. ibid., 78; 83, note 50. Details of the various manuscripts are to be found there.

9. Cited in Vázquez de Prada, 425f.

10. Ibid., 70; *Works*, 1348.

11. Ibid., 70f; *Works*, 1349.

12. Ibid., 71; *Works*, 1264.

For More, at the end of his life, the Body of Christ becomes an all-encompassing reality of his interior life. He kneels with Jesus in the Garden of Gethsemane, shudders with him, shares his sadness unto death. He asks the Trinity to make him, "by the bitter Passion of Christ . . . part of his eternal happiness."[13] And this is the reply: "Fear not, for I myself, the Lord of all this world, have felt even greater fear, sadness, and exhaustion. . . . The brave may find a thousand glorious martyrs whose example they can follow happily. But you, my little, frightened, weak, ingenuous lamb, believe it is sufficient for you to follow me, your shepherd, who looks after you. Do not rely on yourself, but put your trust in me."[14]

---

13. Vázquez de Prada, 443f.; *Works*, 1273.
14. *Works*, 1357f.

CHAPTER ELEVEN

The King's Path

1.

Roper tells of walking with his father-in-law along the banks of the Thames, when More said to him: "Roper, my son, I wish to God that they would put me in a sack and throw me into the Thames this minute, if thereby three things were put right with Christianity." What things were those? "First, that the majority of Christian princes, who tear one another to pieces in mortal battles, lived in universal peace. Second, that the Church of Christ, greatly troubled at present by errors and heresies, found peace and total unity reconciled in the faith. And third, that the matter of the King's marriage, which has now become a problem, found a happy solution for the glory of God and to the satisfaction of all concerned."[1]

The matrimonial catastrophe of Henry VIII (if one bears in mind its consequences, it is no exaggeration to call it that), determined the history of England and the Anglo-Saxon world and the fate of Thomas More. Let us look again at this familiar affair, concentrating this time on Queen Catherine. Only with the publication of the excellent biography by Garrett Mattingly has she begun to receive the attention she deserves.[2]

Catherine, born in 1485, was the last child of Ferdinand of Aragon and Isabel of Castile. Charles I of Spain, in time Emperor Charles V, was her nephew. The marriage between Arthur, heir to the British throne, and this Spanish princess had provided the upstart Tudor dynasty with legitimacy it urgently needed and enabled the Tutors to penetrate the closed circle of royal families who for the next three hundred years

---

1. Roper, 24f.; Chambers, 297; Vázquez de Prada, 299f.
2. New York, 1941; German edition: Stuttgart, 1962 (referred to as: Mattingly).

would rule on the Continent. This young woman of sixteen in 1501 was welcomed in England with jubilation. Whether her marriage with the frail Arthur was consummated was to become a crucial question years later. Catherine said no, and insisted that she was a virgin when she married Henry; but the King and his witnesses (nobles recalled Arthur's boasting on the morning after the wedding night) said yes in order to support Henry's scruples of conscience about marriage between a brother- and sister-in-law.

Prince Arthur died on April 2, 1502. Henry, on whom the dynasty exclusively depended, was not yet twelve. In this delicate situation, political and economic considerations led to the signing of a new nuptial contract fourteen months after Arthur's demise, on June 23, 1503. Since from a canonical point of view Catherine and Henry, six years her junior, were related as in-laws, a papal dispensation was required for the new marriage to take place. Agreement by both parties that the dispensation was necessary presupposed acceptance of the prior marriage as valid and consummated, and therefore not to be lightly annulled. Since the new marriage was not to be celebrated until Henry turned fifteen, and then only provided the second part of Catherine's dowry was received and the dispensation was forthcoming, the poor young widow found herself in the unpleasant situation of a bride who is the established, uninvited guest of the father of her betrothed.[3]

Pope Julius II granted the necessary dispensation in 1504, but the situation of young Catherine did not change. The years prior to Henry's accession to the throne in 1509 were for her a time of humiliation, penury, and dependence on her tight-fisted father-in-law. In these very difficult years of widowhood she exhibited one of her most important qualities: unshakable determination to persevere in what she considered just, not only for herself but also in regard to the divine order. Though treated more as a prisoner than a future queen, she declared that she would sooner die in England than abandon her marriage to Henry, which at the time was no more than a declaration of intent. This remained her position when, twenty-three years later, she was forcibly divorced and repudiated.

Whether marriages contracted between princely houses succeeded or failed largely depended on whether or not they produced numerous, healthy offspring including both sons and daughters. Political relations between the dynasties of the countries of origin of the spouses also were

---

3. Mattingly, 73.

a factor, and it was the women especially who suffered in the event of political conflicts and wars as well as childlessness, the death of infants, and the absence of sons. King Henry loved and respected his wife for years, at times even seeking her support and advice, but Queen Catherine's eventual fate is a typical instance. Strained relations between England and Spain, together with the absence of descendants to ensure the survival of the house of Tudor darkened her life to the point that it became a tragedy. After several other children, including males, were stillborn or died shortly after birth, she gave birth to her daughter, Mary, in 1516. Now, seven years after the wedding, the King's hopes were renewed. "We are both still young," he said, "and although this time it may have been only a daughter, there will be others, with the grace of God."[4] But that particular grace and the much-desired sons failed to materialize.

One should not make light of Henry's concern. In those days, the absence of a male heir to the throne spelled the end of the Tudors. That would have meant internal disorder in addition to the transfer of the monarchy to a foreign lineage, as indeed happened in the case of the Stuarts. To accept all this as well as the indissolubility of the marriage to Catherine would have required a set of priorities very different from those of any sovereign then living. To understand Henry VIII, one must see him as driven by three forces: unavoidable and legitimate concern for the succession, passion for Anne Boleyn inextricably bound up in that concern, and the depravity of his personality, inextricably linked with the other two. Perhaps what happened would have happened anyway. But had not all three factors come together at the same time, Henry's affair would have been a sad and abhorrent but essentially private episode.

The matrimonial crisis, when it came, was hardly a complete surprise. As early as the summer of 1514, the Venetian envoy had reported: "They say the King intends to cast aside his wife, daughter of the king of Spain, and his brother's widow, because he cannot have any children by her; that he has it in mind to marry the daughter of the French Duke of Bourbon. He is intending to annul the marriage and will get what he wants from the Pope."[5]

Thus what eventually happened had been thought out fifteen years before it took place. It should be noted, too, that at one stage the King

---

4. Chambers, 270f.
5. Jacobs, 109.

apparently toyed with the idea of declaring his natural son (by Elizabeth Blount), young Henry Fitzroy, the heir to the throne. More took part in the solemn elevations of the boy as Earl of Nottingham and later Duke of Richmond and Somerset. He perused the elevation documents, and the King subsequently consulted him about his son's education. The father made his six-year old son Grand Admiral and bestowed on him two more titles that he himself had enjoyed when he was young, that of Lord Warden of the Marshes and Governor of Ireland.

We do not know for certain who first suggested the divorce or when. Wolsey, the Bishop of Tarbes, who was temporarily in London, or the King's confessor, John Longland? Did one of them insinuate to the King that his marriage was illegitimate because he had married his brother's wife, and that he was being punished for this sin by the death of his children in infancy and the absence of male progeny? Or did the monarch, well-versed in the Bible and with theological training, think of these things for himself?

❧ ❧ ❧

In 1527, as the power of Charles V reached a peak, England changed sides, from the Spanish to the French. By now Henry's Spanish wife, aged forty, had become exhausted from so often giving birth and was prematurely aging; Henry, in his mid-thirties, was sensual, licentious, and accustomed to the immediate satisfaction of his desires. For some time now he had desired Anne Boleyn, daughter of a member of his Councils, and she had refused to be his concubine. Mary, his eleven-year-old daughter, cannot inherit the throne. Little wonder, then, that desire for Anne and concern for the succession should become merged in Henry's mind.

The Boleyns belonged to the class of newly arrived social climbers. Starting as small London merchants, they managed to amass a fortune and through tactical marriages pushed their way into the ranks of the English higher nobility, such as the Hastings, Ormonde-Butlers, and Howards. Thomas Boleyn, Anne's father and the King's diligent servant, was knighted after his eldest daughter Mary showed herself docile to the sovereign's desires. Anne, who had returned from France in 1521, made several courtiers happy, among them the poet Thomas Wyatt, before attracting the King's attention. She was described as follows: "Her figure was in no way comely, the color of her skin dull, her neck exceedingly elongated; her mouth, wide but more wily than frank and clearly sensual. She had a dense mass of black hair and black almond-shaped eyes that some found beautiful, but these alone were not enough to make her stand out among the beauties at Court. . . . She did possess one special characteristic: an atrophied sixth finger on her left hand, something that made the pious make the sign of the cross to protect themselves from the evil eye whilst the more superstitious spoke of her as a creature of the devil and the unmistakable sign of a witch."

Aspiring to more than the dubious and ephemeral position of royal concubine and observing that Henry became more addicted to her the more he was separated from her, she decided to play for high stakes. What price was the King prepared to pay? Even she must have been surprised to discover that he would go as high as to share the throne with her.

To be sure, Henry would have denied all this and insisted that conscience forced him to separate from Catherine.[6] And his conscience had been awakened by the Bible, where, in the third book of Moses (Leviticus 20:21), he read: "The man who lies with his brother's wife is something abominable; he has uncovered his brother's nakedness, and they will die childless." There was also this, however, in the fifth book of Moses (Deuteronomy 25:5): "When brothers live under the same roof and one of them dies childless, the wife must not marry a stranger. Her husband's brother must accept her and make her his wife and thus fulfill his duty as brother-in-law." On the whole, the Bible seems to be rather more in favor of the marriage between Henry and Catherine than opposed to it.

All England—indeed all Europe—discussed these passages of Scripture endlessly; and soon not only the scriptural passages but also the papal dispensation that had suppressed the impediment. There was no shortage of arguments on both sides. For years the question was treated as a judicial issue in canon law, and in part it was that. But only when looked at from the outside. Henry, however, was not just a husband with a troubled conscience, but a sovereign concerned for his dynasty. Moreover, he was tired of his wife and courting another woman. This was no son of the Church prepared to obey Rome, but a proud ruler in a new era, who saw himself as both temporal and spiritual head of his country, determined to have the papal ruling he wanted and sure he could get it. From the outset, therefore, the canonical question was only

---

6. Mattingly, 260f.

a cover for a power struggle conducted ever more brutally by Henry by the methods of blackmail. In Henry VIII, even before Philip II of Spain, we see the founder of European absolutism, determined to ensure that the Church be dependent on the Crown. As events were to show, a break with Rome, as in the case of England, was not absolutely required; the same end could be achieved, as in the case of France, Spain, and Portugal, with the consent of the Holy See, grown timid and wary because of the English example.

Still, from the moment he definitely decided to divorce Catherine, Henry truly believed in the legality, orthodoxy, and sincerity of his decision. His will obviously was God's will, and if he desired a divorce from Catherine, certainly God wanted the same result. There was no correcting a King whose conscience worked like this. Nor did he ever speak of separating himself from the Church of Rome. Why should he? The Pope, kept informed by the English envoy, knew Henry's mind. The Pope had only one thing to do: declare the marriage with Catherine invalid. That anyone, pope or bishop or whoever, should withstand him in this was inconceivable to Henry. And anyone who might dare do that had to be a traitor, a renegade, a usurper of the power of Christ. Any such resistance turned him into a human beast, totally wanton but with an untroubled conscience. Yet it was important to him that he prevail in a canonically legal manner, supported by a broad consensus of public opinion in England and Europe and by his princely colleagues and the hierarchy. This was important not only to his pride but also for reasons of state. Wishing to ensure that the legality of his new marriage and its progeny could not be impugned, Henry knew that it was incomparably more useful to have the Pope's blessing than to get what he wanted by force.

2.

It was while the King was still seeking his broad consensus that Thomas More became involved. The question, to be precise, was not whether Henry could divorce Catherine but whether he was really married to her or, unmarried, was living with her in incestuous fornication, as would have been the case if the consanguinity impediment had been beyond the power of any papal dispensation to remove. Through Roper, we know the details of More's conversations on the subject with his King.

Realizing the explosive power of the issue, Sir Thomas pretended not to understand such intricate problems and said he was not competent to express an opinion. When Henry insisted, however, and suggested he seek the advice of Tunstall and Clerk, bishops of Durham and Bath, he asked for time to reflect. The opinion of the three men, when delivered, did not meet Henry's expectations. More proffered it in his best courtly manner:

> To tell the truth to your Majesty in this matter, neither the Bishops of Durham and Bath, whom I know to be prudent, virtuous, wise, and honorable princes of the Church, nor I or the other members of your councils, are the proper counsellors to advise your Majesty in this issue, albeit that we are all your loyal servants and extremely grateful for the kindnesses that you have so frequently shown us. But if you wish, Sire, to hear the truth, permit those who do not seek to mislead you for worldly advantage or fear of your royal wrath to counsel you.[7]
>
> And afterwards, he spoke about Jerome, Augustine, and other saintly Fathers, both Greek and Latin. He then set out the opinion he had arrived at after having studied the documents. This pleased the King but little, as it was contrary to his wishes. But Sir Thomas More, who always acted prudently in this affair vis-à-vis the King, put forward his arguments in such an intelligent way that Henry quickly accepted them in a conciliatory spirit and thereafter continued to ask him for advice frequently.[8]

In reality, of course, the King was not looking for advice but consent. This was not true only of More. Seeking to enlist the sympathy of all, he sought as well a speedy solution by Rome that met his royal wishes. Unbeknown to each other, his envoys and Wolsey's bombarded the Pope with dubious and even grotesque requests. Thus, Wolsey, then fighting for his political life, demanded of Clement VII full executive powers to issue a binding and final ruling that would settle the question. Behind his Lord Chancellor's back, the King also put some very odd proposals to the Holy Father, such as that he be allowed, in the manner of the Patriarchs of the Old Testament, to replace an aging, infertile wife with a young, fertile one.[9] In time, too, he would ask for a dispensation declaring his new marriage "valid in the highest degree

---

7. Roper, 32; Chambers, 275.
8. Ibid.
9. Ibid.

of affinity"—i.e., since Anne's older sister Mary had been his mistress, his projected relationship to Anne was, in the eyes of canon law, the same as his relationship to Catherine, supposing the latter's marriage to his brother has been consummated. Thus, to ensure the legality of his remarriage, Henry conceded the Pope precisely the power to grant dispensations that he denied him in the case of his first marriage.

Abstruse as all this may seem, it reflects the fact that Catherine and Henry were probably the only ones to recognize the critical point in the whole dispute. The Queen declared that she had been married to Prince Arthur in name only, the marriage had not been consummated, and therefore it had not existed. When she married Henry, she further stated she was still a virgin. But if Catherine was telling the truth, there was no possibility of the Church granting a divorce or annulment, and the question of the validity or otherwise of Pope Julius's dispensation was beside the point. Henry would have had either to give up his plan to marry Anne Boleyn or else move on to an open break: repudiation of the Queen, and divorce and remarriage on his own authority, in violation of the Sacrament of Matrimony.

Wolsey, as envoy in England, and Cardinal Campeggio, who arrived in London in 1529 as Rome's representative, enjoyed papal powers to reach a decision on whether Henry and Catherine's marriage was valid or not. Fully aware of the fatal consequences should they fail to achieve an amicable and conciliatory arrangement between the spouses, they used every means to achieve this. They tried to put the idea of a divorce out of Henry's head. They also sought to persuade the Queen to enter a convent. The latter solution, as explained by Cardinal Campeggio during numerous meetings, would be to everyone's advantage. And there was a precedent ready at hand: the case of the queen of France who in 1498 entered a convent in order to enable Louis XII to marry Anne of Brittany.[10] Catherine would serve her country, the Church, and Christianity by thus sacrificing herself. On her selfless decision now depended the social order and peace of innumerable people.

But these attempts failed, and there was no help for it but to start legal proceedings. They began on May 31, 1529, in Blackfriars. At the second sitting, the King was represented by proxy, while the Queen appeared in person to declare that the tribunal was not competent and appeal to the Holy See. The third hearing, on June 21, brought

---

10. Pope Alexander VI annulled the marriage and allowed the King's remarriage.

a dramatic climax to the proceedings. Henry, now present, testified to his allegiance to the Holy See. Catherine prostrated herself before her husband, entreated him fervently to restrain his impulses and retrace his steps, and reminded him that he knew well how he had welcomed her as his bride. The King made no further appearances in court after that. The fourth and fifth days of the hearing were dominated by a courageous protest by Bishop Fisher in opposition to the illegal and un-Christian farce of the divorce. He also expressed his opinion in a memorandum to the two envoys, declaring that he was prepared to die for the legal rights and honor due to the Queen.

On July 22, Campeggio decreed the adjournment of the proceedings until October. At almost the same time, the Pope acceded to an appeal by Catherine and her nephew, Emperor Charles V, and transferred the case to Rome. On October 10, the Italian cardinal left England, his luggage, contrary to diplomatic protocol, having first been searched in vain hopes of finding some papal document authorizing Wolsey to proceed to the divorce. Henry was furious. Anne Boleyn threw a tantrum. Wolsey was blamed for everything and fell from power. The Queen seemed to grow in stature with her triumph. But before we go on to examine the series of events which then implacably follows, we need to pause and consider certain questions of human motivations.

3.

The leading role in this drama was not Henry's, or even Anne's, as might be thought, but Catherine's. She was convinced that her husband would accept defeat and eventually submit to a ruling from Rome that she had no doubt would be favorable to her. Here, then, was her first mistake: Henry's character had changed in the years since their marriage. The error presumably strengthened her determination not to give way. Thus she rejected the supposedly elegant solution of entering a convent, just as she did any concession casting doubt on the absolute validity of her marriage. With historical hindsight, it is easy to say Catherine should have made the sacrifice in order to prevent the schism and also to keep Henry from committing other, graver sins—not just those of an adulterer but those of an executioner, tyrant, and destroyer of the Church in England. All this sounds plausible, but it is wrong. There was no "elegant" solution that did not mean denying the Sacrament of Matrimony, and no circumstantial pretext could justify that.

Thus the decision fell to the Pope. This Medici pontiff was a personally pious, but vacillating, weak, and nervous man, cultured and well-versed in diplomacy but unskilled as a politician and unable to distinguish in particular cases between what was more important and what was less, and act accordingly. In sum, he simply did not measure up to the seriousness and complexity of the problems of the day: Protestantism, the English question, the rivalry between France and the Austrians, the Turkish threat. It made sense for Catherine to appeal to him and Campeggio to urge him to take up the case personally, for who but he was competent in matrimonial litigation between Catholic monarchs? But what could he do? The power of binding and putting asunder vested by Christ in Simon Peter, the other apostles, and their successors was not a spiritual blank check. As representatives of the Lord, they could only act according to the law he himself had given them. And the marriage between Henry and Catherine was valid however one looked at it. And if this was so, how could Clement VII dissolve the Sacrament of Matrimony? No pope could annul a validly administered sacrament—unbaptize someone who had been baptized, make a married person single again, unordain an ordained priest. As laicization is possible in the case of a priest, but not the return of his soul to its state prior to ordination, so in the case of marriage separation is possible, but not another marriage while the two spouses are living (which is why, incidentally, even the solution offered by the convent was problematic at best).

It has often been said that Pope Clement's hands were politically tied. Out of consideration for the all-powerful Charles V, he could not have pronounced against the Emperor's aunt. Yet, Charles had no intention of going to war with England for Catherine's sake, and as a practical matter he could not impose a decision on the Pope regarding this matrimonial question.

In fact, it seems likely that Clement VII was as little aware of the enormous significance of the matter as his predecessor Leo X had been of the importance of the rebellion of an Augustinian monk named Martin Luther in far-away Wittenberg. When the Pope, in the spring of 1534, declared the marriage between Henry and Catherine to be valid, the King had already been married for a year to Anne Boleyn. Anne had been crowned Queen of England, and Mary, offspring of Henry's first marriage, declared a bastard. A female child from the new union, Elizabeth, was six months old. When in the summer of 1535, Pope Paul III, Clement's successor, signed the bull excommunicating Henry VIII,

Henry already had been head of the Church of England for some time, and the first martyrs—the Carthusian monks, Bishop Fisher, Sir Thomas More—had paid with their lives for their fidelity to the papacy.

4.

Once the divorce proceedings were transferred to Rome, Henry realized that he had to act for himself or, sooner or later, submit to a ruling that was likely to go against him. That meant divorce, remarriage, and establishing rules for the succession unilaterally. A judicial structure conferring legality on his conduct was required. Several steps were now taken.

1. In no way should it appear that the King was interested only in his own carnal pleasures with Anne, which, as things stood, could not be achieved other than through marriage. The religiously inspired judgment of his conscience required theological justification and confirmation. Thomas Cranmer, a professor of theology at Cambridge who later became Archbishop of Canterbury, advised him to canvass theological faculties. Not only Oxford and Cambridge but also French and Italian universities (among them Padua, Ferrara, and Bologna) sided with the King. But other Italian, German, and Spanish schools opposed him. Nevertheless he could now cite various weighty authorities in his support.

2. On November 3, 1529, the parliamentary session opened by Sir Thomas More met for the first time in six years. Realizing the prevailing anticlerical mood, Henry meant to put the fight against the Church's irregularities and abuses at the top of its agenda. Strongly represented in Commons were people who stood to benefit in the matter from an increase in the value of their estates by the confiscation of Church property, especially the monasteries.[11] The Seven Year Parliament (in operation until 1536), docile to Henry and Thomas Cromwell, provided the royal desires with requisite legal form. The most significant pieces of constitutional legislation, changing the course of English history, were the Acts of Succession and Supremacy of 1534. The Law of Succession declared princess Mary illegitimate, and settled the succession to the throne on the children of Anne Boleyn. The Law of Supremacy solemnly and with no reservations constituted the King head of the Church of England.

---

11. Chambers, 296.

3. Other steps were taken earlier. From 1530 onward, there was an increase in court proceedings instituted by the Royal Supreme Court against bishops or theologians who had sided with the Queen in the hearings conducted by the envoys. In December 1530, the government, with great show, accused the entire body of English clergy of exercising spiritual jurisdiction illegitimately and unlawfully. Convocations of prelates from the ecclesiastical provinces of Canterbury and York purchased royal pardon, confirmed by an act of Parliament, by paying heavy fines in February 1531.

At the same time, questions arose concerning the King's headship of the Church. Henry was demanding that he be recognized as "supreme Head after God." The convocations accepted the new title, with a caveat—"as far as the law of God allows"—proposed by Bishop Fisher. The definitive break with Rome was thus avoided, since the formula, accepted by the King, left acceptance of the spiritual supremacy of the pope intact. But the submission of the Church to the state and the break with Rome were by now well underway.

Since the summer of 1531, Catherine had been exiled to various country houses. She was never again to see her husband. Henry had found an ally, Thomas Cromwell, who knew how to join the widespread anticlerical feelings and greed among the Commons to the King's passions, thus forging an alliance between the requirements of the Crown and the impulses of the spirit of the times that pointed the way to the creation of modern England. Cromwell's historical importance lay in transforming a widespread but unfocused desire for change into the political impetus for a monarchical, oligarchic, unified state.

First it was necessary to destroy the ecclesiastical legal order of the Middle Ages. The Church's laws—such was Cromwell's central premise— had not been sanctioned by the Crown; and without that approval they were not proper laws. Indeed, the ecclesiastical legislator was a foreign lawmaker operating within the state. In the spring of 1532 Henry told a Commons delegation: "We believed that the clergy of our realm were wholly our subjects, but we have now seen clearly that they are only half subjects of ours, that is, that they are really not subjects at all, for all clergy swear an oath to the pope on their ordination that totally contradicts the one they give to us, so that they appear to be more his subjects than ours."[12]

⚜ ⚜ ⚜ ⚜

---

12. Jacobs, 129.

The bishops' convocations were in a way naïve gestures imploring the protection of the Crown because of their justified fear of the anticlerical Parliament. But where forcing the submission of the Church was concerned, Crown and Parliament were hand in glove, and on May 15, 1532, in a move that caused Thomas More to resign, Henry made himself supreme and sole legislator for the English Church.[13] Even so, the ties with Rome had not yet been severed. All new bishops were required to pay a third of their first year's income to the Roman See. Parliament floated the idea of canceling the requirement, but it left the final decision to the King, thereby giving a means to put pressure on the pope.

Close to her goal and sure the King could not back out again, Anne Boleyn had by now surrendered herself to her admirer. She was pregnant and sought a speedy marriage, arguing that the King's interest required not just offspring but a successor to the throne. Henry married Anne in secret on January 25, 1533, without divorcing Catherine. That same month he appointed Thomas Cranmer Archbishop of Canterbury, obtaining papal confirmation using the bishops' payment as a threat. In March Parliament approved an act prohibiting appeals by episcopal tribunals to the Holy See in matters of testamentary litigation and marital law. Implied in this was the granting of power to Cranmer, now head of the supreme ecclesiastical tribunal in England, to rule in the King's matrimonial proceedings. On May 23, the marriage to Catherine was declared null and void and the marriage to Anne Boleyn valid. On June 1, in a very advanced stage of her pregnancy, she was crowned queen. Other laws soon followed prohibiting all payments to Rome and specifying that newly elected bishops and abbots be approved by the King.

Despite the consensus between Crown and Parliament, a great deal of sympathy for Queen Catherine and for the old Church order persisted among the people. But the Act of Supremacy asserted the illegitimacy of Princess Mary and the legitimacy of the child Anne Boleyn was to bear, and compelled subjects to fall in line. To deny the validity of the new marriage was high treason, punishable by a cruel death. Even voicing doubts or raising objections was treason, with imprisonment for an indefinite length of time and confiscation of property the penalties. Since the universal taking of an oath of loyalty to the Acts of Succession and Supremacy was not practical, the King and Cromwell had the option of selecting whom to compel. And here was the really

---

13. For this, and what follows, see Kurt Kluxen, op. cit., 187ff.

shrewd stroke: for they knew very well whose oaths would be useful to them and who could be broken in this way.

By the end of 1534 everything was complete. The Church of England had been wrenched away from Rome and handed over to the state. Money that previously had gone to Rome went to the government, which demanded and received much more than the Pope had. Anyone who even hinted that Henry was a schismatic risked his life. The last pockets of resistance were the monasteries, most of them exempt, that is, outside episcopal jurisdiction, and tied to Rome. Their reputation had gone from bad to worse, and their privileges and wealth were envied. So why not dissolve them and divide up their wealth— with the lion's share going to the Crown? The new Vicar General of the Church of England, Thomas Cromwell, moved first against small monasteries, confiscating them and sending their monks to larger monasteries or parishes, or simply retiring them with small pensions. Next came the abbeys, which were treated less gently. By 1540 every abbey, monastery, convent, and priory in England was gone.[14]

5.

Up to now, not much has been said in this account of events about Thomas More, but it all has a bearing on his fate. His only way of escape from the new situation created by Cromwell with the help of the King and a Parliament blind to the consequences of its decisions lay in flight, inward or outward as the case might be. Yet at first many of Henry's subjects, especially a substantial majority of prelates, believed that a kind of every-man-for-himself tolerance would keep them safe while allowing things to settle down in due course. The date of Queen Anne's coronation was fixed for June 1. No bishop or abbot could prevent it, and it would serve no good purpose to provoke the King's wrath. Not even Bishops Tunstall, Clerk, and Gardiner of Durham, Bath, and Winchester, respectively, could be blind to such realistic considerations, nor should good Sir Thomas be.

Knowing him to be short of money, Roper reports, these gentlemen, who appreciated him and truly admired him, sent him twenty pounds to buy new clothes worthy of the festive occasion. More kept the money, and stayed home on coronation day. Later he explained to his surprised and perplexed benefactors that his presence at the coronation

---

14. Ibid., 191.

would soon have been followed by a demand that he actively defend the new order. "May it please God," he told Roper, "that the acceptance of these new things may not need soon to be confirmed by the taking of an oath."[15]

Humility and prudence were the strands of the rope by which More dangled between the obedience that rendered the King what was his and an opposition that refused him what was not. He did not publicly condemn the path the King had chosen, but neither did he do anything suggesting his consent. He increasingly drew apart from public life.

Here, in More's view, was a difference between himself and Fisher: A bishop was obliged to speak up in defense of the apostolic faith of the Church and the Church itself; but the laity had a right to remain silent as long as silence did not mean explicit collaboration with injustice. Nobody had to go looking for martyrdom. He writes: "Although Christ, Our Redeemer may require of us to suffer death freely if this is inevitable; he prefers not to command us to do anything that is contrary to nature, but he does allow us to fear death. Neither can I advise anyone to expose himself recklessly to danger or put himself forward unless he is able to do so with measured steps and in a dignified manner, for if he cannot climb to the top of the mountain he runs the risk of crashing down to the bottom of the steepest abyss."[16]

If permitted, More would have gladly remained silent until he died quietly at home in his bed. But that did not satisfy Cromwell and the King. A trial for high treason unrelated to the supremacy issue would have done the trick, but Cromwell failed in his attempt to show More opposed to the Nine Articles. Something else was needed, something completely new.

Born in 1485 of humble origins, Thomas Cromwell had spent his youth as a soldier in Italy and a merchant in the Low Countries. Eventually he became a somewhat shady lawyer in London. Wolsey took him into his service in 1520. Cromwell learned rapidly. To finance construction of a college in Oxford, he forced smaller monasteries to close while seizing their property and income for his master's benefit.

After Wolsey's fall from grace, he quickly discerned the best route to promotion—and to the King's corruption: total submissiveness to

---

15. Roper, 57ff.; Chambers, 354f.
16. *Works*, 1355; Vázquez de Prada, 444f.

the plans, wishes, whims, and cravings of the sovereign. During More's chancellorship, in 1530, he became Henry's secret adviser and the real administrative power. Morality aside, he is an important figure in English history—superior to More in organizing ability, the founder of the English state church, and a co-founder of modern England. He also provided the legal window dressing of the reign of terror that brought the liquidation of Fisher, More, and many others. In 1540, in an ironic and macabre twist of history, he was tried as a traitor and with little ceremony executed, just as his own laws prescribed.

In his second attempt to get rid of More and also Fisher, Cromwell realized that the case of Elizabeth Barton, the "nun of Kent," would serve very well. This poor creature, a servant somewhere in the county of Kent, had become mentally disturbed, and saw visions and spoke in tongues. Common people considered her simple and saintly. In 1527 she entered the Convent of the Holy Sepulcher in Canterbury and there her visions took a dangerous turn: God condemned the King's divorce and his marriage to Anne Boleyn, and the King was destined soon to die. Certain clergy encouraged her to spread her prophecies, and the affair began to acquire some urgency. In 1533, on the King's orders, the nun was brought before Archbishop Cranmer, to whom she confessed that she had had no visions but had made it all up. Barton, her spiritual director, the Franciscan Resbye, and other clergy who had taken a charitable view of her activities were condemned for high treason and on April 20, 1534, sentenced to a brutal death.

By then, More had already been three days in the Tower of London, implicated in the affair of the "nun of Kent." Cromwell knew he was innocent, but the facts were of little importance. More had corresponded with the woman and spoken with her. That was enough. And even if More's complicity could not be proved, some other crime deserving death could surely be found. But More had no intention of falling without a fight, and he meant to use all his lawyerly skill and cunning in his own defense just as he had done in defending others. He wrote to Cromwell:

> I should be grateful if you would let me have a copy of the charges made against me. I would like to peruse it as it is hard to believe that it does not contain false accusations against me. As soon as I learn with what I am charged, I shall address a humble request to His Majesty the King. To him or the person to whom he may direct me

I shall set out the whole truth as I see it. . . . . He cannot deny me his benevolence once he hears the whole truth, just as no honest citizen should deny me a just sentence. But even if I received neither one nor the other, and were sentenced unfairly, I would not be offended. God and I myself are the best judge of my innocence. Come what may, whatever happens it will only be in accordance with his will. May he keep you body and soul.[17]

Eight or nine years before, for official reasons, More had looked into the case of that "unworthy woman" (as he called her after her confession before Archbishop Cranmer). He found nothing remarkable then in Elizabeth Barton's so-called revelations,[18] and to the best of his knowledge the King had not taken the matter seriously after that, although he and Wolsey did receive Barton, whether out of mistrust or curiosity. More only came into contact with the matter again when the Franciscan Resbye, his guest at Chelsea at Christmas 1532, "highly praised her holiness." He was pleased to hear it, Thomas told Cromwell, but when Resbye brought up the question of Henry's divorce, he added, he said he wished to hear no more. "I expressed the hope that God in his bounty would deign to guide His Majesty in grace and wisdom and see this great issue through to a solution to his personal satisfaction in the interests of the security of the realm."

Still later, acceding to the requests of some monks who expressed doubts about the authenticity of Barton's revelations, he himself had interviewed the nun. This incident, in the spring of 1533, was undoubtedly a mistake on his part. "I spoke with her in a tiny chapel," he wrote. "There was nobody else present." He told her he was not interested in her revelations but in her reputation for holiness, and asked for her prayers. "To this she replied virtuously: 'God works in me better than I, miserable creature, deserve.'" She made a favorable impression on him, but neither then nor later, in conversation with others, did he discuss her revelations. Here are the defense tactics of an expert lawyer: he readily admits acquaintance with Elizabeth Barton in her spiritual and religious aspects but only that. The in-depth examination of the woman was Cromwell's responsibility. And: "You deserve the

---

17. Blarer, 122; letter from Chelsea, Saturday, February 1534.
18. Concerning this, and what follows: Blarer, 122–133, letter to Thomas Cromwell, dated March 1534.

highest commendation, for the fact of bringing out into the light such an abominable fraud is undoubtedly a very meritorious feat. Let every rascal be warned so that it never enters their heads to spread such devilish phantasmagoria dressed up as divine revelation."

The heart of More's defense was that in speaking of and with the nun, he had never discussed politics. And in testimony to the truth of this, he provided Cromwell with a copy of a letter he had written her immediately after their interview—very likely to protect himself against just such an eventuality as had now arisen. He wrote: "I assured you that I did not want, neither now or in the future, to learn anything about other people through you. And that above all I feared any revelations concerning the Prince or matters of state. . . . I made it clear on purpose that such things were of no interest to me, that I wanted to know absolutely nothing about them."[19]

In the eyes of Cromwell and the King, however, such protestations failed to exonerate More, for he said nothing expressing approval of the new state of affairs. On the contrary, More's unspoken "no" was clear. Could anything have saved him by then? Shortly before More's imprisonment, the gruff, trouble-making Duke of Norfolk, who was fond of him, exhorted him: "By all the saints, Master More, it is highly dangerous to oppose the sovereign. I should be glad if you would give in to the King's wishes. By the Body of Christ, Master More: *Indignatio principis mors est.*" Quite so. The Prince's anger meant death.

⚜ ⚜ ⚜

But as was becoming clear, not even servility and submission suffered any longer to ward off that fate. It was all up to Henry. And More replied to Norfolk: "Is that all, my lord? If so, the only difference between us is that I shall die today and you not till tomorrow."[20] Although his name was deleted from the list of those accused of high treason because of complicity with the nun, he was brought before a commission of inquiry made up of Archbishop Cranmer, the Lord Chancellor Audley, the Duke of Norfolk, and Thomas Cromwell. Now he was told what was really expected of him: a clear statement, sworn before witnesses, acknowledging the King as sole supreme head of the Church of England, together with assent to the legality of the new marriage. Thus, early in March 1534, the final phase of More's journey began.

---

19. Blarer, 128ff. The letter is dated: Chelsea, Tuesday, 1533.
20. Roper, 71f., Vázquez de Prada, 426.

He pointed out that he had communicated his opinion to Henry at the very start, and the King had then declared he would make no further demands on him in the matter.[21] At that the gentlemen dropped their friendly tone and informed him that "never before had a servant proceeded so infamously against his lord and master, nor a subject acted so treacherously against his prince as he had."[22] The treason lay in *Assertio Septem Sacramentorum* of 1521. Very likely More was dumbfounded. Everyone knew the history of that book of Henry's, the King better than anyone else. More replied: "Gentlemen, these threats are for children, not me."

Thus ended the first interrogation. The defendant was still free. Obviously they could not bend him, so they would have to break him and, if necessary, crush him.

Knowing what lay ahead for him, could he not have fled to the Continent? What prevented him? Consideration for his wife and family, who would have been the targets of reprisals? Love of country? Horror of life in exile? Loyalty to the King? There is no indication that More ever thought of fleeing. When he returned home after his interrogation, Roper asked why he was in such good humor. "Because I have prepared a defeat for the devil," was the reply, "and because I have reached a point with those gentlemen from which I could not draw back without dishonor."[23]

Immediately after returning to Chelsea, he wrote Henry:

> I prostrate myself at your feet with utter humility. I beseech you to consider the case and judge its transcendent importance with the wisdom and goodness that we recognize in Your Majesty. . . . May God prevent that false charges be heeded. I beg Your Highness most humbly in your well-known mercy to defend a poor man's honor and not to permit that he be assassinated by false allegations. The souls of those who would condemn me would be put in great danger, for when all is said and done the salvation of my soul could but little be damaged by all such injustices. My feared and beloved Lord, I wish to implore the Most Holy Trinity to protect the body and soul of Your Majesty and all your faithful servants, and punish all your adversaries.[24]

21. Roper, 66; Chambers, 359.
22. Roper, 68f.; Chambers, ibid.
23. Roper, ibid.; Chambers, 360.
24. Blarer, 134–137; *Corr.*, 198

The King was not impressed. The letter went unanswered while Henry grew more wrathful toward this man who had enjoyed his confidence. No doubt he had also read the long statement of principles More addressed on the same date, March 5, to Cromwell in which he set out an extended defense even before the machinery of the law was set in motion. Here Thomas summarized everything he had to say about the question of the marriage, the supremacy issue, and the Kentish nun.

Yes, More's name was removed from the list of those accused of high treason, but to the King it was becoming increasingly clear that this man had to be destroyed. Thomas knew that, too. The Act of Succession, approved by Parliament toward the end of March, not only laid down the Henry/Anne Boleyn line of succession but also envisaged that all adult subjects be made to swear an oath subscribing to the prescription of the law. Refusal to swear was punishable by prison and confiscation of property.

On April 12, the Sunday after Easter, as More was visiting John Clement and Margaret Giggs at their old residence in Bucklersbury, he was summoned to appear next day before the King's commission of inquiry convened in Lambeth. He returned to Chelsea, said goodnight to his family, went to church early the next morning, made his confession, heard Mass, and went to Communion. Forbidding his family to accompany him to the boat, Roper writes: "He closed the main door behind him and left them. With a heavy heart, as his face showed, he went with me and our four servants by boat to Lambeth. After remaining sad and silent for some time, he suddenly turned to me and said: 'Roper, my son, I thank the Lord because the field has been won.' I did not know then what he was trying to say, but not wanting to show ignorance replied: 'Sir, that makes me very happy.'"[25]

There could have been no better answer.

---

25. Roper, 73; Chambers, 363f.

CHAPTER TWELVE

Consolation in Suffering

1.

In his preamble to the "Tower Works" of More, Martz relates that he went with a friend to see the film *Anne of a Thousand Days*. In one scene the King orders Bishop Fisher, the Carthusian prior, and Thomas More to sign the oath of loyalty to the succession, which also implied acknowledgement of the Crown's supremacy over the Church. Fisher and the prior refuse and protest against both being coerced and the oath's objectionable content. But More replies softly to Henry: "I shall read the document and trust that my conscience will allow me to sign it."

At that moment, Martz recalls, his friend leaned over to him and asked: "Why can't More be as brave as the others?" It is a good question. More probably asked it himself many times. In his Latin treatise on the Passion, he takes Christ's mortal fear in the garden of Gethsemane and his words "Let the chalice pass me by" as encouragement to other martyrs filled with dread and a sign that it is no sin to look for an honorable way out.[1]

Still, it is precisely the limits on this right to save oneself that place the greatest demands on conscience. One must see with the eyes of God to stay on the right side of the line separating honorable evasion from betrayal of God and destruction of oneself. More's words to Roper, "The field has been won," signified not the conquest of his dread but his decision to accept it and to travel his own long, slow road to Calvary. Even in the case of Henry, he meant it when he wrote Cromwell, "Among my earthly assets it has been the King's affection that I have coveted most. I regret that the King should consider me obstinate and assume that in

---

1. Cf. Martz, op. cit. in the chapter "Corpus Christi", note, p. 77.

the important matter of his marriage or concerning the Pope's primacy I am going across to the side of his opponents."[2] Even when he had to resist the King, his concern was for the welfare of Henry's soul.

His letter of March 5 dealt in great detail with two issues on which his life depended: the King's marriage and the royal supremacy over the Church. He relates that in the summer of 1527, after accompanying Wolsey on a trip as envoy to Francis I, he presented himself before the King at Hampton Court: "I walked with the King in the gallery from one end to the other; there he suddenly started to talk to me about his great affair. He explained that it had now been confirmed that his first marriage was not only contrary to the positive law of the Church and against God's written law but also entirely incompatible with the laws of Nature with which not even the Church could dispense."[3] This was the first he heard of the "great affair."

Relating how he came to be entrusted with the matter of the marriage, More says: "The King put the Bible in front of me, and read me the words which had given rise to doubts in him as well as in several scholars. He then asked my opinion on the whole of this affair. . . . The King graciously received my hasty off-the-cuff reply and instructed me to get in touch with Edward Fox, the Royal Almoner, to discuss with him the book which dealt with the whole problem."

But although More continued to hone and elaborated his "hasty and off-the-cuff" opinion, he did not alter it, and his initial, tentative negative response became in time a settled "no." He attempted to make it as palatable as he could, and he never questioned the motives of the King and his advisers. But Henry wanted to win him over at all costs, and More therefore found himself ever more deeply embroiled in a compromising situation. Even that very first difference of opinion, between two men alone with each other in the gallery at Hampton Court, became known to those intimate royal counselors who would eventually interrogate Thomas: the Bishops of Canterbury and York, Thomas Cranmer and Edward Lee, Dr. Edward Fox, the Royal Almoner, and the Italian Franciscan, Nicola de Burgo. More recalled: "I read all sorts of things; everything that was relevant to the divorce interested me. I tried to weigh it all up and draw my own conclusions according to my poor intelligence. I looked up everything that might at some time in the past

---

2. Blarer, 138.
3. Blarer, 139–143; *Corr.*, 199.

have been written in similar cases. And above all I spoke to the above-mentioned royal advisers. We kept up a sincere and affectionate friendship between us. I am sure that they said only favorable things about me to the King, for I was neither obstinate nor adamant, but showed myself adaptable in everything in as far as such a controversial matter allowed."

But it can be extremely difficult to establish a universally binding formula in a matter of conscience. More always spoke with great care, tact, and charity about people whose views on the subjects of marriage and the supremacy differed from his. Similarly he is speaking with unquestionable sincerity when he says of Henry: "The King accepted everything indulgently and never for a moment doubted my loyalty. . . . In his bounty he decided to choose, to handle his matrimonial affairs, only people who in all conscience were convinced of the legitimacy of the divorce. . . . He was a benevolent sovereign toward all his subjects; he would never have forced any one of them to follow a course of action that would have placed a burden on their conscience."

By the time that was written, however, the tolerant Henry had long ceased to exist. We do not know if More finally grasped that the King's "plenteous bounty" had only been cold calculation. He had a virtually limitless belief in the good motives of others.

On the matrimonial issue More insists that he "looked deeply only into the books written by friends of the King." Yet he does not take the final small step on which his life depends: declaring his agreement with those books. He closes his preliminary defense with a passage that has caused the experts enormous difficulties of interpretation: "I only wish to be the King's subject. He has already remarried, his wife is the true anointed queen of England. I shall not grumble or argue about it; I have never done so to this day, and I do not propose to start in the future. I wish to remain on the sidelines of the whole affair. I want to pray, with the rest of the loyal subjects, for the King and Queen, that God may grant them and their noble progeny, according to His will, glory and security; and to the realm tranquility, peace, welfare, and prosperity."

From the context it is clear that by the "Queen" More means Queen Anne. The argument that, because he considered the marriage invalid, he must have been referring to Catherine ignores precisely one of the constituent elements of More's greatness: that the judicial precision of his words never descends into sophistry or hypocritical double-talk. Yet neither does he express any opinion on the new marriage, the anointing, and the coronation; and he uses the word "wife" without entering into the question of the term's ecclesial legitimacy, and speaks of the "true anointed queen of England" without declaring his position on the legalities of the case. Is it an open question whether England now perhaps has two "truly anointed" queens? It was precisely what he left unsaid that was to lead him to the scaffold.

The third point of the accusation against More—his position on the supremacy question—also had to have a place in his letter of March 5. Here, too, he defends his right not to get involved, but with a very important difference from the marriage question. On that he keeps quiet. But on supremacy he reiterates his convictions.

First, More recalls that in the book against Luther he had been in favor of turning down passages that stressed papal primacy. But then he adds:

> I later considered in greater detail the work of the King, and over the past ten years numerous writings on the subject of the Pope's primacy. I was thus able to confirm that all the learned men of the Church, from St. Ignatius, pupil of the Apostle John, down to our day, whether they wrote in Greek or Latin, were at one on this point. The Pope's supremacy has been ratified at various councils. . . . The whole of Christendom supports the Primacy, and this for the following very weighty reason: [the pope] has been put there for the purpose of preventing schisms and ensuring a regular succession at the See of St. Peter. This conviction must have been [held] for at least one thousand years now, given that one thousand years have passed since the death of St. Gregory.[4]

In line with thinking current at that time, More insisted he had never held the view that "the Pope should be above a universal council." Still, he added, on the subject of the primacy "I side with the whole of Christianity, in that I do not speak much about the problem, do not think about it or make any unnecessary efforts to find proofs." This concedes nothing to Henry VIII's hopes of supremacy. Perhaps More was hoping for a miracle: the Act of Supremacy declaring the

---

4. Gregory the Great governed the Church from 590 to 604. A saint and doctor of the Church, he is one of the greatest figures in papal history. He laid down the bases for the future papal State, reordering the administration of the pontifical lands; he initiated the mission to England (596), was the first pope to call himself *Servus Servorum Dei* (Servant of the servants of God), wrote the *Regula Pastoralis*, and had a permanent influence on the Church through his homilies, lives of the saints, reform of the liturgy of the Mass, and liturgical chant.

King spiritual head on earth of the Church of England was not passed by Parliament until November 3, 1534; Pope Clement VII died on December 25, 1534. But his successor, Pope Paul III (1534–1549), did not negotiate with Henry but only implemented the bull of excommunication against the Tudor King, issued on August 30, 1535, but not promulgated until December 1538. It would be centuries before, in our own time, a dialogue was established between Rome and the Church of England.

Thomas More had said all he had to say. "I cannot speak in a manner different from what my conscience tells me," he concluded. "I do not oppose my King from sheer obstinacy. . . . I value the King's benevolence more than anything else; I would willingly give up all my worldly goods, but not my soul, to retain thus his esteem."

2.

More had barely arrived at the archbishop's palace in Lambeth before he was pressed to swear his assent to the Act of Succession promulgated by Parliament after Pope Clement declared Henry's first marriage valid.[5] Since the oath had a preamble asserting that marriage to be null and void and rejecting the Pope's supremacy over the Church in England, More refused to swear. This happened twice on April 13, and again on other occasions after the Act of Supremacy was passed in December. More's reasons for refusing did not change. "Truly," he assured the gentlemen present that first time, "my conscience tells me that I can indeed swear to the succession but not to the supremacy, for in so doing I would be exposing my soul to the peril of eternal damnation."[6]

In no way should it be thought that the distinguished members of More's commission were wicked men. Except for Cromwell, they were not even anti-Roman fanatics. They were merely subjects of the King who had to comply in order to keep on enjoying comfortable lives. Their harassment of Thomas took two forms: repeatedly telling him that an overwhelming majority had sworn and were still swearing the oath; and reproaching him for being obstinate in the face of the King's wish and the royal patience.

---

5. This decision of the Pope was made known to the country on April 4, making the situation, particularly that of the "rebels," more difficult still.

6. Concerning this and what follows see: Blarer, 148–153; *Corr.*, 200 (Letter from the Tower, dated April 17, to his daughter Margaret Roper).

Thomas More's martyrdom did not consist only of prison and death. He also was afraid: of pain, of being weak, of offending God, of loneliness. Continually he was tempted through the mouths of those he loved most, including his daughter Margaret. They accused him of being arrogant and proud. Did he think he understood these difficult and complex issues better than so many learned and high-ranking men? Did he consider himself to have a more discerning conscience? They kept up their recriminations for over a year and a half. The pressure on a sensitive and delicate conscience can only be imagined.

More declined to explain himself. His interrogators demanded that he set out his objections or else be considered maliciously silent. Here was the second and more dangerous probing. If he kept silent about his reasons, he exposed himself to imputations of harboring wicked motives or of cowardice. Yet in stating his reasons he would seal his fate. To say the King was an adulterer and his second marriage concubinage would bring him a gruesome death. And more than that: Sir Thomas's loyalty to his King forbade him to speak such things. Instead he prayed day and night for Henry Tudor, England, and Christianity, as well as for his own soul, his family, and his friends.

He kept quiet right up to the time he was condemned on the basis of false testimony. When the Archbishop of Canterbury exhorted him, "Obey your King's orders and swear," he replied: "I cannot permit myself to do that, for according to my conscience this is precisely one of those cases in which I do not owe obedience to my prince. . . . My lord Archbishop, if your argument were to be accepted, any dissension would easily be avoided, for as soon as any difference of opinion were to arise . . . the King could remove it at a stroke by means of a completely arbitrary mandate."

In fact, just that happened soon after his death. The King, backed by Parliament, announced "what the people were obliged to believe under pain of death."[7] When More made his prescient remark, however, Cranmer sidestepped the issue and appealed to numbers instead: "He said that I had to fear that my opinion could be mistaken because I was in opposition to the entire Privy Council." But what is that? "I do not feel bound to mould my conscience to the orders of the Council Royal, seeing that the opinion of all Christianity is opposed to it."

Cromwell weighed in, claiming he would prefer to see his only son lose his head than that More should refuse to swear the oath.

---

7. Chambers, 366.

More repeated that he did not care to avoid trouble at the cost of losing his soul.

The Chancellor then read the record of the interrogation. The Archbishop repeated that More had declared himself ready to swear his acceptance of the Act of Succession. More interjected that he wanted a draft of the text that did not violate his conscience. The prelate turned to Cromwell, saying, "Secretary, Sir, remember to underline this particular remark. You have heard him say that he also wants to swear this oath subject to certain stipulations." Not so, More insisted. "I only wish to know the text in advance so that I do not swear falsely and act contrary to my conscience. I cannot see any danger in ensuring the succession of the children of Henry's second marriage. . . . [But] I leave everything to the dictates of the conscience of each individual, and I think it only fair that I should be allowed to choose my own personal position."

~&~&~&

They were deadlocked. More was taken into custody and handed over to the Abbot of Westminster, William Benson, for four days. Cranmer used the time seeking an acceptable compromise, which meant presenting More and Fisher with a considerably amended version of the oath. It was his idea that they be asked to swear only to the Act of Succession—that is, to support the accession to the throne of Anne Boleyn's children— but without specifically rejecting the first marriage and the Pope's primacy. The understanding would be that they keep the contents of this oath to themselves.[8] Cranmer's intentions were good insofar as he sought a way out for More and Fisher. What they would have had to swear to accept, however, was not just the accession of Henry's children but the accession of his legitimate children, the offspring of Anne, who at that time included Elizabeth: which unavoidably meant that the marriage to Catherine had been invalid and the position of the papacy could be overridden.

In any case, the King and his secretary had no intention of letting More and Fisher off with a secret partial oath that could not be kept secret very long. Cranmer was told to say nothing about his inopportune and possibly dangerous ideas. Henry demanded the oath whole and entire—period.

---

8. Ibid., 366ff.; *L.P.* (*Letters and Papers, Foreign and Domestic, of the Reign of Henry VIII.* Preserved in the Public Records Office, the British Museum, and elsewhere in England. Arranged and catalogued by I. S. Brewer, James Gairdner, and R. W. Brodye, 23 Vols. London 1862–1932; revised edition by Brewer-Bodie, London, 1920), Vol. VII, 499.

Besides the lengthy report noted above, More sent Margaret a brief note containing affectionate prayers for the people at home and closing with the footnote: "May the Lord always keep me faithful, believing, and sincere, and I implore him with all my heart to permit that I die rather than fall into an attitude that may be contrary to that. Meg, as I have often told you, I have never prayed for a long life. Truly, I do not wish that even now, and if God were to call me tomorrow I would be content."[9]

⚓ ⚓ ⚓

His imprisonment in the Tower of London was to last 445 days. He gave no thought to the historical significance of his case or its present or future influence on anyone. It is that modesty which has made him so attractive for centuries and continues to do so. His dry comments never give the impression of being affectations; they are reasonable reactions to particular situations. As was his habit, he wore a golden chain around his neck. On the way to the Tower of London, Richard Cromwell, a nephew of Sir Thomas Cromwell, had been instructed to accompany him. He advised More to remove the chain and send it home. "No," More replied, "I shall not do that, for if I am taken prisoner in the field of battle, I would like my enemy to keep something of mine."[10] The Governor of the Tower of London, Sir Edward Walsingham, was an old acquaintance. He apologized for not being able to provide more pleasant accommodations lest the King be angry. "Rest assured, Sir Governor," More replied, "that the treatment does not displease me, but if at any time I appear unhappy with it, you are at liberty to evict me from your premises!"[11] When visited by Lady Alice, who nagged him to take the oath, he asked: "Well, now, Alice how much longer do you think I have left to enjoy life?" "Twenty years at least, God willing." "My dear wife, you have no head for business—would you really like me to trade eternity for a mere twenty years?"[12]

As such anecdotes suggest, More's time in prison was fruitful for him and those who came into contact with him. As his end drew near, Thomas took it as an enormous privilege that he should travel on the *via crucis* of Jesus Christ. And as none of those present at Christ's

---

9. *Corr.*, 201; Blarer, 153f.

10. Roper, 741.

11. Ibid., 744ff; Chambers, 371.

12. Vázquez de Prada, 424, Stapleton, Folio 1010, chapter VI.

Passion remained unaffected, so too More's martyrdom left its mark on those who had dealings with him.

Undoubtedly the one most affected was his eldest daughter, Margaret. Never had the inner closeness of father and daughter been so intense as during the final months of More's life. No one was left empty-handed, whether it was a prayer for the King and his judges, a smiling word of comfort for Lady Alice, a joke with the executioner, his disarming defense before the Commission of Inquiry, his sensible advice to his companions in misfortune. But Margaret Roper is his truest confidante—although even to her he does not reveal his real reasons for refusing to swear the oath. Yet their relationship was under a heartbreaking strain. Margaret's repeated efforts to make her father change his mind and swear the oath have been construed by some as guileful maneuvers to convince Cromwell to permit her visits, but everything seems to indicate that she was utterly serious in urging him to swear. Finally, though, loving him as she did, she accepted, and even inwardly shared, his attitude, albeit without ever fully comprehending it—which only sharpened More's pain.

Knowing that Cromwell intercepted and read their correspondence, Margaret and Thomas did not put in writing all that they wished, but what they did write was sincere. In one letter he writes: "I no longer have it in my power to do anything for you; I can only commend you to God. I want to beseech God to let me enter into the eternal happiness of heaven when He shall deem it appropriate, and that he meanwhile, amidst all these horrors and perils, grants you grace to pray humbly in remembrance of his bitter fear on the Mount of Olives."[13] Margaret replies expressing hope for his release: "I ask God most fervently that he may grant us this joy; but above all I want to submit myself entirely to his will."[14] She managed to visit her father in prison on May 20, 1534, and was able to continue visiting with some regularity in the months that followed. He maintained contact with the outside world through her.

In a manner as natural as when he wore his gold chain of office and ermine cloak and dined with royalty, More now sought help from his friends, including material assistance. "As I am now kept under strict vigilance, I cannot tell you what I shall need in the future. I do not even know what difficulties are in store for me. That is why I very much beg you all to grant my daughter Margaret all the assistance that she may ask of you in my cause. She is the only one of all my friends and relations

---

13. Ibid.
14. Blarer, 157.

who has obtained permission to visit me in prison. Please give her all your attention just as if I were the petitioner turning to you in person. I beg of you all not to forget me in your prayers, I think of you daily. Your faithful friend and poor mendicant, Thomas More, knight, prisoner."[15]

Louis L. Martz describes as a "marvel" a letter to Lady Alice Alington, dated August 1534. Here an explanation is in order.[16] During a hunting party on the estate of her husband, Sir Giles Alington, More's stepdaughter, Lady Alice, took the opportunity to ask Lord-Chancellor Audley to intercede for her stepfather. Saying that he was responsible for having More's name removed from the list of those accused of high treason for dealings with the nun of Kent, Audley added that he now could neither understand nor condone Sir Thomas's obstinacy. By way of illustration, he told two allegorical fables that supposedly illustrated his point. Writing to her stepsister, Lady Alington related with sadness the failure of her request. Margaret took the letter with her when she went to visit her father in the Tower, and we must suppose they discussed it.

The reply took the form of a dialogue, a jewel among More's works. In the sixteenth century the question was asked whether it was the work of Margaret or Thomas, or father and daughter jointly? I side with Martz in supposing that More was the real author, although, Margaret no doubt collaborated, either by taking notes or completing sections he had begun or coauthoring more important passages. In any case, the spirit, the art, and style of Thomas More give the dialogue its exceptional quality.

It opens up no new lines of argument, focusing not on swearing or not swearing but on the right to decide for oneself according to one's personal conscience. More defends this right while rejecting the charge that disobedience to the King is disobedience to God's commandments, a sin that makes it impossible for friends to help him. More says: "I really do not see any way out. God has put before me these alternatives: either I fatally offend against him, or I have to take on my shoulders every human misfortune that he may wish to send me by way of penance for all my remaining sins."

The letter devotes a great deal of space to Audley's fables. Of the poor, stupid ass in one More remarks:

His Lordship could only have referred to me, as already his other affirmations about my scruples allude to my person. With such a

---

15. Ibid., *Corr.*, 205.
16. Cf. regarding: Martz, *St. Thomas More: Action and Contemplation Corr.*, 206; Blarer, 158–180.

comparison he means that it is only due to stupidity and blindness that my wary conscience considers it a danger to my soul to swear the oath. By all accounts, he obviously thinks of it as something of no importance. Yes, I believe you; many other people, both lay and religious, see it the same way. Perhaps, too, many that I hold in high esteem because of their great learning hold the same view, but I am not convinced that those words express their true thinking. And even if they did think that in all sincerity, I would not be impressed or change my mind, not even if His Lordship, the Bishop of Rochester, could be made to change his.

Then follows this passage of the utmost significance:

> It could happen to anyone at any time to become involved in a conflict situation in which he finds himself totally alone before God, with no one able to help him and no one to act on his behalf. The fact that he can get into such a situation, that is, one in which he is able to recognize the dilemma of moral values and competing course of action he is in, is the sign of the existence of an internal compass. It is part of our insuperable weakness stemming from original sin that this compass, which we call conscience, does not clearly and unequivocally, much less in a way binding on everybody, delineates this situation of conflict and it's resolution.

Thomas listed ways in which a man can keep his conscience from causing him suffering in this world.

> There are some who bend their consciences at will and believe that later God will make allowances, given that they have acted out of fear. Others trust in being able to repent and confess, whereby, of course, they will be granted forgiveness for their sins. And, finally, there are a few who think that, without running any risk, they can say one thing and think the opposite, because God, after all, looks into their hearts rather than listening to what their tongues are saying. They are firmly convinced that an oath applies only to what is in their minds. That, at least, is how a lady I happen to know explained the problem to herself.

More is speaking of his wife Alice, who sought to persuade him to swear with a "mental reservation."

When father and daughter had this conversation in August, 1534, the Act of Supremacy had not yet been passed nor had Parliament made the Act of Succession obligatory along with the preamble that Thomas and Fisher found unacceptable. Thus the two men were unlawfully imprisoned because Cromwell and the other advisors sought favor by laying the oaths of his principal adversaries at the King's feet. They had been jailed with the full knowledge and approval of Henry, who, under the influence of his secretary and the Boleyn clan, no longer bothered with legalities and judicial formalities. Parliament did not retroactively legitimatize the trial of the Bishop of Rochester and the ex-Chancellor until November. Margaret's comment at the end of the conversation, that the secretary, "as a good friend, sends a message that Parliament is still sitting," refers to the existing situation as it then stood.

Yet her question—"But father, why do you refuse to take the oath?"—must have come as a blow to More. Had all that talk, all those explanations, been in vain? More responds: "It may sound odd to you if I say that it is possible for a man to lose his head without suffering any damage to his soul; and although I trust God will not allow that a good and wise prince repay the services of a faithful subject over so many years with such ingratitude, I do not forget that such cases are not in the least impossible in this world. . . . On many occasions, steeped in such thoughts, my heart felt heavy, yet not even the deepest anguish could make me change my opinion."

And still the daughter does not understand. In the worst case, she points out, he might yet change his mind, but by then it could be too late. "Too late, daughter of mine? I pray God that if I decided to change my mind there would not be any practical possibility of being saved. For any other stance could only endanger the salvation of my soul, especially if it stems from fear. May God, therefore, grant me the fortitude to remain faithful to my present thinking."

These words do not express the speaker's sense of his strength but his desire to remain faithful. He says: "By the grace of the Most High I want to bear everything with patience, even joy; in that way (added to the merits of his bitter passion, which contribute much more to my salvation than all my merits), my torment in Purgatory will be reduced at the same time that my reward in Heaven will be increased."

If he does not waver, he knows it is because Christ supports him; and if his strength deserts him, Christ will lift him up as he did St. Peter: "I assure you, Margaret, I shall not sink except through my own fault. . . . But, Margaret, I truly have faith that in his loving compassion [God] will deign to save my soul. . . . Nothing happens against the will of God. The fate he has prepared for me can only be for the best, no matter how hard it may appear by human standards."

More's love, trust, and longing for God radiated out to anyone who sought his counsel. Dr. Nicholas Wilson, former Court chaplain and confessor of Henry VIII, had been detained in the Tower of London for the same reasons as More. Wilson apparently had shown himself prepared to swear the oath, but feeling troubled, he asked More for some words of comfort.[17] The reply was concise:

> I have never advised anyone against taking the oath on the new legisla-
> tion. I never placed the burden of scruples on the conscience of others
> concerning this matter. I do not wish to discuss my convictions with
> others. Let each one square it with his own conscience; as for myself, with
> God's help I want to comply with what he shows me to be just. I would
> be exposing myself to the risk of eternal damnation if I were to swear
> against my convictions. I cannot tell what will happen to me tomorrow;
> I do not even know if I shall be granted the grace of constancy till the
> end of my days; that depends not on me but on God's mercifulness.[18]

Wilson seems not to have understood, and asked for clarification, and out of compassion Thomas wrote again. After stating again his sentiments, especially his firm determination to remain silent on the reasons for his decisions and his right to make them, he continued: "When I met you in London, before the form of oath was put before us, I told you that I did not wish to have anything further to do with the matter, but simply obey my conscience, for I have to account for it before God. That is still my conviction today, and I venture to tell you sincerely that this possibility is open to you too."

The letter concludes:

> I pray the Lord that he may grant you peace and tranquility accord-
> ing to his will for your soul's sake. As for myself, I ask God to grant
> me the grace to submit patiently to his wishes, so that his mercy will
> enable me to reach the safe destination of heavenly bliss, after the dif-
> ficult storms of a life full of tribulations; that he may deign to take,

---

17. In the Blarer edition of the letters, this short reply from More appears after an exhaustive letter on the same question. In fact, the brief answer preceded the lengthy letter. Wilson, following More's "swift reply," wrote back to him, and only then did Thomas write the long letter. Cf. *SL*, 58–59. *Corr.*, 207–208.

18. Blarer, 187f.

according to his will, also my enemies (if I have any) to the place where we may all meet again in love. . . . I do not ask anything worse for my enemies than for my friends, and nothing more disagreeable for the former than for myself, God willing. Well, Master Wilson, pray for me, as I will for you, sometimes during the night when I would be sorry to think that you may not be asleep.[19]

Fear adds an especially horrible dimension to suffering. In a letter to Margaret, More wrote: "By nature I tend to scare at the slightest flick, and to complain. Yet through the horrible fear of death which—as you know, I have often experienced, heavy in heart and all hope lost—before I was brought to the Tower, I stayed awake for hours thinking when my wife thought I slumbered; yet despite all that I was never reconciled to the idea of agreeing to something that went against my conscience and which would bring down on me God's deepest disapproval."[20]

Fear never has the last word with Thomas, but neither is it ever entirely overcome. "I do not want to be so rash as to give a definite guarantee here and now to remain constant come what may. But I shall pray, and ask my good daughter to pray with me, so that God may hold me true to the conviction that he has deigned to give me."

Often, forgetting his surroundings, the Privy Council, the succession, the supremacy, and the oath, More wants simply to speak to Margaret about God. Recalling the words of St. Paul *"There is nothing I cannot overcome with the help of the One who gives me strength,"* he speaks of his own hope: "Meg, to be sure, your heart is not as timid as mine. But I trust in God's mercy; he will protect me, for I am entirely in his hands. He will not permit me to miserably forsake him and he will likewise take you by the hand, dear daughter of mine."[21]

3.

The prologue to the German edition of the *Dialogue of Comfort Against Tribulation*[22] speaks of the affinity between this work and Boethius's

---

19. Ibid., 180–187.

20. Blarer, 191; *SL*, 60; *Corr.*, 210 (Letter to Margaret Roper, from the Tower, 1534).

21. Ibid.

22. Cf. chapter "The Poor Souls," note 3. Citations will be taken from this edition. Also cf. Louis L. Martz, "The Design of More's *Dialogue of Comfort*," in Moreana, 15–16, (1967), 331–346; Joaquin Kuhn, "The Function of Psalm 90 in Thomas More's *A Dialogue of Comfort*" in Moreana, 22 (1969), 61–67.

dialogue *The Consolation of Philosophy*. Indeed, there are superficial likenesses: Boethius and More both were representative figures of their cultures and stood at the thresholds of new eras—Boethius at the frontier between the Antiquity and the Middle Ages, More at the transition from the Middle Ages to the Modern Age. Both had been the highest-ranking civil servants of their realms, and both were imprisoned by the arbitrariness of their sovereigns—Boethius by the Ostrogoth King Theodoric. The death sentence for high treason awaited them both, making them victims of judicial assassination.[23]

However, the similarities end. Although Boethius, too, was a Christian, the source of his comfort lay in stoicism's counsel to accept the inevitable with quiet dignity. The dialogue—in fact, a monologue—is between the prisoner and the noble lady Philosophy. For the reader of later times, the value of this tract, with all its poetic beauty, lies in its extolling noble self-reliance in the face of suffering and death. Boethius's work has had wider circulation and incomparably more effect than More's, and has been translated numerous times—for example, into English by King Alfred (849–899) and by Chaucer.

But even though More's *Dialogue*, written in 1534, is little known even today, in its humor and knowledge of human nature, it is superior to the work of the philosopher of late Antiquity. Rather than composing elegant, high-sounding generalities on standing up to suffering, he looks to Christ mocked and scourged, his heart as deeply pierced by compassion for the human condition as his head was by thorns.

Even here, of course, More abides by the literary conventions of his time. Instead of launching into a sermon, he begins by setting the stage, telling the reader that the *Dialogue* was composed in Latin by a Hungarian, later translated into French, and then into English. The nephew, Vincent, visits his ailing uncle, to be strengthened and comforted himself. The Turks are approaching with a huge army, having already conquered a large section of Hungary; news of frightening cruelties and persecution of Christians precedes them. Nothing can stop them, and the worst is expected. What to do—flee, stand and fight, pray, give up in despair?

The setting of Hungary, mortally threatened by the Turks, was not chosen at random. After the Turkish victory at Mohacz in 1526, the greater part of the country succumbed to Ottoman power, with only a narrow band in the Northeast remaining in the hands of the

---

23. *Consolation in Suffering*, prologue, 10–24.

House of Austria. In 1529 the Turks arrived at the gates of Vienna. Although unable to conquer the city, they were repelled only with great difficulty by the imperial army, as was to be the case again in 1683. The inhabitants of Austrian Hungary were in constant danger; devastation by war and the sufferings of the Christian population of the Ottoman-controlled part of Hungary were constant realities.

More's situation was simple: on the one hand, loyalty to the King, liberty, life; on the other, fidelity to conscience, which meant fidelity to the Church, the Pope, the Sacrament of Matrimony, and the love of Christ; in the end, a choice between eternal damnation and eternal life. Very simple, but not at all easy. The Tempter stood before him and pointed ways out, and, not succeeding, showed his face as torturer and executioner.

More understood all this very well, and *The Dialogue* deals with it—with More in his own land, the England of Henry VIII, with More face to face with death, and with all those who at some time might find themselves in comparable situations. There will always be tyrants requiring good men to worship their idols or pay the price.

All suffering entails a temptation to evade it. To the man of our time this seems natural, and frequently the word "temptation" in this context would even be rejected. Anyone used to looking on suffering and pain as enemies, and these cannot be seen in any other light outside the relationship of God's love, penance, and salvation of the soul, will fight against them with every means and, if possible, will avoid them entirely. On the other hand, he will feel deeply dismayed if he cannot avoid them by taking the necessary precautions or overcome them in the struggle. He will then feel totally overwhelmed, fall prey to fear and probably lose hope if he gets into a situation in which he should freely opt for pain and suffering, even though he could avoid them. When does such a situation arise? When do circumstances converge so that life itself, or even only well-being, has to be bought at a price the payment of which could devalue and perhaps destroy life and comfort? Although the question may be theoretical, it has always been and continues to be timely. It has been repeated in every generation, from Macchabees to the martyrs of today. And it will always be so, for there will never be a lack of idols and dictators who demand this sacrifice.

A book of consolation like this also had to be a book of instructions. Extreme situations tend to build up gradually, almost unnoticed at first.

The capacity to judge and resist develops slowly, and small surrenders—leading in the end to final surrender—are easy. More sought to show in the first place who the enemy is and how he operates: "The Devil pursues us through temptation, and tempts us by persecution. Just as persecution means suffering for all of us indiscriminately, temptation means suffering for good people too. And even though in both cases it may be the Devil, our spiritual enemy, who joins battle against man, there is a difference between ordinary temptation and persecution as such. Temptation is, so to speak, a preliminary skirmish, while persecution is open, all-out battle."[24] But this only comes at the end; and how a man resists then depends largely on how he has conducted himself earlier in the skirmishes, the temptations.

Various kinds of temptation are considered in great detail. The aim is to give consolation and foster courage. He follows Psalm 91: "*God's truth will protect you like a shield, you need not fear the terrors of the night, the arrow that flies in the daytime, the plague that stalks in the dark, the scourge that wreaks havoc in broad daylight.*" Here are four general categories of human tribulation. The first is the terror, the sadness, of the night—the night of literal, natural darkness, and also the darkness of the soul, melancholy.

Pusillanimity is the state of the darkened soul. A person without fortitude first becomes impatient and then often moves on to contradiction, obstinacy, and opposition to God; often, too, he neglects to do the good he should and would do if he trusted in God's help.[25] Pusillanimity, Anthony notes, has a daughter named Scrupulousness. And the scrupulous person falls "easily from one grave error into a much graver one, if he embraces a new doctrine that preaches a false sense of freedom because of the calm and relief he finds therein. His conscience now is as wide as it was narrow before."[26] Undoubtedly, the uncle adds, a somewhat" narrow" conscience is preferable to a "wide" one.

More gives surprisingly exhaustive treatment to "suicide" as the terminus of the mortal sin of despair. He is worried, too, by the complex vice of disguised spiritual pride and the distinction, often so difficult to draw, between authentic revelations and demonic delusions. The link to the author's situation is clear. Often, when praying before the tabernacle,

---

24. Ibid., 73.
25. *Consolation in Suffering*, 84f.
26. Ibid., 88.

he must have asked if he was toying with suicide in opposing the King? Acting out of spiritual arrogance? Heeding the voice of God or Satan?

Like Anthony in faraway Hungary, Sir Thomas in the Tower of London is ill, wracked with a cough, fever, and cardiac pains. These physical sufferings are among the temptations of the night. He closes this part of the meditation with some concrete advice: "The most effective way of fighting someone who is harassed and tempted is to pray to God for help, pray for himself, and ask others to pray for him: the poor, to thank God for alms received, and other good people, out of Christian charity, especially good priests in the liturgy of the Holy Mass. He should also invoke his guardian angel and other saints to whom he may have a special devotion. . . . But there is no prayer that is more efficacious, and which God accepts with greater pleasure, than the words our own Redeemer taught us: 'Lead us not into temptation but deliver us from evil.' "[27]

Next More turns to the psalm's "arrow that flies in the daytime." This is the arrow of pride, which, during the "short wintry day" that is life in this world "transfixes our hearts and carries us up into the clouds." And there "considering our own glory, we think of those other poor souls, perhaps former companions of ours, as silly miserable ants."[28] Of course More is thinking of himself and his own brief day, now so soon to end. Didn't he look down in humanist superiority on those "silly miserable ants," the ignorant monks who did not know Latin or Greek? Didn't he enjoy being a successful writer and being painted by Holbein? What about that splendid, warm, fur-trimmed garment of office? "It is extraordinarily difficult to handle fish without getting smelly fingers or to pin a snake to the ground and fend off its venomous bite, to put a young man and a young woman together without the potential danger of lust. Just so difficult is it for anyone, whether man or woman, to live amidst great material wealth and comfort yet remain immune to the desire of vainglory, to which the Devil leads us at every opportunity."[29]

On the face of it, it might seem that there is not much consolation in meditating. But this arrow does wound, and the wounds do ache and grow infected at night. Moreover, the good Anthony reminds his nephew: "Apart from the darkness of night, there are other times

---

27. Ibid., 140ff.
28. Ibid., 143ff.
29. Ibid., 148.

of gloom. One is before the break of day and the other is at twilight. There are two parallel times of gloom in the soul of man: one before the light of grace has entered fully into his heart, and the other when the light of grace begins to disappear from his soul."[30] Thus More turns to the *negotium perambulans in tenebris*—the pestilence that goes abroad in darkness.

He has much to say about the ceaseless, feverish "busy-ness" that can arrest itself and become a source of pleasure. Unlike the work it often imitates, it lacks the spirit of service and self-effacement. In his decades of public and private life, he has met this particular devil within himself, in the hour between light and dark, tempting to a kind of greed. For one of the main motives driving ceaseless activity is the ceaseless accumulation of material goods. Young Vincent remarks: "I cannot quite understand how a man can make himself rich and continue to be rich, the world being what it is, with so many poor in it, without running the risk of damnation. If there were no poor, he might keep his wealth and remain in God's grace like Abraham and so many other rich people since then. But since there are countless numbers of poor people in the country nowadays, all those who keep a little wealth for themselves must perforce have an inordinate attachment to it because they do not give it away to the poor and needy, as they are seriously enjoined to do out of charity."

Anthony replies, "My dear nephew, there are certain matters in which it is difficult to order or prohibit, affirm or deny, censure or confirm. . . . To be able to say precisely, 'This is, or this is not, good' the exact circumstances have to be taken into consideration also."[31]

This sentence is noteworthy for its rejection of oversimplification. Once again we were reminded that More is a spiritual writer who elevates his craft to a level beyond polemics. To be sure, in inviting men to imitate him, Christ commends evangelical poverty; but he is not threatening the condemnation of those attached to worldly things, but only seeking to clarify the proper priority of attachments. "Christ teaches us to love God above all else, and he who holds on to part of his goods at the risk of displeasing God does not, therefore, love God above all else. . . . But, giving up everything so that no one becomes rich and owns a fortune, that is something that I have not found to be a precept anywhere. The Lord says: 'There are many mansions in my

---

30. Ibid., 157.
31. Ibid., 164.

Father's house and happy is he who lives in one of them, even if it only happens to be the very last one.'"[32]

More's Anthony next turns to the gospel account of Jesus' encounter with the publican Zacchaeus (Luke 19:1–10): "Zacchaeus, come down—hurry! I want to stay at your house today." But the people grumbled, for tax collectors had a bad name for thieving, blackmail, and corruption, and this Zacchaeus, a man of immense wealth, was considered a terrible sinner. Yet already the Lord had transformed him: "Master, I am going to give half my property away to the poor, and if I have cheated anybody I will pay him back four times the amount."[33]

Here Vincent interrupts: "In my view, he should have spoken first about giving their property back to those he had cheated, and then he could have spoken of giving alms. Restitution, as we all know, is an obligation, whilst giving alms is an act of free will."[34] From a legalistic point of view, perfectly correct. Sometimes, however, as in the case of Zacchaeus, what is intrinsically good and immediate takes priority over the theoretically and abstractly correct. "He who has enough," replies the uncle, "should likewise give alms to the poor around him who ask for help, before going to all his debtors and those against whom he has committed some injustice and perhaps live some distance from one another." Act on a good intention while the good intention exists. "It is always a good thing," says Anthony, "to do what is right as far as we are able."[35]

More seems to leave the subject of wealth with difficulty, and one might ask oneself whether he is digressing, as is his custom, or whether our perception of suffering and consolation is too limited. He was not a poor person, and at one time had a considerable income. His home in Chelsea was a stately mansion; the King had given him land; he had pensions and endowments. Is this what Christ asks of those who follow him? For the few fortunate enough to be called by God to absolute poverty, in chastity and complete obedience, the path, though difficult and filled with sacrifice, is clearly and unambiguously defined. But the path for the rest is not easy either; and it can be equivocal. Without the help of God, no one can be poor and at the same time live in comfort, clean-living amidst pleasure, obedient while being careful to look

---

32. Ibid., 167f.
33. Ibid., 170.
34. Ibid., 171.
35. Ibid.

out for himself. Yet this is what More had tried to do, bearing tension within himself for nearly forty years. And although only he, God,
and Margaret knew it, he had never entirely lost a hankering for the
world's way. So this dialogue was bound to become an examination of
conscience for him, and he drew consolation from Jesus' words to Zacchaeus: "Today salvation has come to this house!" We can live "in the
world" and at the same time be in a state of grace and in God's favor.

The *Dialogue* up to this point has been a preparation for what
comes next. The temptations of daily life are only preliminary skirmishes before the decisive battle. Now that battle is joined *ab incursu,
et daemonio meridiano,* "with the devil in broad daylight" (Psalm 91).
It consists of persecution, and from Good Friday to the end of time it
takes place when the Devil drops pretense and shows himself the brutal
executioner he is, seeking by naked terror to cause treason and apostasy
from Christ. The dialogue between Anthony and Vincent now speaks
of the horrors of a persecution, including terror and the false testimonies of renegades. Now More is foreseeing his own fate and very likely
the fates of so many English Catholics after him.

In many passages the "Turkish" motif of the dialogue merges with
English reality. Anthony says: "Of course, in this country, there is no
shortage of Turks, who under various pretexts roam the land and, no
doubt, report on everything to the Grand Turk."[36] Vincent then asks
whether "it is advisable to look into your heart, consider in advance
and decide whether in the event of falling into the hands of the Turk,
it would be preferable to die rather than deny the faith." To which
the uncle replies that it is not allowable for a Christian, in order to
evade martyrdom, to "deny Christ through his lips but keep faith in
his heart."[37]

On the contrary, the obligation of a Christian under persecution
is clear: "Christ frequently and explicitly said that every man is obliged
under pain of eternal damnation, to openly confess his faith, even where
he is compelled and threatened with death and they try to force him to
act to the contrary. . . . In the face of torture, his heart trembling with
dread, he should remember what great pain Christ suffered for us."[38]

This *incursu a daemonio meridiano* envisages the most perilous of
temptations. Who can be strong when he can easily evade torture and

---

36. *Comfort in Tribulation,* 199.
37. Ibid., 201.
38. Ibid., 202.

death by simply offering sacrifice before the Emperor's image, or giving lip service to the prophet or swearing an oath to an act of Parliament? More writes: "By temptation on account of the faith I do not refer to the struggle in the field of battle, where a believer must risk his person in defense of his faith and the non-believer must bear his share of fear and terror. I mean the persecution in which he is seized and cast into captivity, yet by apostatizing and distancing himself from his faith could free himself and live in peace, sometimes even in luxury. . . . That is an extremely dangerous occasion of his falling into the sin that the Devil tries to lead him into: the denial of his faith."[39]

It is easy—rationally speaking—to see how far superior the supreme good is to the goods one may gain by disloyalty or apostasy. But when one comes face to face with the irrational fear of physical suffering, Vincent says: "Were the Turk to take away everything, including my shirt, if I did not give up my faith, and were he to offer me everything fivefold on condition I embraced his faith, I would not hesitate for a single second and would prefer to lose everything rather than desert the holy faith of Christ. But if I then start to think of the torments and pain that threaten my body, dread enters into me and makes me tremble."[40]

One can only imagine how that dread must have plagued More. He has Anthony say: "If we were not the obtuse and silly individuals we are, meditating on the incomparable love and bountifulness of Christ and his Passion would ignite our cold hearts. Then we would not only be prepared to suffer death for him but would long for it. How many people over the centuries have died for spent causes—glory, honor, country or even an ideal, for a personal earthly love, often under great torture? That being so, is it not more than shameful that Christ should see Catholics prefer to deny their faith in him than bear everything for heaven and true glory?"[41]

At the end of the *Dialogue*, More weighs the most extreme earthly affliction in relation to heaven and hell. As to the latter: if people facing the worst the Turks could do suddenly glimpsed hell, "such a vision would frighten us to such an extent that we would hardly remember even having seen the Turks."[42] As to heaven: "If there came into view the great glory of God, the Trinity, in its sovereign and marvelous majesty,

---

39. Ibid., 206f.
40. Ibid., 244f.
41. Ibid., 253.
42. Ibid., 254.

and our Lord in his glorious humanity seated on his throne, with his immaculate Mother and the entire glorious community, and he called to us, even if the way lay through a valley of horrible, tormented death, not a single person, seeing such glory, would hesitate for a second. All would hasten to run toward it, no matter how much all the Turkish torturers and demons from Hell stood in the way."[43]

By now More had settled his accounts with life. He knew he faced a cruel death. Yet he has Anthony say that in bringing a man safely home to heaven God "helps someone more by releasing him from this wretched world through a very painful death . . . than by simply saving him from a horrible plight."[44]

4.

It should be clear to people who lived through the events of the twentieth century that the response to the harsh terror inflicted by the midday demon separates saints from ordinary people. Henry and Cromwell felt secure in the thought that, for every martyr, there were ten others who applauded what they did, and for everyone who took a stand there were thousands who kept quiet. This latter group, the "silent majority," make possible the cruelties of history, but they suffer nothing for it in earthly tribunals. As for those who applaud, most probably are not hypocrites. Often they really believe in what they bestow their praise upon. There was no shortage of such people, especially among the professors and the prelates, at that time. On March 2, 1534, Cambridge University unanimously rejected papal authority. Three days later the convocation of the ecclesiastical province of York did the same. So did Oxford University, led by its Chancellor John Longland, Bishop of London, on July 27.

Meanwhile, Parliament had been busy taking steps to deal with recalcitrant individuals like More and Fisher. Above all, after February 1, 1534, whoever criticized, even by mere allusion, Henry's supremacy in the Church, his marriage, the succession legislation, or the King's person, was guilty of high treason[45] and could expect punishment by disemboweling. Chambers believes the House of Commons showed courage in specifying those who were "maliciously" guilty of high treason. Alas, the word "maliciously" never saved anyone.

---

43. Ibid.
44. Ibid., 260.
45. Chambers, 385.

Very soon the Carthusians of London were put to the test. With the full agreement of the entire Chapter, the prior of the London charterhouse and head of the English Carthusians, John Houghton, made the decision to refuse to take the oath accepting the Act of Supremacy. Houghton knew what this meant. After asking his brothers' pardon on his knees and saying Mass, he went, accompanied by the priors Augustine Webster of Lincolnshire charterhouse and Robert Lawrence of Beauvale charterhouse in Nottinghamshire, to see Thomas Cromwell and tell him they could not take the oath. In early April the three were taken to the Tower. Already there for refusing the oath was Father Reynolds, a Bridgetine monk of the Abbey of Sion and reputedly the most cultured monk in England.[46] After several interrogations, during which the accused stood their ground, they were tried on April 29 before a special commission consisting of Chancellor Audley, the Duke of Norfolk (quite docile by now), and Cromwell, together with about twenty other nobles and advisors who had legal backgrounds of some sort.

Rastell describes the trial in his biography of More.

> The Carthusians, through their spokesman John Houghton, confessed to rejecting the King's supremacy, though not maliciously. The jury could not agree to condemn these four religious, believing they did not refuse to assent out of maliciousness. The judges' reply, however, was that anyone who rejected the concept of supremacy did so from malice. . . . Despite everything, the members of the jury were not disposed to condemn them. At that point Cromwell flew into a rage and threatened the jury with "grave misfortune" if they did not agree to their condemnation. Thus, overcome by threats, they sentenced the accused and thereby received an ample reward. Subsequently they were ashamed even to show their faces in public, and many were seriously distressed at what they had done.[47]

Everyone knew the trial was a sham. To accept the idea of anyone's rejecting the new order "without malice" would have set a precedent that halted the whole apparatus of terror. But the trial of the Carthusians was meant to intimidate and terrify. Joined by the vicar of Isleworth, John Hale,[48] the condemned suffered a horrible fate. Four days

---

46. Ibid., 388 (cf. Reginald Pole: *Pro Unitatis Ecclesiae Defensione*, 1538).

47. Ibid, 390.

48. He fell victim to a certain Robert Feron, who, as a young priest, spied for the government and provoked Hale to write a harsh criticism of the King. Cf. Jacob, 168f.

after their execution on May 8, 1535, the Emperor's envoy wrote his superior, Secretary of State Antoine Granvelle: "After being dragged to the gallows, they made the condemned men climb one by one onto a cart that was then pulled away from under their feet, leaving them dangling in the air. They then immediately cut the rope, put them in a place prepared for the purpose, and, while they were still standing, cut off their private parts, which were thrown on the fire. Then they cut open their stomachs and ripped out their entrails; finally, they were decapitated and their bodies quartered before their hearts were removed and their mouths and faces wiped with them."[49]

Meanwhile, More's trial had begun. The authorities hoped to exploit the horror of the Carthusians' deaths, reasoning that if they could not now succeed in making the headstrong ex-Chancellor and Bishop Fisher swear the oath, they never would. Swift execution then would follow, since the possibility of any resistance by two such famous men raised a specter far more threatening than the deaths of the newly slaughtered clerics. This is why, on April 30, the day after the Carthusians were condemned, Cromwell and some royal counselors went to More to urge him for the last time to submit. In effect, as More told his daughter, his trial for high treason began with this interrogation. On July 11 he was pronounced guilty and sentenced.

The trials of Bishop Fisher and other Carthusians, the Fathers Middlemore, Exmewe, and Newdigate (a former courtier and favorite of Henry) took place simultaneously. The monks, who refused to swear the oath, were tortured hideously, with More standing nearby in the courtyard of the Tower. From May 25 to June 11, when they were sentenced to death "they were kept on their feet, with an iron collar round their necks, tied to a post with heavy chains around their legs, and during the whole of that time they were never moved from that position, not even to answer the calls of nature."[50] Two days before, Fisher had been condemned to death, and three days later he was beheaded. Pope Paul III's gesture on May 21 in bestowing on him the red hat of a cardinal, in the vain hope that it might provide some kind of protection, only accelerated Fisher's end, since it was alleged—unjustly—that he had secretly asked for the cardinal's hat. Chapuys reported to the Emperor that the King had promised several times to send the bishop's head to Rome to receive the hat. He also joked that the Bishop of

---

49. Ibid.
50. Chambers, 398f.

Rochester would have to wear the hat on his shoulders "for a head he will have none."

Searches and interrogations of Fisher's servants had yielded nothing useful against him, nor had the arrests of Fisher's relatives and protectors. Instead the elderly bishop, less versed in legal matters than the experienced lawyer More, had personally handed his enemies the weapon they needed to destroy him. On May 7, assured by the King's messenger, the Solicitor General and senior lawyer Richard Rich, that he would not suffer for it, Fisher was induced to sign a statement declaring that he rejected Henry's supremacy. That made easy the work of the special commission set up to bring the traitors to trial.

As the interrogations of Fisher and More proceeded, Thomas several times warned the bishop, by notes conveyed via the servant of the governor of the Tower of London, to say nothing suggesting collusion between them. More had no expectation of a happy outcome, but he was determined to uphold his professional reputation and put up the best defense he could. But Fisher's assertion that he had been promised "discretion" regarding the statement he had made was of no use. Said Rich: "Even if I had spoken to you as you claim, that would not exonerate you before the law."[51]

Sentence was passed on June 7 at Westminster: Guilty of high treason and condemned as the law prescribed. Bishop Fisher died, his sentence commuted to "simple decapitation," on the morning of June 22, 1535. He asked those standing around the scaffold to pray for him. "I never feared death until now, but I realize that I am but a man, and that St. Peter, for fear of death, denied our Lord three times. So, I beg of you to help me with your prayers, that at the moment of death I may have no doubts through fear on any point of the Catholic faith,[52] and that God's infinite mercy may deign to save the King and his realm."[53]

For fourteen days, Rastell relates, Fisher's head, raised above the bridge over the Thames, looked as if it were alive to the people who came en masse to London. When it was time to make room for More's head, the executioner unceremoniously flung the Bishop's head into the river.

---

51. The documents relating to the trial and death of Fisher and More are contained in *L.P.*, Vol. VIII.
52. Chambers, 403.
53. Vázquez de Prada, 452.

Fisher and More were canonized in 1935, and the liturgical calendar designates the same day, June 22, as their feast. St. Thomas More and St. John Fisher were leading lights of humanism and scholars of international standing. They brought humanism and Catholicism together in a way that was to the advantage of each. Like More, the bishop had stood at different times both with and against the King. He lashed out against Luther in the tracts *Assertionis Lutheranae Confutatio* (1523) and *Assertionum Regis Angliae Defensio* (1525). Like More, along with praying and meditating, he used his time in prison to compose religious texts in his mother tongue: *A Spiritual Consolation* and *The Ways to Perfect Religion*. The difference between them was the difference between layman and priest. Fisher was obliged to resist the regime's aberrations directly. In this sense, his position was easier than More's. Priests who come into conflict with the state and wish to remain faithful to the Church will invoke St. John Fisher as their patron; whereas perplexed Christians entangled in the complexities and intrigues of the social apparatus and in need of an example and intercessor, will turn to St. Thomas More.

CHAPTER THIRTEEN

In Conversation with God

1.

Although sixty-six days followed More's interrogation on April 30, his fate was sealed then. He gives Margaret an account of it in a letter dated May 2 or 3.

Cromwell, with the malice that characterized the interrogation, asked the prisoner, "From whom does the King of England derive his power? His Majesty and his heirs have become the head of the Church of England by an act of Parliament, and now derive their authority directly from Christ just as it should always have been in justice and as it will continue to be henceforth." The first article of the Act of Supremacy stated as much. Cromwell: "The King wants to know Sir Thomas' opinion and attitude on these words." More: "But from the beginning of the negotiations I have made known, from time to time, my attitude to the King; and you, Secretary, Sir, already know it too from my numerous oral and written explanations. I have striven to put all these matters behind me; I have no desire to discuss the King's or the Pope's titles. I am the King's loyal subject and will always be. I shall pray daily for him and his own. I shall also remember you, his counselors, and will commend the whole kingdom to the Lord. I shall in no other way involve myself further in worldly affairs."[1]

After stating "that such a reply would not do for the King and that he would be compelled to give a more specific one," Cromwell started to treat his former colleague like an obstinate child. Far from being severe, he insisted, Henry was generous and merciful, always ready to welcome back a subject who had offended against him but

---

1. Blarer, 200–204.

who returned and showed himself docile; this was particularly true in More's case, he added.

More had heard it all before, but he still felt under immense pressure. He was not obstinate but sensitive. He loved the world, Chelsea, and his family, and the Tempter had ample material to work on. But: "Having recovered my composure, I replied concisely that I had no intention of getting involved again in temporal matters at any price, since I had firmly resolved I would direct my thoughts entirely towards Christ's Passion and with such thoughts prepare myself for my own death."[2]

More was subjected to further interrogations on May 7 and June 3. The commission was composed of the Archbishop of Canterbury, the Lord Chancellor, the Earl of Suffolk (Charles Brandon, brother-in-law of Henry VIII), the Earl of Wiltshire (Thomas Boleyn, Keeper of the Royal Seal), and Cromwell. Told yet again that the King had the authority to insist that he state his position unequivocally, More replied: "Do you consider it fair to force me to adopt a firm position, since I find myself having to decide whether to approve the law and thereby lose my soul, or speak out against it under pain of death?"

Interesting as the interrogation may have been as a lawyer's duel, it yielded nothing new. More continued to insist on his right to silence where assent was impossible for reasons of conscience that no one can be compelled to explain. Cromwell sidestepped the issue of conscience while pointing to an apparently logical connection between More's interrogation procedures as a judge when dealing with "heretics, thieves, and evildoers" and the present situation. More simply replied that where the penalty in either case was death, it made no difference from the point of view of conscience whether one was condemned for saying something deemed unacceptable or for not saying what was considered acceptable.

As for why now, when death no longer frightened him, he did not oppose the law openly and sincerely, the reply was: "I have not led such an exemplary life that I could offer myself up to death without giving it a thought. God could punish me for such presumption. For that reason, I do not wish to be in a rush but to take my time." Rebuked by the members of the commission for his treacherous and ungrateful attitude, he was taken back to his cell. There, saddened by Margaret's letter begging him to give way, he spent a few quiet days.

---

2. Ibid., 205. For the following: 204–209.

On June 12, Rich, the lawyer for the Crown, visited him accompanied by several gentlemen who immediately set about searching his cell. "Master More," Rich began ingratiatingly, "everybody knows you are a quiet and wise man, well-versed in the laws of the land. Please, therefore, forgive my audacity, Sir, in putting a question to you without malice aforethought. Let us take, Sir, a hypothetical situation in which, by an act of Parliament, I am crowned king. Would you then accept me as such, Master More?" "Yes, I would, Sir." "Suppose now that the act of Parliament made me pope, would you acknowledge me as such, Master More?" "Regarding the first case you put to me, Master Rich, I would say that Parliament may well intervene in the status of temporal sovereigns, but as to the second instance, I answer as follows: Imagine that Parliament passed a law decreeing that God should not be God. Would you, therefore, maintain that God is not God, Master Rich?" "No, Sir, I would not say that, for no Parliament can pass such a law."[3]

Since 1963, we have also had another document concerning this conversation that cost More his life. It reports that as Rich prepared to leave, he warned that his silence placed him in grave danger: "And may Jesus therefore grant you better judgment." With that the visitors departed, taking with them books, manuscripts, paper and ink, in order to cut More off from contact with the outside world. Sir Thomas immediately closed the shutters, leaving his cell in darkness. When the jailer asked why, he answered: "When they take away the serving counter and the tools of the trade as well, it is time to close the shop."[4] Among the confiscated manuscripts was the Latin text of the meditation on the Passion known as *Expositio passionis Domini, ex contextu quatuor evangelistarum usque ad comprehensum Christum.*[5] Thomas had completed it up to the words *iniecerunt manus in Jesum* ("They laid their hands on Jesus").

On June 14, two days after the conversation with Rich, More was again interrogated. Three questions were put to him: 1) Did he acknowledge the King as supreme head of the Church? 2) Did he acknowledge the marriage of the King and Queen Anne as legitimate and, by implication, the one with Lady Catherine as illegitimate? 3) Why, supposing him to be a loyal subject of the King, was he not obliged in law like all other subjects to answer these questions and acknowledge the King's

---

3. Roper, 84ff.; Vázquez de Prada, 450f.; Chambers, 408; Reynolds, 341f. and Appendix II, 385f.; PRO., S.P.2/R, folios 24 and 25.

4. Vázquez de Prada, 451; Stapleton, folio 1031 (Chapter 13).

5. Cf. Vázquez de Prada, 526–529 (Manuscript of Our Lord's Passion); *Works*, 1350.

supremacy? As to the first question, the record states: "He is unable to give an answer." As to the second: "He neither speaks against nor gives a reply." As to the third: "He cannot give an answer."[6] He was reserving that of course for the session on July 1 at Westminster.

Utopia is the best-known of More's works, but his trial and death are the best-known events of his life. Among his contemporaries, and even in our day, the story of the dramatic trial and execution has often been told.[7] This list of charges against him contained nothing new. More, weakened by imprisonment and illness, was allowed to remain seated. He kept his calm while repeating yet again: "I tell you that your statute cannot condemn me to death because of my silence; there is no law in the whole world, not even this new English law, that can execute anyone who has not done or said anything but simply remained silent." In response to the response that such silence showed bad faith, inasmuch as "every loyal and faithful subject of the King was duty-bound to acknowledge categorically and sincerely that this statute was good and holy," he called attention to the Roman principle of law: *Qui tacet consentire videtur* (Silence seems to imply consent): his silence upheld the Act of Parliament and subsidiary legislation, and he did not condemn them. Later he reiterates his plea for the right of silence: "You must understand that in all matters that touch our conscience, every good and loyal subject has to take account of his conscience and soul more than anything else in this world."[8]

The judges called the chief witness, the prosecution lawyer Sir Richard Rich. He repeated the conversation already mentioned, then claimed to have told More: "You are aware that our King has been declared head of the Church; why then do you not recognize him as such, in the same way that you might recognize me as king?" More supposedly replied that Parliament could indeed designate and then remove a king but it could not make and unmake the head of the Church. Rich knew as well as More that he was lying under oath. "If the statement you have submitted here under oath is true, Master Rich," More told him, "I do not ever want to come face to face with God;

---

6. Reynolds, 344; L.P. VIII, 867.

7. Cf. *L.P.* VIII, 996; Jacob, 168–175; Chambers, 405–414; Reynolds, 358–371; Vázquez de Prada, 454–466. And of course the corresponding sections of Roper, Rastell, Harpsfield, and Stapleton. And also the *Acta Thomae Mori: History of the Reports of his Trial and Death with an Unedited Contemporary Narrative*, by Henry de Vocht (Louvain, 1947); E. E. Reynolds, *The Trial of St. Thomas More* (London, 1964).

8. Harpsfield, 186; Chambers, 406f.

and . . . nothing in the world would ever make me utter these words."[9] He then set out what had happened during that visit on June 12. He noted Rich's dubious character and asked whether it was credible that he would have confided in such a man something he was not prepared to reveal even to the King and his counselors. Even supposing he had in fact denied the King's supremacy, he added, he would certainly not have done that with "malicious" intent, and therefore, according to the law, would not have committed a crime carrying the death sentence. "In truth, Master Rich," he concluded, "the false testimony that you have given saddens me more than the peril that now threatens me."

The secondary witnesses for the prosecution, Richard Southwell and Palmer, who had accompanied Rich and removed the prisoner's personal effects, were either unable or unwilling to remember the exact words spoken on June 12. Both said they had not been paying attention because they were otherwise occupied. All that remained then, was the sworn statement of Sir Richard Rich containing More's alleged denial of the royal supremacy. No matter, it was time for the show to end. The judges retired for a quarter of an hour, then returned and announced their verdict: "Guilty." The penalty was death. The Lord Chancellor pronounced sentence according to the wording of the new law.

Only the King could change the butchery awaiting the accused at Tyburn to the more humane death by beheading. Among the nine previous executions, that favor was granted only to Bishop Fisher. Knowing all that More knew that the time had finally come when it was his duty to speak out. Interrupting Lord Audley, who evidently wished to finish quickly, he said: "Chancellor, Sir, when I was a judge I used to ask the accused, before imposing punishment, if there was any reason why they should not be condemned." Audley paused and asked More whether he had anything to say.

"Since it is obvious," he began, "that you are ready to condemn me (God only knows how), I would now like, to set my conscience at rest, to express in a clear and open manner my opinion on the accusation and your legislation. The accusation is based on an Act of Parliament which is in direct contradiction with the laws of God and his holy Church, and whose supreme direction, whether totally or in part, no sovereign in pursuance of any statute may lay claim to. That belongs to the Holy See in Rome by a special privilege which our own Savior,

---

9. Roper, 87.

while he was alive in this world, granted exclusively to Saint Peter and his successors, that is, the bishops of the Holy See. Hence, this is not a law under which a Christian can accuse another Christian."[10]

Finally he had said it. It must have been a great joy and relief for him.

Audley responded by citing the votes of bishops, scholars, and universities. "I would question," said More, "whether it is not more certain, perhaps not in this realm, but certainly in the rest of Christendom, that the majority of learned bishops and virtuous men are of the same opinion in this matter as myself. And if I had to speak of those who have died, I am absolutely sure that the majority of them thought exactly the same way I do now. For that reason I am not obliged, my Lord, to accommodate my conscience against the universal council of Christians, to the council of just one kingdom. For every one of your bishops I can put forward a hundred holy bishops; and ranged alongside your council or Parliament—God knows what that is—are the councils which have stood the test of the past thousand years. And against this realm are set all the other Christian kingdoms. For that reason I invoke God, whose eyes are the only ones that can penetrate into the depths of the human heart, to be my witness. Be that as it may: you are baying for my blood not so much on account of the supremacy issue as because I have not deigned to approve the marriage."

Audley: "Master More, you are presuming to be deemed wiser and with a better conscience than all the bishops and noblemen; than the whole of the realm."

Norfolk: "More, now is your malice shown quite clearly."

More: "My Lord, what I am saying here is necessary both to reveal my conscience as well as to soothe my soul, and I therefore call on God to be my witness, who is the only one who knows the hearts of men."

The Lord Chancellor was rattled, afraid he might be called to account for lax conduct of the hearing. Although the fourteen jurymen had already pronounced the guilty verdict, he now put to the Royal Supreme Judge, Fitzjames, the astonishing question whether the charge was sufficient to warrant the sentence! Fitzjames replied, oddly: "I have to acknowledge, Sir, that if the law is not unlawful in itself, then the

---

10. Harpsfield, 193.

accusation is not, according to my conscience, insufficient."[11] There is no knowing what, if anything, the judges made of that. Probably they, too, simply wanted it to end. Audley swiftly pronounced sentence: this man guilty of high treason was to be dragged to Tyburn, hanged, his limbs amputated while still alive, slashed—and so on. Did More have anything to say in his own defense? More rose. "No more than the following: as we can read in the *Acts of the Apostles*, Paul was present at the death of Saint Stephen and kept their garments for those who stoned him. Despite that, today they are both saints in heaven, and there they shall be friends for ever and ever. So, I hope—and will pray with all my heart for it—that although you have condemned me here on earth, we shall meet for our eternal salvation in heaven."[12]

On the way from Westminster Hall back to the Tower, the executioner carried his axe in front of him with the edge toward More as a sign he had been sentenced to death. His son John stood by the roadside and knelt to ask his blessing; his daughter Margaret and Margaret Clement (Giggs), who had been waiting near the Tower, did the same. Later Margaret Roper could no longer contain herself and "made her way through the guards who surrounded him closely with their halberds and lances, threw herself on his bosom, put her arms around his neck and kissed him."[13] Calmly and deliberately her father said: "Have patience, Margaret, do not distress yourself: it is God's will. You have known the secrets of my heart for a long time." Margaret drew back but then again flung herself on him, embraced him, and kissed him repeatedly. More quietly told her to pray for his soul.

Very likely he heaved a sigh of relief when the door of his cell finally closed behind him and he was by himself. Not knowing how or when the execution would take place, he expected the worst, but hoped it would go speedily. Now he turned his attention to writing the prayers that Rastell included in the 1557 edition of his works. His words have moved even hardened hearts.

> Holy Trinity, [begins the last prayer] Father, Son and Holy Spirit—three equal persons and equally eternal in one all-powerful divinity, take pity on me, a miserable, despicable, and detestable sinner, who before your sovereign majesty confesses his ever-sinful life. Just as you

---

11. Chambers, 412.
12. Roper, 96; Chambers, 413.
13. Roper, 98f.

make a gift to me, good and clement Lord, of the grace to acknowledge my sins, grant me also that I may lament them not only in words but also with all my heart, and that I may forsake them entirely. Forgive, I beseech you, also those sins which, through my own fault, my bad qualities, and low habits, I fail to recognize as such because my reasoning is so blinded by sensuality. Illuminate, Lord, my heart; grant me your grace to recognize and see all my sins, and forgive those I have forgotten through carelessness; in your clemency recall them to my mind so that I may be purified of them completely.[14]

His eagerness to go home, growing for so long, was transparent as death drew near. "Glorious God, grant me the grace, without casting another look at the world, to unite my heart completely with yours in anticipation . . . so that with the Apostle Paul I may say: 'The world has been crucified on my account, and I for it. I long to end it and be with Christ.' All-powerful God: teach me how to do your will!"[15]

He prays for the grace to be able to offer up his physical fear, so that it too will bear fruit along with his other sufferings.

Lord, grant me the grace, in my fear of death, to think of the great dread and agony of death which you, my Redeemer, suffered on the Mount of Olives, so that by meditating on such sufferings I may receive comfort and consolation for the salvation of my soul. All-powerful God, take away from me all vanity, all desire for praise, all indolence, greed, lust, and sensuality, all anger, all thought of vengeance, all enjoyment of the downfall of others, all pleasure in irritating and provoking any religious, or any pleasure at the confiscation of any priest's goods or his being insulted.

Grant me, O Lord, an irreducibly staunch faith, a sure hope, vigorous charity, and a love of God incomparably greater than my love of self. Make me love everything that concerns you, and may I not love anything displeasing to you.

Forgive, bountiful Father, my temerity in making such great requests, for I am a sinner unworthy to receive even the least of them. But, Lord, the nature of these petitions is such that I must perforce express them; and they would be greater still were it not for my many sins.

---

14. *CW* 13, 228-231; *Works*, 1471; Vázquez de Prada, 468.
15. Ibid.

Take away from me, O Lord, this lukewarmness, this half-hearted and indifferent attitude with which I now pray to you. Give me warmth, joy, and spiritual alertness of thought in contemplating you. And grant me the grace to yearn for your sacraments, but above all that I may feel happy in the presence of your Sacred Body, beloved Savior Jesus Christ, in the Sacrament of the Altar.[16]

Almighty God, have pity on (N.) and (N.) and all who wish me evil and want to cause me harm. Be considerate toward their short-comings and mine, and make us all better with the gentle and clement means that your infinite wisdom can devise, so that as redeemed souls we may live with you and your saints in heaven.[17]

More's old friend Antonio Bonvisi remained faithful to him throughout his time in prison. Still considered a foreigner, even though his family, from Lucca, had settled in London toward the end of the fifteenth century, he was permitted to send food to Fisher and More three times a week and to provide them with warm winter clothing. In his next to last letter, Thomas thanks him movingly: "Dear Antonio, the most beloved of my friends, I beseech the Most High—I cannot do more—to reward you in abundance for all the benefits that you render to me daily, that he may take pity on us and, from this troubled life, make us reach out to the peace of heaven where there is no need to write letters, where no walls separate us, where no jailer overhears our conversations."[18]

To the very end, Dorothy Colly, Margaret Roper's maid, was allowed to take food and wine to the condemned man. Thus it was she who received his last letter, written in charcoal, dated July 5, and addressed to his beloved daughter. After sending blessings to his children, grandchildren, godchildren, and friends, giving some instructions and requesting some favors, he writes:

I am sure, my good Margaret, that I am becoming a burden to you, and would be sorry if it were all to last beyond this morning. But tomorrow is the eve of St. Thomas and the octave of St. Peter. I would like to die on that day, as it would be very fitting.

I never valued your love for me any higher than when you kissed me for the last time. I was overjoyed to see your unconcern

---

16. *Works*, 1417ff; Chambers, 415.
17. Ibid.
18. Blarer, 210ff.

for the conventions of this world. I bid you farewell, my beloved daughter, pray for me, as I pray for you and all our friends and that we may merrily meet again in heaven. Thank you for all the burden that you have taken on your shoulders on my account.[19]

Together with this letter Margaret received a few souvenirs as well as his hair shirt, which she had so often secretly washed for him. Roper relates how one summer evening, More's sister-in-law had found him "at supper, wearing only a doublet and hose and a plain shirt without ruff or collar. My sister More (Anne Cresacre), noticing his hair shirt showing, began to giggle. Then when my wife saw this she quietly drew his attention to it, and he quickly finished dressing, regretting that his daughter-in-law should have glimpsed the hair shirt."[20]

More had always avoided exhibiting his inner world, especially his relationship with God. Nor was there any need for Henry's admonition, delivered via Thomas Pope, to show discretion in delivering the customary condemned man's final remarks: "At your execution you shall not use many words."

Pope, an officer of the law, whom More had been friendly with for years, appeared like an angel from heaven in the early hours of July 6, a Tuesday, with the message that the King deigned that the execution—that very morning at nine—should take place by the axe. Truly this was a great and unexpected favor. More's gratitude was undoubtedly sincere: "Master Pope, I am cordially grateful for your good news. I have owed the King a debt of gratitude for a very long time for the many favors and honors he has bestowed on me. I am even more grateful to him for having brought me to this place where I have had time and opportunity to contemplate my end. And, by God I tell you, Master Pope, that I am obliged to his Majesty for wanting to release me so soon from the sufferings of this sad world. For that I shall not forget to pray for him here and in the next world."[21]

<hr>

19. Ibid., 214f. In England the feast of the "Transference of the Bones of St. Thomas of Canterbury" (Thomas à Becket) was celebrated on July 7. Thomas à Becket was murdered on December 29, 1170, in Canterbury cathedral at the instigation of King Henry II. He died because he would not give in to the unjustified demands of the King for power over the English Church.

20. Roper, 49; Chambers, 149.

21. Roper, 100ff.

There are many anecdotes surrounding More's last hours.[22] More gave the executioner the silk cloak Bonvisi had given him; the Governor then called the man "a knave without honor," and it is said that More replied: "Am I to call someone who renders me such a great service a 'knave?'" Sayings also have come down to us from the scaffold. "Governor, Sir," asked the condemned man as he stepped on the rickety steps, "please help me up safely, for on the way down I shall manage on my own." He encouraged the executioner, saying: "Have courage, lad, do not be afraid to carry out your duty. I have a short neck; so be careful to strike a sure blow so that you are not taken for a mere beginner at your job." Kneeling down, he carefully tucked in his beard, which had grown much in prison. "This has not committed high treason," he explained.

These may all be true recollections. They are typical of More. But the only eyewitness from among those close to him present at the execution—though unknown to him, was Margaret Clement. From her we know that the saint came out of the Tower into the open air looking pale and thin, his beard long and tangled, wearing a coarse grey garment and holding a red cross in his hands. A woman in the crowd offered him a glass of wine, which he declined politely: "They offered Our Lord vinegar and gall but not wine."

He climbed the scaffold's rickety steps with great effort. Reaching the top, he asked those present to pray for him in this world as he would for them in the next, and to bear witness that he was dying in and for the faith of the holy Catholic Church. He strongly exhorted them to include the King in their prayers, so that God might send him good counselors. "I die as a faithful servant of the King," he concluded, "but first and foremost as a servant of God." He fell to his knees and recited Psalm 51: *"Have mercy on me, O God, in your goodness, in your great tenderness wipe away my faults, wash me clean of my guilt to the end, purify me from my sin."* He embraced the executioner, who, as was the custom, knelt to ask his forgiveness. Blindfolding himself with a small handkerchief he had brought with him, he placed his neck on the block.

More's body was first buried in the Church of St. Peter in Chains within the Tower. His head took the place of Fisher's on London Bridge.

---

22. *L'Univers*, 509.

2.

During the long hours of solitude in his cell, More turned often to the Book of Psalms for consolation, jotting annotations in the margins— random ideas, associations, and inspirations.[23] These provide a deep insight into his soul which, in a way, makes up for gaps in what we know about the last few months of his life.

For instance, we do not know if there was a priest present at the execution, or whether More was able to receive the last sacraments, or what in general had been done to provide for the prisoner's spiritual welfare. Surely Roper and others would have said so if, as a special form of cruelty, he was not allowed to receive the Sacraments? Was not this minimal pastoral care something so obvious that there was no need to mention it? However that may be, as death approached More lived in a state of constant spiritual communion. And in that state he composed two moving documents.

More commented on forty-seven of the one hundred and fifty psalms. Often he wrote only a few words, but sometimes short phrases and occasionally longer ones. There is no need to consider their philosophical aspect here: Martz and Sylvester have done excellent work on that.[24] But a few remarks from a religious point of view are appropriate here.

Especially striking to today's Christians is how present and real the supernatural world was for Thomas More. The great tug-of-war between God and Satan, the battle between two kingdoms that runs throughout the whole of history and through every soul, is the central fact of human life. For More this conclusion is not the result of a set of ideas or historical experience or his own experience of life. It is the consequence of a reality as perceptible to him as the beating of his heart. God was ever present to him as his father; Jesus Christ reached out to him; the Holy Spirit spoke to him in his soul; his guardian angel was always at his side. But no less real was the presence of the Devil and his henchmen, the evil spirits perpetually lying in wait, the fallen angels ever seeking by seductive wiles to destroy men's awareness of their divine sonship.

---

23. Cf. in this regard: *Thomas More's Prayer Book*. A Facsimile Reproduction of the Annotated Pages. Transcription and Translation with an introduction by Louis L. Martz and Richard S. Sylvester (New Haven and London, 1969). This is a scholarly edition of great value. Since 1976 the corresponding volume 13 of the Yale edition (*CW* 13), edited by Gerry E. Haupt, has also been available.

24. *Prayer Book*, 13–45.

Moved by particular verses, More refers more than forty times to the constant threat posed by the *diabolus* and the evil spirits that go about the world. He has been warned about them and strengthened against them.[25] A few examples will suffice.

Next to the verse *"Safe in God's hand I lay down and slept, and now, though tens of thousands of enemies surround me on every side, I shall not be afraid"* (Ps 3:5–6), the prisoner scribbles: "Declaration of war against the demons." Besides *"Their throats are yawning graves; they make their tongues so silken"* (Ps 5:9), he notes: "Against the snares of the Devil." Alongside *"But I tottered and they crowded around in glee, flocking together to jeer at me, to punish the innocent"* (Ps 35:16), he comments: "The devils mock us but we want to be humble, serene, without impatience, fasting and praying." And of the same psalm's *"Let not those rejoice over me who are wrongfully my foes; and let not those wink the eye who hate me without cause,"* he says: "The demons too show us their false adulation."

False accusations have brought More down. Beside Psalm 27:12 *"Do not abandon me to the will of my foes, for lying witnesses rise up against me, and breathe out violence,"* he writes the single word: *"Calumnia"*— calumny. It is not just his own harassment that he protests. *"Display your marvelous merciful kindness, O Savior of fugitives, for you save from the enemy those who hide under the shadow of your wing"* (Ps 17:7) draws the comment: "Prayer of the Christian people against the power of the Turks." Of *"Let not those who hope in thee be put to shame through me, O Lord God of hosts"* (Ps 69:6) he says: "For the Hungarian faithful to pray in times of oppression, when the power of the Turks increases and many Hungarians fall into the false faith of the Turks."

More's affection for his family and household was expressed above all through education based on the tenets of the faith. Now he admonishes those who act differently toward their own. Concerning *"They sacrificed their own sons and daughters to demons"* (Ps 106:37) he writes in the margin: "This is what people who educate their children badly do." And on Psalm 49:16 *"Do not be afraid when a man grows rich"* he notes what experience has taught him: "Pride of the rich—worthy of compassion." There is human solidarity not only in original sin, but also in personal guilt and penitence. All the members of the Mystical Body of Christ share one another's pain and suffering.

---

25. For example Psalms 3:7; 7:7; 7:16; 9:4; 13:3; 17:15 etc.; cf. Note 23, *Prayer Book*, 189–203.

The other great theme of More's marginal notes on the Psalms is therefore "penitence for sins committed." He repeatedly hears the call to repent in the psalmist's words. In regard to *"I lie down and sleep; I wake again, for the Lord sustains me"* (Ps 3:5), he applies "sleep" and "getting up again" to the life of the soul and comments: "He who rises from his sin." The entreaty *"Do not rebuke me in your wrath, Lord; in your ire do not punish me"* (Ps 6:1) is interpreted as "asking for the forgiveness of sins."

Of Psalm 32:5, *"At last I admitted to you I had sinned; no longer concealing my guilt,"* he writes: *"Confessio peccati,* Confession of sin." The supplicant plea *"How much longer, Lord will you ignore me?"* (Ps 13:1) is understood as a prayer to make good confession that brings peace: "He who has scruples in confession, and does not feel cleansed within, let him pray this psalm." He advises those who leave the confessional worrying that they may not have confessed everything and so may not have been forgiven, to say to the Lord in all simplicity *"Give light to my eyes, or I shall sleep in death, and my enemy may boast saying: I have beaten him"* (Ps 13:3–4). Far from making light of such problems as is commonly done today, he counsels sincere prayer for enlightenment.

That was always his way. He did not comfort people by encouraging them to pooh-pooh truths of faith but by urging them to take those truths seriously, with reverence and filial trust. In More's psalm book there are many expressions of *"maiestas Dei"* (God's majesty)[26] and *"fiducia in Deum"* (faith in God).[27] Thanksgiving is always in order, as when he comments on Psalm 85's *"You have granted grace to your country, Lord"*: "Prayer after victory over the Turks or over the evil spirits of temptation, or as thanksgiving following the plague, drought, the rains." So, too, with prayer that expresses yearning for God—for example, Psalm 84, *"Lord of hosts, how I love your dwelling-place, for the courts of the Lord's house my soul faints with longing."* More writes: "Prayer of prisoner or patient confined to his sickbed yearning for God's house, or a believer longing for heaven."

More's lowest marginal comment concerns Psalm 38:12–13: *"Those intent on taking my life lay down traps for me; others, hoping to hurt me threaten my downfall, hatching treacherous plots; but I am like the deaf, I do not hear; like a dumb man who does not open his mouth."* Of this he says: "The gentle of heart must behave like this in tribulation; he must

---

26. As in 88:7; 95:4; 96:1.
27. As in 19:8; 22:4; 26:1; 55:5.

neither make vain speeches, nor respond to wicked words, but should bless those who despise him and gladly accept suffering for the sake of justice if he has deserved it, or for God's sake if he has not."

Now, at the end, he is "the gentle of heart," but he was not always so. There was a time when he was proud, condescending, and self-satisfied, but such attitudes have melted away. And if from the cross the unblemished One had asked his Father to forgive his persecutors, then those unjustly condemned but not altogether blameless, had likewise to forgive.

❧ ❧ ❧ ❧

Even intrigues and enmity, pain and harassment, called for gratitude as contributing to his salvation. There is no more heartfelt expression of this sentiment than More's marginal notes in his Book of Hours.[28] These thirty-seven verses, comprising the so-called "Godly Meditation," were written in English in the top and bottom margins of this book of Marian prayers which contains hymns and psalms, as well as prayers specifically dedicated to the Virgin.

The Marian hours were prayed at the times of the canonical hours. More's comments are found on the pages containing the first, third, and sixth hours, 6 a.m., 9 a.m., and noon. Accompanying each hour are contrasting images of the beginning and end of Jesus' life: three large engravings representing the birth of the Lord, the annunciation to the shepherds, and the adoration of the Magi, and three smaller engravings depicting Christ before Pilate, crowned with thorns, and carrying the cross.

One can understand More's feelings properly only by attending to these images. At the manger, where Mary and Joseph, together with the ox and the donkey, bow their heads before the newborn Child, he writes: "Grant me your grace, good Lord, that I may place little value on things of this world." At the picture of Christ bound and standing before Pilate: "Make it so, dear Lord, that when filled with joy, I may think of you and that I may devoutly ask for your help." And at the depiction of the angels and shepherds: "Acknowledge my wickedness, my misery, and in your hands make me humble." The Man of sorrows is the Redeemer. The crown of thorns signifies *gaudium magnum* (great joy). More writes: "Grant that I may keep my final hour at the

---

28. *CW* 13, 226f.; *Prayer Book*, 37f.

forefront of my mind, that I may always see before me my traveling companion: death."

The third engraving, occupying an entire page, shows the Three Kings, bearers of the world's wisdom, splendor, and wealth, adoring the child whose helplessness conceals the omnipotence of God. More asks God to prepare him well for death: "That I may never lose sight of hell, ask forgiveness before the Judge approaches and consider in my heart what Jesus Christ went through for me."

Thomas More knew full well what he needed. He asked for it in these words:

> Grant me your grace, good Lord, that I may attach little value to earthly things. Bind my soul close to you that I may not trust what men say and do. Help me to accept isolation without longing for companionship here on earth. Grant that every step that removes me away from it will remove my heart from temporal desires, and permit, dear Lord, that, filled with joy, I shall think of you and devoutly turn to you for help. May I trust entirely in your consolation. May loving you be the reward for my efforts. May I admit to my wickedness and wretchedness, and in your hands show humility. Lord, let me feel remorse for my sins and, repenting of them, patiently bear pain. Lord, I praise what purifies me on earth. Help me seek to bear misery and adversity cheerfully, tread the straight and narrow path that leads to life, lend my shoulder to bear Christ's cross, and at my final hour think of you with eyes fixed upon my traveling companion, death. Keep it always before me, Lord, so that I may persistently contemplate Hell and ask forgiveness before the arbiter approaches, treasuring in my heart all that Christ suffered on my account. Grant that throughout my life I may show gratitude for the good he has done me and make up for the time I have lost. Save me from idle chatter and gossip, from mindless and scandalous pursuits. Keep me from foolish, vain pastimes and the worldly merriment, friendships, freedom, and joy of living that we so much desire; let me deem it all nothing as compared with attaining Christ. May I see in my worst enemy my best friend. The brothers of Joseph could not have done him a greater favor by showing him love and sympathy than they did with their hatred and envy. To bear all this in mind is worth infinitely more than all the riches of this world's princes, than all the goods and wealth of Christians and pagans piled up to the sky.

Epilogue

On July 6, 1973, the anniversary of More's death, I promised the priest of my parish, St. Thomas More in Cologne, to write a book about this "modern" saint. I didn't know what I was getting myself into. Besides difficulties relating to the sources and the fact that I am not an expert on English history or the early modern age, there was a deeper problem: Despite my admiration and sympathy for the great Englishman, I could not find the key to his personality and work. The project was at risk of turning into a conventional biography. Only my intellectual and spiritual encounter with St. Josemaría Escrivá, founder of Opus Dei,[1] showed me the Christian perspective that makes it possible for someone today really to understand More.

This perspective, which I have attempted to convey in this book, depends upon two central concepts: *unity of life* and *divine filiation*. These are inseparable realities shaping the life and doctrine of Josemaría Escrivá.

From the Middle Ages until now, Christian spirituality has been characterized by a dichotomy: on the one hand, the *active life*, the path of the laity in the world; on the other, fleeing the world in order to live a *contemplative life*, the path of the cleric, the religious. The former way was the ordinary way: the latter the way of the elite, the perfect. Very gradually the revolution that will always be linked to the name of Josemaría Escrivá has begun to show us how enormously important it is to overcome that split.

This young priest, Escrivá, who in 1928 founded Opus Dei, recalled to Catholics something practically forgotten for centuries and made it a way of life for an increasing number. In doing so, he effectively paved the way for The Second Vatican Council's formal proclamation of these rediscovered truths, especially that, in accordance with the Lord's words "Be perfect as your Father in Heaven is perfect" all are called to the sanctity that begins with Baptism. The universal call applies to those

---

1. He died in 1975 and was canonized by Pope John Paul II in 2002.

living "in the midst of the world" and can be realized precisely there. This is meant to be the normal path of Christians. "I am speaking," said Msgr. Escrivá, "of the interior life of ordinary Christians who regularly find themselves in the hubbub of the city, in the light of day, in the street, at work, with their families or simply relaxing; they are centered on Jesus all day long."[2] Elsewhere he said, "All of your life will be full of God—in its sentiments, its works, its thoughts, and its words. . . . These great horizons of our Christian vocation, this unity of life built on the presence of God our Father, can and ought to be a daily reality."[3]

In practice, it had been supposed for centuries that lay people were called to follow Christ, and could only follow him at a lower level, with complete commitment and the path to sanctity reserved for religious and clerics. Even today, relatively few fathers and mothers of families have been canonized as saints. Thomas More is one. But his canonization came about because he was martyred and not primarily because of his holiness as a husband and father or a professional man. More himself regarded these roles almost as impediments—increasingly so—and not the way to sanctity. In this he was a child of his time. Only those who grasp this can grasp the liberating character of the demonstration by the founder of Opus Dei that our sanctification takes place in the sanctification of the world from within, with the desire of restoring it, not withdrawing from it.

More was deeply conscious of his *divine filiation*. That fundamental stance of love situated by Christ himself at the center of his teaching: "I tell you solemnly unless you change and become like little children, you will never enter the kingdom of heaven" (Mt 18:2–3). Both in pastoral doctrine and the everyday life of the Christian, it had almost been forgotten until St. Josemaría Escrivá brought it once again to the fore. He wrote: "If we let ourselves be guided by this lifegiving principle, who is the Holy Spirit in us, our spiritual vitality will grow. We will place ourselves in the hands of our Father God, with the same spontaneity and confidence with which a child abandons himself to his father's care. . . . This is the old and well-known 'way of childhood,' which is not sentimentality or lack of human maturity."[4] Thomas More traveled this route.

---

2. St. Josemaría Escrivá, *Christ Is Passing By* (New Rochelle, NY, 1985), no. 8.

3. Ibid., no. 11.

4. Ibid., no. 135.

Up to now, no recent, extensive biography of More from the pen of a German author has dealt in sufficient detail with all aspects of this extraordinary personality and his era. To be sure, there have been many studies, articles, and conferences; in particular, much has been written about his *Utopia* (unlike his other works). Even in this book it has not been feasible to take account of all his writings, such as *Dialogue Concerning Heresies* or *The Debellation of Salem and Byzance*; while others have only been mentioned in passing—for example, his *Apology* and the *Treatise on the Passion* or *The Sadness of Christ*. In those cases where a usable German version of a text exists, I have used it. Among the key works in the rich bibliography on More there are the biographies by Bremond, Chambers, Vázquez de Prada, and Reynolds. I am especially indebted to Chambers and Vázquez de Prada. In particular I am grateful to Germain Marc'Hadour, without whose research the writing of this book would have been far more difficult.

For their suggestions, advice, and continual encouragement, I thank my friends, Father Joaquin Alonso and Father Rolf Thomas, both in Rome; also Father Gustav van de Loo, priest of St. Thomas More Parish in Cologne, who placed his rich Morean library at my disposal. I am also sincerely indebted to my collaborators in the very extensive translation work: Emanuel Kolly (Cologne), who collaborated in the translation of the French version of *Supplication of Souls*; Widmar Puhl (Cologne), who translated part of the biography by Vázquez de Prada from the Spanish; and especially Gerda Traxl (Vienna) and Wendelin Wetzel (Heidelberg), who translated into German for the first time a good part of More's works and the relevant commentaries.

Index